Brooklyn's Dodgers

Brooklyn's Dodgers

The Bums, the Borough, and the
Best of Baseball
1947–1957

Carl E. Prince

OXFORD UNIVERSITY PRESS
New York   Oxford

Oxford University Press

Oxford   New York
Athens   Auckland   Bangkok   Bogotá   Bombay
Calcutta   Cape Town   Dar es Salaam   Delhi
Florence   Hong Kong   Istanbul   Karachi
Kuala Lumpur   Madras   Madrid   Melbourne
Mexico City   Nairobi   Paris   Singapore
Taipei   Tokyo   Toronto

and associated companies in
Berlin   Ibadan

Copyright © 1996 by Carl E. Prince

First published by Oxford University Press, Inc., 1996
198 Madison Avenue, New York, New York   10016

First issued as an Oxford University Press paperback, 1997

Oxford is a registered trademark of Oxford University Press

Library of Congress Cataloging-in-Publication Data
Prince, Carl E.
Brooklyn's Dodgers : the Bums, the borough, and the best of baseball
1947–1957 / Carl E. Prince.
p.   cm. Includes bibliographical references and index.
ISBN 0-19-509927-3
ISBN 0-19-511578-3   (Pbk.)
1. Brooklyn Dodgers (Baseball team)—History.   2. Brooklyn (New
York, N.Y.)—Social life and customs.   3. Brooklyn (New York, N.Y.)—
History.   I. Title.
GV875.B7P75   1996
796.357'64'0974723—dc20   95-26483

1 3 5 7 9 10 8 6 4 2

Printed in the United States of America

For Jon, Liz, and Marcia

Contents

Introduction

When Bobby Thomson's home run cleared the high left field wall in the Polo Grounds in 1951, my mother, a normally voluble woman, got up from the sofa, turned the tiny television off, and went into the bedroom, closing the door behind her. When my father, white-faced, came home from work two hours later, he entered the apartment with an equally unusual silence. He asked us (I was sixteen; my sister thirteen) where our mother was. We pointed to the bedroom; he peeked in, backed out, closed the door, and for the only time I can remember, made supper. I never before or since saw him at a stove. True, he only heated up four cans of Spaghetti-O's, and opened three bottles of Royal Crown, but it was supper. My mother stayed in the bedroom for sixteen hours. She appeared the next day to take up her usual domestic responsibilities. She never said a word about that loss, that season, that home run. Not ever.

We took our baseball seriously; it was a common basis for communication in a family that needed it. I still take it seriously as a means of communication. Now, on another coast where I spend my summers, my grown children and I share season tickets to a major league club. No, heaven forbid, not the L.A. Dodgers. That is no team of mine. Now I follow the Oakland Athletics, who play in a yuppy, smoke-free stadium that is as far from the subculture of Ebbets Field as a stadium can be.

Around New York and across America, Brooklyn's Dodgers remain familiar figures. Prime-time television's *Brooklyn Bridge* introduced them in a local context to a national audience. Feature stories on *The Boys of Summer* abound. Even twenty years later, Roger Kahn's memorable book still moves me and, I know, many others. And when the Los Angeles Dodgers, beginning in 1990, tried to force "The Brooklyn Dodger Sports Bar" to change its name, it became a David and Goliath struggle in the nation's media. (See Chapter 9.) The *New Yorker's* cover of March 7, 1994, featured at its center a banner in a deco collage of New York reading WELCOME BACK DODGERS! That visual spoof was filled with other references to the unattainable for New Yorkers, like polite cab drivers, a portrait of complete racial harmony, and omnipresent street cleaners and sanitation men.

Jackie Robinson's name, and now the legend surrounding him, is a part of most discussions when race progress or the lack of it is the subject. Robinson, Duke Snider, Gil Hodges, Roy Campanella, Leo Durocher, Don Drysdale, Sandy Koufax, and Branch Rickey have all written books or had books written about them—or both.

So the Brooklyn Dodgers remain alive and well in memory, as the last chapter of this book recounts. The team is now seen through a nostalgic haze, a special team playing in a distinctive decade that is the focus of this book. It was distinctive because it was the team's last and most successful decade in the borough. In the years 1947 to 1957 the Dodgers formed a vital, bonded, winning team, but when October rolled around, its flaws surfaced painfully. As a unit, the ball club was tagged a "choke" team. In a macho game, Dodger manhood was always suspect. This stigma is common in sports, and recently in passing it has been the property of the Buffalo Bills' football team. The Dodgers' case was special because it locked into its unique role as pioneers in race integration. Thus both race and male culture form important focuses of this study. The Dodgers did play out, over a decade, a kind of racial and macho *Oberammergau*.

In this book, male acting-out is described both on and off the field. It is as well a broader study of Brooklyn and its people, not only the men, but the community's women and adolescents as well. For many if not most Brooklynites, baseball was a central focus in their lives. Kahn's *Boys of Summer*, Peter Golenbock's *Bums*, and Jules Tygiel's *Baseball's Great Experiment: Jackie Robinson and His Legacy*, have all helped entrench in the American mind this uniquely legendary team. My study explores some realities of life on the ballclub, looks in depth into the community in which it played, and tries to place both in the broad social and political context of the postwar era of which the Dodger team was a part. Jackie Robinson's presence stirred up deep-seated racial tensions, within the team, with other teams, and among the public. But the Dodgers developed an uncanny ability to overcome their own prejudices and to unite in the face of race-baiting from other teams, the St. Louis Cardinals and Milwaukee Braves in particular.

Reflecting the times and the Brooklyn community, the Dodger team was probably more consistently anticommunist than any other professional team of that Cold War decade. Right-wing management, in the persons of Branch Rickey and Walter O'Malley, resonated well with both the team and most of the Brooklyn community. For example, several Dodgers revered Douglas MacArthur and Richard Nixon, both frequent visitors to Ebbets Field. Jackie Robinson, a radical activist in seeking national integration, nevertheless was strongly anticommunist and, in general terms outside race issues, politically conservative. For many in that era, the Dodgers appeared politically larger than life and were publicly identified with national issues in ways few teams have been before or since. In that political context, the Dodger club was very much a part of the conformist culture of the 1950s.

This was true as well in its inevitable bouts with gender matters. Typically macho, several Dodger players, like many male athletes of that generation, mimed the values of the society from which they were spawned. Their relationships with women were no less complex than woman fans' relationships with the team. Male attitudes and the prices they exacted from the players form an important part of this story. Recently, scholars have concluded that the ways that organized male sports are played "influence developing masculine identities" and provoke sexual aggression.*

---

*See notes at the end of the book. Each note is keyed to the page number and paragraph to which it refers by italicizing the first four words of the paragraph.

Gender, then, is an important part of this story. Instances of male sexual aggression on the Dodgers was evident in some team members' involvement with "Baseball Annies" (groupies) on the one hand, and the handling of paternity suits by management on the other. Gender is also a factor in woman fans' relationship to the team. The identities of women like Pulitzer Prize poet Marianne Moore and working-class stiff Hilda Chester, for example, help reveal the complexities of gender roles in sports in the insular fifties.

This book is also about Brooklyn. Serendipitously or not, the team reflected the scrappy working-class culture of that borough. The close relationship between deeply ethnic Brooklyn and its team was perhaps most evident in its schools and on the Parade Grounds, a mammoth athletic field, probably the best-appointed in the nation, where most organized amateur sports were played. The Dodgers shrewdly signed as many as ten Brooklyn boys each year, grooming them in the intricately organized Parade Grounds sandlot programs. The team knowingly renewed fan identification annually by keeping alive a dream every kid cherished. A few, such as Sandy Koufax and Chuck Connors, Cal Abrams and Bill Antonello, actually made it to the Dodgers. In a community of very clearly defined racial, ethnic, or religious neighborhoods, this Dodger involvement with local boys was no small element in providing the borough with its central identity.

Racial, ethnic, and religious community tensions form distinct parts of this story. Race excepted, these didn't manifest themselves much on the Parade Grounds, but were very evident in Brooklyn bars, churches, and civic organizations. The pervasive Dodger presence was an ameliorating force in all these institutions. Brooklyn's deeply embedded working-class bar culture did not spawn any melting pots, immigrant lore notwithstanding. Neither did the ubiquitous veterans' organizations, severely separated as they were by religious affiliation. And Jackie Robinson notwithstanding, African Americans were rigorously segregated in Brooklyn from the Parade Grounds' playing fields to the final honors conferred in the houses of God in the "Borough of Churches." So while even the Dodgers could not prevent separate spheres in Brooklyn life, the team did inject a generally soothing common ground, one where at least some level of urban civility survived.

I tell my story whenever possible via an on-the-field/off-the-field matrix, drawing on both the copious oral histories amassed so skillfully by others and my own grand and enjoyable re-reading of the sports pages and popular periodicals of my youth. On re-reading what I have wrought, I find it nostalgic, even as I have tried to deal with real historical questions in a dispassionate way. On this occasion, I am probably a bad example to my graduate students, for I do not follow an early learned professional canon that dictates that professional historians should strive for objectivity when writing serious history. I think this is serious history, but I'm not sure it's very objective. I just couldn't do it this time.

As much as any American team, the Brooklyn Dodgers symbolized the flawed greatness of the postwar decade. Baseball mirrors some part of the American character, and in several ways the Dodgers were central to shaping and reflecting America's postwar national image. Throughout the book, I have tried to be as specific as possible on these matters. The Brooklyn Dodgers' story, after all, comprehends important elements of Cold War politics, the racial tensions building after World War II, the American brand of macho sports culture, the transitional gender tensions evident in the wake of the war, and the emerging pressures on the sense of community that followed the war.

Several friends at New York University have read portions of the manuscript, and their comments have helped shape it. In particular, I want to thank Esther Katz, Michael Lutzker, and David Reimers. Other friends at NYU, notably Paul Baker, Leslie Berlowitz, David Hicks, Philip Hosay, Molly Nolan, Evelynne Patterson, Jeffrey Sammons, Kenneth Silverman, Arthur Tannenbaum, Daniel Walkowitz, Randall White, and Marilyn Young, have talked theory, baseball, and Dodgers with me over the years. Lorry Greenberg of Hunter College helped enormously with the end game in readying this book for press. Dena and Robert Scally have not only engaged our common interest in New York baseball, they have often fed me in the process. Debra Michals, a doctoral candidate and Assistant Director of the Woman's Studies Program at NYU, provided invaluable assistance, especially in making important suggestions on how to improve my take on gender theory as it applied in Chapter Five. Several former students, now academics themselves, have encouraged me in my intermittent escapes from early American history, and remain important people in my life; Norma Basch, Philip Coombe, Julianna Gilheany, Paul Gilje, Graham Hodges, Melvin Kalfus, Aryeh Maidenbaum, Howard Rock, Michael Russo, and Lola Van Wagenen have all contributed directly or indirectly to this project.

Former history editor and now Senior Vice President of Oxford University Press Sheldon Meyer gave this manuscript a cogent and important reading, causing me to re-think and re-write in several places, something he has done for many others over the years. Andrew Albanese, my editor at Oxford, not only did all the usual stuff with great skill, he also applied his knowledge of New York baseball to help me choose illustrations. Peter Levine of Michigan State, a long-time friend, read the manuscript twice, each reading leaving it better than it was before. He provided important aid and encouragement in other ways as well.

Marcia Freedman, a good friend as well as my sister, improved this book with her personal insight. Her encouragement has meant much to me over the years. Bill Freedman, ex-brother-in-law and still close friend, also read parts of this manuscript, much to my advantage. Andrew Cooper, as both a professional editor and author of sports-related psychology studies, both read the manuscript and talked through key points of it along the way, and made himself indispensable in its conceptualization.

My daughter Elizabeth has surfaced in her adult years as a great and knowing baseball fan, and is a frequent companion at the Oakland Coliseum, helping me to indulge my second childhood. My son Jonathan does that only occasionally, but he indulged that second childhood during his first, he told me later, by continuing to play little league ball primarily so that I could continue to manage his teams as league rules mandated. Not for nothing are both of them psychologists.

New York University
May 1995

C.E.P.

1
Integration: Dodgers' Dilemma, Dodgers' Response

Baseball Hall of Famer Hank Aaron recalled recently that as the Dodgers and Braves moved northward in his rookie year of 1954, barnstorming at the end of spring training, black players on both teams stayed in the same hotels. The northward bound athletes were segregated not by team, but by race. "I always managed to find my way to Jackie's room. He and Newcombe and Campanella... had strategy sessions on how to cope with the racial situation."

As the ranking black ball player in the major leagues, Jack Robinson was the national symbol of baseball's integration. With seven great years in the major leagues behind him, he still felt he had to explain to the current crop of "colored" rookies "what to do if a guy spit at them for instance, or whether to join in if there was a fight on the field." For Robinson and for his longtime Dodger teammates both black and white, 1947 was a beginning, not an end. The close of that much-written-about season did not shut the door on baseball's confrontation with race. That war had not yet been won, not in the majors, not in the minors, not even on the Dodgers.

The veteran Dodger regulars of the 1950s responded well to the notion of destiny imposed on them by Robbie's presence.

Some of his 1947 teammates had not, and many bench-warmers in the 1950s didn't either, so there were recurrent Dodger race problems during the entire decade Robinson played. To deal with the issue initially, Dodgers' owner Branch Rickey "northern-ized" the team between 1947 and 1949. That purge reduced the tension, but did not make it go away.

Because the South's temperate climate and consequently longer baseball seasons produced a disproportionate number of major leaguers, half of the 1947 Dodger team were southerners. This was true of the major leagues generally. Fortunately, on the Dodgers, northern and western-born players Duke Snider, Ralph Branca, Rex Barney, Carl Erskine, George Shuba, Gene Herman-ski, Gil Hodges, and especially one southerner, Kentuckian Pee Wee Reese, were all consistently supportive of Robinson and the other black ballplayers who followed. Many others, including most of the southerners present in 1947, were gone by 1950. These included Bobby Bragan, Hugh Casey, Kirbe Higbe, Pete Reiser, Ed Stanky, Ed Stevens, Dixie Walker, and Preston Ward. Some were just over the hill and slated to go anyway; others may not have been overtly hostile to Robinson. But all were ambiva-lent. Most felt pressured by friends in baseball or their families at home, and they were glad to play elsewhere.

Opposing teams certainly never let Dodger southerners forget about their unwitting roles as integration pioneers. Nor were the Dodgers from the South allowed to forget their degra-dation off the field. As Pee Wee Reese thought to himself in 1947, "What will my Louisville friends say about me playing with a colored guy? Probably won't like it, but I say to hell with anyone who doesn't like it." Preacher Roe, from rural Arkansas, had similar hometown problems, which he dealt with as Reese had. Alabaman Dixie Walker, on the other hand, admitted his prob-lems at home, would not confront them, and, like others, asked to be traded.

Jackie Robinson was always in the middle of these grating race tensions, no matter how many black ballplayers followed him into the majors. Both his symbolic presence and his political activism made that so. What made these racial bumps so meaningful at the time was his national visibility from the first moment he signed

Branch Rickey's contract. Paradoxically, even as the grinding race-baiting he experienced bothered many of his teammates, his increasingly outspoken, rejection of racism generated internal tensions among these same teammates. Race-related stress continued to plague the Dodgers as the club added other African Americans to its roster in the early 1950s. In particular, Jim Gilliam's displacement of Billy Cox in the infield in 1953 provoked a major race-tainted controversy on the Brooklyn team. And Jackie Robinson, as contentious and symbolically significant as ever, could not help but be at the heart of confrontations like this.

Robinson at the storm center was only half the story. In another ironic twist, the Dodger team always came together with remarkable cohesion when outsiders engaged in race-baiting, wherever and whenever it happened. This was true even in 1947, Jackie's rookie year, as such writers as Jules Tygiel, Roger Kahn, and Peter Golenbock make clear. That Dodger unity in the face of outside prejudice remained a hallmark of the club to the end of its years in Brooklyn. If this was a response by regulars who accepted their media-imposed roles as nationally acknowledged integrationists, it was as well an expression of the reality of the deep bonding the longtime players achieved over the years. Race, in short, added depth to the unity the Dodgers manifested, and Robinson was at the center of that, too. He and Reese made that Dodger team one of the most remarkable major league clubs ever to play baseball.

But the going wasn't easy. Jackie Robinson's vast importance as a symbol of integration raised the stakes of his political activism for the ball club. When Robinson sneezed politically, the rest of the Dodgers were expected to say, "God bless you." It was sometimes hard to take. Still, respect for his ability as a player, an up-close appreciation of the pain race-baiting inflicted on him almost daily, and a growing sense among the regulars of the greater story of which they were a part all softened the problems Robbie created for his teammates. And for the most part, Pee Wee Reese's presence, humanity, and leadership checkmated the remaining racists on the team.

In the real world, team bonding did not automatically make everyone consistent on the issue. Baseball, academic Michael

Kimmel reminded us, has been a race-divided sport since the 1880s, and that fact did not disappear overnight because some black integration had occurred. "The baseball diamond," he concluded, "became more than a verdant patch of pastoral nostalgia; it was . . . a contest between the races, in which the exclusion of non-whites and non-European immigrants from participation was reflected in the bleachers, as racial discrimination further assuaged the white working class." Baseball, in the words of Bart Giamatti, owned "a racist past." As well as has anyone, David Halberstam exploded that myth. Nearly a quarter-century after Robinson broke the color line, Halberstam addressed the persistent myth that sports heals racism: "White boy meets black boy, doesn't like him; black boy doubles in white boy with two out in the bottom of the ninth; lasting friendship is forged." Not true, Halberstam concluded. The "friendship" did not survive the moment.

Bearing this out, Robinson's on- and off-the-field aggression didn't always sit well with his strongest admirers on the team. Even Duke Snider, always one of Robinson's closest Dodger friends, occasionally vented some annoyance. In 1954, the day after Bethune-Cookman College awarded the aging star an honorary doctorate of laws degree, his teammates kidded him around the batting cage. Snider tartly rode the second baseman, reminding him that finally his prowess as a clubhouse lawyer had gained the recognition it deserved. When, in 1952, Robinson publicly charged Cardinal manager Eddie Stanky with tossing off racial epithets from his dugout, Dodger pitcher Clem Labine, like Snider always supportive of Robbie, told reporter Roger Kahn, "Look, maybe if someone called me a French-Catholic bastard, I'd tell him to go fuck himself. I wouldn't come crying to you." In that same summer, Jackie had to be restrained from going after the Cubs' Phil Cavarretta who, Robinson thought, was baiting him. In the clubhouse later, an indignant Cavarretta told the press he would never call Robinson a nigger. Several embarrassed Dodgers confirmed Cavarretta's version, and Robinson a day later publicly apologized through the press.

Jackie Robinson could be perverse even when he was right. Edward R. Murrow used his television show to assault segregation from time to time, and Robinson of course approved. But the

Dodger was anticommunist, and he did not like Murrow's television denunciation of Senator Joseph McCarthy. When Dodger public relations director Irving Rudd brought Murrow to the Dodger locker room in 1952, he was told off by some Dodger players and sportswriters for bringing a "Red" around. Several players dressing for the game pointedly told Rudd not to bring Murrow around again. Robinson, according to the Dodger public relations man, at that point said, "Irving, any time Edward R. Murrow wants to enter the Dodger locker room, dugout or anyplace else, he's my guest." "It got quiet fast," according to Rudd. Robinson, who agreed with his teammates on the evils of communism, nevertheless deliberately elevated the tension level in the clubhouse to make a political point larger than baseball. "That's where it was at with Jackie," Rudd concluded. (For Dodger politics, see Chapter 2.)

Jackie Robinson did not hesitate to turn his anger toward the baseball establishment as well. In the case of the New York Yankees, he provoked the confrontation; in the case of National League President Warren Giles, it was forced on him.

Robinson initiated a running battle with the Yankees in 1953 when he accused the team of deliberately excluding blacks. For good measure, he made the charge in a sensitive forum, the *Youth Wants to Know* television show. The indictment against the class team of baseball was of course widely denied at the time, and Robinson was called on the carpet by Baseball Commissioner Ford Frick for speaking out against "the best interests of baseball." Robinson thought otherwise. "I felt deep in my heart for years that the Yankees had been giving Negroes the runaround." Yankee management, Robbie said, did not want Yankee Stadium "deluged by Negroes and Puerto Ricans who would chase away all their . . . good customers from Westchester." Yankee players were no better, Robinson hinted, although he could not prove it beyond the evidence of his eyes. Years later, however, Yankee outfielder Gene Woodling confirmed that the 1950s team was one "filled with Red Asses," as Robinson had long ago believed.

Even as Robinson willingly took on the Yankees, he was forced into a running feud with National League president Warren Giles.

Giles came to his position in 1952, after owning the Cincinnati Reds, a team, a front office, and a city all strongly resistant to racial change. Shortly after assuming the National League office, Giles fired the first shot, exploding at Jackie on the field in Cincinnati. He was present as Robinson, as he so often did, challenged an umpire's decision. "Jackie Robinson was a greater offender than the others," Giles told the press. When Robinson was openly contemptuous at being singled out, the *Brooklyn Eagle* agreed, inflaming local public opinion. Giles quickly backed off. At Ebbets Field a week later, as Giles presented Roy Campanella with his Most Valuable Player trophy for 1951, he patronizingly praised Robinson as an icon for the game and nation. Roger Kahn said that later, as Giles spoke, "I watched Robinson's face . . . and his smile was hate."

Estrangement between Giles and Robinson persisted until the latter's retirement, but Giles was unable to confront the Dodger openly without underscoring his insider reputation as a bigot. In 1954, for example, he fined both Reese and Robinson for umpire-baiting, but singled Robinson out yet again as the instigator. Robbie's response was violent and public, and again he told the press Giles "has singled me out." The contretemps was submerged once more, with Robinson paying a small fine and Giles backing off a threat to suspend him.

Yet to see Robinson only as the center of controversy on his team would be to gravely misread the more complex reality. The Dodgers formed a unit that coalesced over a decade. Robinson the player was a big part of it. He pushed many Dodgers to face their humanity, and the most important of them came through. He also brought fans into Ebbets Field and every other ball park in which he played, thus pushing a reluctant ownership to pay everyone more. Finally, in six of the ten years he played for the team, Robinson helped put World Series shares in all Dodger pockets, no small matter when for most even a losing share could equal 20 percent or more of a year's salary.

Money apart, the black star's teammates came to embrace him for what he stood for. In 1953, pitcher Carl Erskine put it best when he said that "race relations on the team are a model the whole country could learn from." Duke Snider felt much the same way. The team, he said, meaning Dodger regulars and explicitly excluding most southern teammates, "genuinely cared for each other." Even Carl Furillo, the most ambivalent of the Dodger cadre, told Maury Allen thirty years later that, whatever doubts he may have voiced, Jackie "was one of us." Writing at the end of Brooklyn's golden era in 1957, Robert Creamer caught a central reason. "No other group of stars . . . has played together so many years so successfully as the eight man nucleus of the modern Dodgers: Reese, Furillo, Gil Hodges, Snider, Campanella, Newcombe, Erskine and . . . Jackie Robinson." The "sheer greatness" of that team core made it a contemporary living legend.

At least one southerner was an exception to the inherent prejudices southern ball players as a rule brought to the table of baseball integration. Pee Wee Reese did not consider himself the "social revolutionary" some writers made him out to be, but he did move often reluctant Dodgers to both unify into the great team they became and to accommodate themselves to a growing black presence. What Reese did mattered most because at the time Robinson arrived, the shortstop emerged, in the words of Duke Snider, as "the unquestioned leader" of the young ballclub. Command passed to him when veteran Dixie Walker abdicated in the face of Robinson's appearance. Managers came and went—Durocher, Shotton, Durocher again, Dressen, Alston. By 1951 Rickey was gone, too. So for ten years, it was Reese, among the white Dodgers, who made integration work.

As team captain, others emulated what he did. Even Robinson deferred to Reese, usually referring to him as either "Captain" or "Colonel" (Reese was, naturally, a Kentucky colonel). The shortstop's "droll cockiness" and quick mouth masked civility, sensitivity, mental depth, and moral courage. Robinson would pointedly remind the world of the realities of race-baiting on the field throughout his playing days by acknowledging Reese's humanity and also using the captain publicly to make race-related points in a positive way. In the summer of 1949, Robinson syndicated a serialized newspaper autobiography circulated in conjunction with the release of *The Jackie Robinson Story,* a movie in which he played himself. The newspaper account signaled a racial theme in the movie. Reese was baited "viciously" as a turncoat by opponents, who called him "some very vile names." Each one, Robinson added, "bounced off of Pee Wee" and "hit me like a machine gun bullet." It was Reese's habit at these times to show the team flag. Robinson wrote in 1955 that Reese invariably "walked over to me, put his arm around me and talked to me in a warm and friendly way, smiling and laughing."

More than any other team, it was the St. Louis Cardinals that punished the Dodgers for its black presence. St. Louis is a southern city, and Sportsman's Park bused in thousands of black fans to fill its bleachers for many otherwise low-attendance dates. This increased an already high level of tension on the field. The hostility of the situation was underscored by the Chase Hotel's refusal to accommodate black ballplayers until 1954. In that city, uniquely, the Dodger team was itself segregated. Finally, the worst death threats Robinson encountered (and he received many) were in St. Louis. In 1953, for example, he was sent a series of ten notes over the course of the season, and he was protected by the FBI whenever he played there that year.

It was no coincidence that it was at St. Louis that the death threats were most ominous. The threatened 1947 Cardinals' strike against Robinson's presence has already received all the attention it needs elsewhere, but it deserves brief mention here only because several Cardinals themselves mirrored the hostility of many local fans in this southern city. Long after the 1947 strike threat, virtually the entire ball club, with its preponderance of southern ballplayers playing in the South, was hostile to Robinson in his rookie year. The most notable exception, among a few others, was the team's star, Stan Musial. Much has been written about Enos Slaughter's viciousness, a sadism he paid for by his long wait for admission to the Hall of Fame. There was a second nemesis. Played down in recent years because of his current fame as a television notable is the equally sadistic role played by Joe Garagiola in 1947. He and Slaughter were the racist leaders of the Cardinals; both were guilty of deliberately spiking Robinson as he played first base. Slaughter's actions are well known; Garagiola deserves a piece of the fame.

Robinson assaulted Garagiola's pride by running on the catcher every chance he got. Garagiola responded with racial epithets. Things came to a head on September 11, 1947, when the Dodger bench, as it always did with the hated Redbirds, loudly got on the catcher. Garagiola "has been a target for the riders from the Brooklyn bench all season," New York *P.M.* reported. Garagiola and Robinson had to be physically separated by the umpires during that game. While hitting into a double play, the catcher stepped on Robinson's heel, forcing Jackie to the bench "for repairs." Garagiola has recently professed to remember "Jackie" warmly, but the record says differently. The late-blooming television pundit no longer remembers any strike threat, and acknowledges only that others "cut" Robinson, not he. Robbie in 1955 recalled the spiking differently, claiming Garagiola did it and did it deliberately.

Robinson's teammates, whatever their individual ambivalence, were clearly moved by the on-the-field treatment meted out to Robinson. His intensity, ability, guts, and that looming World Series check all worked for him. No one reflected that ambivalence more than second baseman Eddie Stanky, an Alabaman who played with Robinson in 1947. He was traded after that season because he was one of those southerners who didn't want to play with the black ballplayer. Stanky was also about to be replaced by Robinson at second base. Stanky, after playing stints with the Braves and Giants, was named manager of the Cardinals in 1952. Leo Durocher picked up on Stanky's ambivalence. He quoted Stanky as having told Robinson at the start of the 1947 season: "You're on this ball club and as far as I'm concerned that makes you one of twenty-five players on my team. . . . I want you to know I don't like it. I want you to know I don't like you." In 1951, when he was playing for the Giants, Stanky called Robinson a "black bastard" in Monte Irvin's presence. Moving over to manage the Cards in 1952, he really went out of control.

Race confrontation erupted anew almost immediately after Stanky took over. He regularly led the team's barrage of taunts from the bench, even in the confines of Ebbets Field. Ironically, he would contribute to the Dodger team's finest hour as a symbol of racial togetherness.

That 1953 moment was a year off, however, when the Dodgers made their first trip of the '52 season to St. Louis. Even as

Stanky denied the story breaking in the papers following the night game of June 10, the *Brooklyn Eagle* reported that the Cardinals' bench shouted "nigger" and other "ugly adjectives" when Joe Black came in to relieve. Robinson heard Stanky himself, and told catcher Del Rice, "I'm sick and tired of that stuff . . . and you can tell that gutless [son of a bitch] that I said so." "Didn't hear a thing," Stanky told New York reporters after the game. "Of course, there was the usual jockeying, but that was just routine riding."

Roger Kahn broke the story that night, covering the team for the *Herald Tribune*. Trying to be fair, he printed Stanky's denial along with Robinson's version. Belatedly realizing Stanky had misled him when he told Kahn he had "heard nothing out of line," Kahn visited the Cardinals' clubhouse the next night. "Here comes Robi'son's li'l bobo," Stanky told his entourage. The manager repeated, "I heard nothing out of line," adding "'black bastard' and 'nigger' are not out of line." Kahn wrote another story, one that the *Tribune* would not publish, lest the paper "be a sounding board for Jackie Robinson."

The Dodger front office responded vigorously even if the New York newspapers did not. Walter O'Malley "declared angrily that something must be done to put a stop to such unsportsmanlike conduct." Team vice president Buzzie Bavasi promised an official protest to the league office, knowing it would be a futile gesture, given Warren Giles's hostility to blacks in general and Robinson in particular. By the early fifties, the public saw the Dodgers as a team victimized by others in the game, a band of brothers facing racist baseball enemies.

But the reality even in 1953 was different from public perception. Race tension on the team still festered, occasionally breaking through to the surface. The Gilliam-Cox contretemps was a case in point. The arrival of Jim Gilliam brought racial conflict on the Dodgers back to the surface, causing teams like St. Louis and Milwaukee to believe they could exploit it on the field. Although there were fewer southerners on the 1953 Dodgers than on other teams, there were still nine on the twenty-five-man roster. That "Klan Contingent" formed a sizable cadre, and it found its cause in fighting the good fight for Pennsylvania-born third baseman Billy Cox. Cox was to be replaced at third by Robinson, with rookie Gilliam taking over second. This move irritated several bench-warming southerners—and two regulars, Preacher Roe and Cox himself.

Cox was known as a "brooder," hypochondriacal, suffering from "depression" after experiencing battle fatigue in World War II. Manager Charley Dressen, with his usual lack of both tact and foresight, mishandled the switch from the beginning. First, "he never did let the brooding Billy in on the secret," according to Arthur Daley, until "Cox discovered it for himself in the newspapers. Without preliminary reassurances from his skipper, the Cox morale was seriously jolted." Dressen also managed to embarrass Jackie. "Everyone knows," Dressen told the press at the end of spring training, that Gilliam "can play second better than Robinson can now, and I don't care what Gilliam is hitting at present."

Gilliam's presence in the infield caused comment in spring training. While working out in his St. Paul uniform, reserve infielder Bob Morgan shouted to several Dodgers, "How come he ain't a Dodger? He's dark enough." A second-string outfielder, probably Dick Williams, responded, "Yeah, they're gonna run us all right out of here." It was the marginal southern players and players whose jobs were threatened, ballplayers trying to keep a spot on one of the best teams ever put together, who saw their slots and World Series shares put in jeopardy by arriving young, black talent. Their reactions were visceral if they came out of segregated cultures, less predictable if they hailed from the north.

Rumors of racial unrest persisted all spring. Even the staid *New York Times* carried the stories. Robinson and Joe Black, Rookie of the Year in 1952, tried to defuse the situation. "I thought the pitchers would miss" Cox's presence in the lineup, the black righthander told the press. "He's the best," Robinson, who was to replace Cox, said of the third baseman. Billy was "the most underrated player in baseball," according to Jackie. The worst sniping came from two front line pitchers, Russ Meyer and Preacher Roe. "The one who was doing the undercutting was Jackie," Meyer believed. "Jackie could get something in his craw, and he'd agitate, instigate until he more or less got what he wanted."

Preacher Roe, the team's most consistently winning pitcher from 1949 to 1953, had arrived with Cox from the Pirates after the 1947 season. Both got along well with Robinson, Campanella, and pitcher Don Newcombe. Cox said it all: his problem wasn't with Robinson, whom he admired, "I mean the nigger, the kid," he told Kahn. For Roe, Gilliam's arrival meant "They're pushin Billuh around."

While the baseball public had only a sketchy idea that Gilliam's presence was proving a minor irritant to the Dodger team, those in the game knew better. The seriousness of the situation was underscored by owner Walter O'Malley. He was, he said, prepared "to remove some players from the Brooklyn club and bring in others from the minor league affiliates." It was in this unsettling climate that Ed Stanky saw an advantage he thought he could exploit. His chance came on August 30, 1953, as the Dodgers were closing in on their second straight pennant. The Cards were in town for a three-game series. The opener, with Robinson playing on a bad leg, was a landmark game, one that suggested strongly that, whatever the internal race problems, the core of that Dodger team knew how best to show its racial commitment.

During the first six innings of a close game, Stanky very crudely and publicly imitated an ape in the visitor's dugout of Ebbets Field. He was taunting the limping Jackie Robinson. The *Eagle* caught him in a series of photos showing the Cards manager in action: fists under armpits, lips out, jaw thrust forward, grunting, shuffling, and scratching as he moved from one end of the dugout to the other whenever Robbie came to bat. At least half the 16,000 fans in intimate Ebbets Field were able to look into the St. Louis dugout to witness the display.

One of them was Hilda Chester, the Dodgers' ultimate fan. (See Chapter 5.) Alerted early to the display, she made her way from her usual center-field bleacher seat to a spot immediately behind the Cardinals' dugout. Robinson led off the seventh. Stanky is shown in the photos on the dugout steps doing his ape routine as the third baseman limped to the plate. Chester is shown in the background waving a white handkerchief. Robinson, moved back by a pitch, finally fanned, as Chester led a localized round of booing directed at Stanky.

The incident was worse than the usual racial taunting both because of the crude visual display and because so many fans were privy to it. But it might have ended there had not a remarkable event occurred. Perhaps it was because they were incensed, perhaps it was only serendipitous, but Robinson's teammates proceeded to make Chester's feeble handkerchief protest matter by scoring twelve runs that inning. Eight Dodgers would bat and six would score before Robinson made the second out of the inning again by striking out. Six more Dodgers would score before the inning was over, breaking the game open and winning by a humiliating 20–4 score. Stanky and the Cards looked on grimly at the murderous parade of regulars—Reese, Snider, Campanella, Hodges, Furillo, Shuba—as they pounded three Cardinal pitchers.

Twice in that inning Stanky, head down, was forced to trudge the twenty miles to the mound to change pitchers. Twice, Chester waved her hanky in Stanky's face as he made the return trip to the dugout. Twice the small stadium rocked with the fans' boos, directed at a former Ebbets Field hero. Hilda orchestrated the chorus from the stands, as the Dodger bench jockeys, a jubilant Robinson prominent among them, joined the outpouring of vituperation. It was a Chester moment; it was a Dodger moment; it was a Brooklyn moment. This one time, a crude, frontal racial assault by the Cardinals had been met with the brute force of Dodger bats. This was the last time St. Louis would openly exercise its anti-black bias against the Dodgers.

There can be no doubt that Stanky's 1953 ape imitation reflected deep-seated racial bias, a peculiar manifestation of it widely recognized in American culture. An ironic reprise indirectly involving Jackie Robinson would occur exactly three decades later. On a 1983 Monday night football telecast Howard Cosell would unthinkingly gloss Alvin Garrett's long run from scrimmage by adding, "that little monkey gets loose, doesn't he?" A "national furor" ensued, according to Cosell, as he was vilified coast to coast for his "innocent" remark. The irony comes in because he subsequently introduced two lines of defense: his closeness to and support for Muhammed Ali and Jackie Robinson; he described the latter as "a symbol of a brave new era." That era was just beginning in 1953 and was far from ended in 1983 when Cosell engaged nearly the same inflammatory metaphor.

The Milwaukee Braves also attempted, via racial provocation, to exploit the turmoil in the Dodger clubhouse that summer of 1953. The Milwaukee club had made the move from Boston at a time when the team was gelling into a first-division competitor. It arrived in a city enthusiastic about a major league presence, one with a settled, oddly ironic German heritage: a community with both a strong socialist egalitarian constituency, on the one hand, and a deeply ingrained white supremist, neo-fascist element, on the other. The latter seems to have dominated at the ball park. At the time of the riotous game of August 3, the powerhouse Dodgers were in the process of beating the Braves out of a pennant.

Jackie Robinson and Roy Campanella were having great years (the former hitting .329, the latter winning his second MVP award), thus subtly annoying a very racist team. Robinson was one of the best bench jockeys ever to play the game, and he needled the Braves often. He took particular pleasure in getting on the Braves because their stars (Warren Spahn, Lew Burdette, and Joe Adcock) were prejudiced, or so the Dodgers, white and black, thought. Pitchers Burdette and Spahn consistently threw more at black players than white ones. The usual justification prevailed: blacks lacked guts and could be intimidated.

At the same time, the Braves' trio baited their few black teammates. Warren Spahn, for example, once said to the clubhouse: "What's black and catches flies? The Braves' outfield." In 1953 Billy Bruton and Jim Pendleton played regularly, and Henry Aaron, in the wings, was only a year away. For Spahn, one of the greatest lefthand pitchers of all time, "Jackie got arrogant after a while," taking advantage of his blackness, as Spahn put it very delicately years later. The stage was set for the August 3 confrontation a week earlier when "Robinson was involved in a quick name-calling episode with Burdette."

Milwaukee fans seemed to know all about their team's attitude toward opposing blacks. Robinson and Campanella were usually booed roundly when they played there. *Brooklyn Eagle* columnist Tommy Holmes was as direct as newsprint allowed when he asked rhetorically: "What were the people in the stands trying to prove with their treatment of Campanella and Robinson—that Milwaukee is a citadel of white supremacy?" Braves players were encouraged in their empathies by the racism in the stands.

The Braves still had long-odds pennant hopes, and the August 3 game was close. As Campanella came to bat, Burdette started him out by calling him a "black mother-fucker." He then got two quick strikes on the furious Dodger catcher. There followed two more pitches at Campy's head, both sending him into the dirt. After the second beanball, Burdette shouted from the mound, "Nigger, get up and hit." Campanella struck out on the next pitch, then took off after Burdette, bat in hand. When Del Crandall, the Braves' catcher, grabbed Campy from behind, the Dodger team "swarmed out of the dugout" and a "melee" ensued. Reporters accurately described the anger of the Dodger players. As in the case of the St. Louis game later that month, it was a defining public moment, for the impression left (correctly) was that while internal racial unrest might afflict the team from time to time, when others threatened it, this Dodger team would strenuously protect its own.

The aftermath bordered on the absurd. Umpire Tom Gorman denied having heard Burdette say anything. Campanella and Burdette, in the denial mode of the early 1950s, were forced publicly to shake hands for photographers the next day. A Brooklyn fan, also in the '50s mode, blamed the whole incident on underground instigation by "intellectuals in the behest of Stalinism and Fascism." (For Brooklyn's and the Dodgers' anticommunism, see Chapter 2.) The last may be hard to credit unless one accepts that in the confined world of Brooklyn in that decade most things could be blamed on those three faces of evil. Only Jackie Robinson made any sense, saying in the aftermath of the game, "There are thoughtless and stupid people in every business and baseball is no exception."

Even that did not end the matter, for the beanball returned. Later in the series, Dodger manager Charley Dressen had to explicitly *order* Russ "Mad Monk" Meyer to absolutely *not* knock down Sid Gordon, the Braves' Jewish second baseman, in retaliation. Meyer was also known as "Russell the Red-Necked Reindeer." This apt monicker was hung on Meyer by Bob Carpenter, owner of the Philadelphia Phillies, the pitcher's previous team. Meyer's first choice for a beanball was Billy Bruton, but even Meyer could figure out that wouldn't do, given who his own black teammates were. A Jew, in Meyer's mind, seemed an adequate stand-in if he couldn't throw at a black.

A payback came a year later. Joe Adcock hit four homers against the Dodgers in a 1954 game, and was sickeningly beaned by Dodger pitcher Clem Labine the next day. Angry Braves in their Ebbets Field dugout yelled loudly that Adcock had been hit deliberately, but prudently, they did not rush the field. Adcock was carried off on a stretcher, but Robinson for one showed no remorse. He reminded the press that, as bad as the beaning was, Adcock had to pay Burdette's bill. The latter was guilty of "throwing at hitters all the time." Nobody on the Dodgers disagreed.

More than any other player then or later, Jackie Robinson remained at or near the center of any racial episode the Dodger team encountered. It was the symbolism he embodied for so many Americans of different backgrounds that served as a constant reminder to his teammates to do the right thing, at least publicly. Robinson was quick to remind his cohorts, subtly or otherwise, of the spotlight under which his presence placed them. The passage of time, the winning percentage, the publicity, the World Series checks, and simple humanity all brought the Dodger regulars finally down the path to integration. It was a cause they consciously came to embrace. And where the first-string stars went, the rest usually followed. Those who didn't, mainly those from the South, were traded. For his part, Robinson forcefully used the national symbolism to which he was umbilically tied to press at every opportunity for national integration. The wall of segregation, undermined first by limited but symbolically important efforts at integration in the armed forces and on the job, was assaulted anew with the Supreme Court's decision on *Brown v. Board of Education* in 1954. The presence of paratroopers escorting black students into a white school in Little Rock, Arkansas, soon thereafter was a signal of more to come.

Much of Robinson's own symbolic role began with his signing, and his mystique grew as his greatness as a ballplayer became clear. In a remarkable 1947 interview published well before she became a singing star, Brooklyn resident Lena Horne indicated clearly what she felt was being played out at Ebbets Field. "Being a successful Negro artist," she told *P.M.* in a Sunday supplement feature, "is an unenviable position to be in." "I'll never forget how frightened I was for Jackie Robinson," she continued, "how we were frightened because we knew that if he made the normal mistakes that any ballplayer made it would be a reflection on his race. We felt, oh God, he must perform magnificently or those white players will scorn him." She saw herself in 1947 "in the same sort of position." When Robinson made it, other outsiders in Brooklyn, including whites, felt vindicated.

Advertising mogul Jerry Della Femina, writing about growing up Italian in Brooklyn, felt that Robinson "was once in a lifetime." His early inherent prejudice over Robinson's blackness was overridden by the latter's greatness; not much racial enlightenment maybe, but a start. Aaron, Alan Lelchuk's fictional young Jewish protagonist in *Brooklyn Boy*, idolized Robinson above all other Dodgers. Kareem Abdul-Jabbar remembered his Brooklyn in 1955, when the Dodgers finally achieved nirvana by beating the Yankees in the Series: "I celebrated the Dodgers' victory the best way I knew. I yelled out the window." Robinson, he said, was virtually his first role model for success.

Many future black major leaguers saw him the same way. Jackie's outspokenness convinced Frank Robinson to address black issues (which he did belatedly, only after he became a manager). "I know what I went through," he said, "and I can't imagine how he survived all that anger." "He didn't have it easy," Dave Winfield said of Jackie, "none of us do." And he added, Robbie "didn't even work for George Steinbrenner." Ed Charles, the Mets' third baseman on the "Miracle Team" of 1969, noted that the most significant thing was that because of Robinson, "the entire black population of America became Dodger fans."

Other evidence exists that there was a wider world outside Brooklyn and baseball drawn to Robinson's drama. Inasmuch as the South was the focus of the earliest civil rights efforts in the late '40s and the '50s, Robinson's travail and ultimate success was tied in the public's mind to the reform of the South. As early as the summer of 1947, it was becoming clear what problems

Robinson's presence on the Dodgers might introduce. Several places in Florida threatened to prevent either training or games when the races were mixed on the field. Both Florida and the entire South would cave in, Charles Mohr predicted. "There are many good reasons to break down these feudalistic traditions and all of them are money. . . . It is entirely within the range of possibility," he continued, "that many major league clubs will move into Arizona, California and other states where there is no racial segregation in sports." He was right. Florida quickly succumbed.

Willie Morris, long-time editor of *Harper's*, remembered that as a twelve-year-old southern white boy, he witnessed the beginning of the end of the South he knew. Robinson's success created for southern blacks an "atmosphere of heady freedom before anyone knew the name of Justice Warren or had heard much of the United States Supreme Court." The Dodgers, it was rumored in Morris's white South, "had Jackie Robinson, Roy Campanella, and Don Newcombe—not to mention . . . God knows how many Chinese and mulattoes being groomed in the minor leagues." Education, a little, anyway, was taking place. "I remember my father turned to some friends at the store one day," Morris recollected. "'Well, you can say what you want about that nigger Robinson, but he's got guts,' and to a man the others nodded, a little reluctantly, but in agreement nonetheless." Reese, they acknowledged, "a good white Southern boy, was the best friend Robinson had on the team, which proved they had chosen the right one to watch after him."

In the end, however, it was how Robinson's white teammates reacted that mattered most, if the symbolic gains Jackie inculcated were to matter. That is to say, if it were not perceived that the Dodgers got along with each other, the experiment would have failed. Duke Snider spoke for several Dodger greats when he said about the Robinson of 1947: "The man put up with far more than the rest of us could have. I was there on the field with him and I heard the taunts and insults, and I saw the fans throw things at him, and other players go out of their way to spike him. . . . Jackie played through it all and became Rookie of the Year."

Pee Wee Reese saw Robinson for the last time at Gil Hodges's funeral in 1972, a few months before Robinson died. He was shocked at Robinson's appearance. "Jackie just seemed to get older faster than the rest of us. It had to be what he went through. I don't think Jack ever stopped carrying that burden. I'm no doctor, but I'm sure it cut his life short." Like Snider, Reese felt deep empathy and clearly got caught up at some level in Robinson's crusade. His teammates respected Robinson even if they didn't always love him.

Much of the respect he engendered was rooted in the bonding of the unit. "The dozen or so athletes who were at the core of the team," Robert Creamer wrote, "knew they were set apart." Robinson stood at the center of that coalescence. The Brooklyn Dodgers were not only set apart, they were driven inward by the racism they played through so successfully. "Every hand is turned against them," columnist Tommy Holmes concluded late in 1949, "and it hasn't affected their play in any way you can see." Indeed, with the perspective that time provides, it is possible to see that, forced in on themselves, the Dodgers played more inspired ball than they might otherwise have.

The Dodgers knew early on they were in a game larger than baseball. Ira Berkow said once that the story of Jackie Robinson breaking into baseball was "the most important social issue in sports history." Maybe the Dodger regulars at the time didn't quite know the full meaning of the events they were part of, but they knew a lot. The majority of them were not the stupid jocks of caricature. They knew, as Duke Snider said later, that they "were a symbol of baseball and of America itself." On balance, the last generation of Brooklyn's Dodgers both played the game superbly and bonded as a team.

"On balance" though, much remains to be explained. Several Dodgers, including some standouts, were probably quite ambivalent about Jackie Robinson, at least personally. He was not only black, he was abrasive. Contemporary observations and later evaluations by those on the team seen as close to Robinson over the long seasons were perforce almost always positive. But the evidence of the continuing racial tensions through 1957 strongly suggests some paradox at work: there were privately more complex responses to black Dodgers, Robinson included, that even longtime teammates could never indulge publicly. For a team so revered and so symbolic, open expressions of ambivalence about Robinson and other African American teammates was not an option open to most Dodger regulars.

So despite the evidence of real team bonding and surface civility, a clear appraisal of Dodgers' racial realities as of now stands unsatisfyingly locked in an historical haze awaiting better evidence. The gap between what the Dodger stars said then and say now, and the contradictory evidence of continuing race problems on the team, at least through 1957, is too great to conclude otherwise.

2
Political Culture: Reds and Dodger Blue

Th' two gr-eat American spoorts are a good deal alike—
polyticks an' baseball. They're both played by professionals,
th' teams ar-re r-un be fellows that cuddn't throw a base-ball
or stuff a ballot box to save their lives an' ar-re on'y
intherested in countin' up the gate receipts. . . . They're
both grand games.

—Mr. Dooley, 100 years ago

After World War II, the Brooklyn Dodgers relentlessly exemplified major league baseball's permanent preoccupation with
American politics. There were three reasons for this. First, where
Branch Rickey reigned, political intrigue followed. He played
anticommunist hardball in defense of the sacred reserve clause,
a contractual nicety that legally kept all professional players in
bondage, and most especially those journeymen ballplayers who
were poorly paid and in career-long servitude. Second, Jackie
Robinson, in his mission to capitalize on his fame and talent to
help end segregation both in and out of the game, thrust himself
into the breach of Cold War politics. Finally, both Rickey and his
successor, Walter O'Malley, consciously courted political influence: conservative Republican connections on the national level,
and the dominant Brooklyn Democratic establishment locally.
These forays cumulatively made the Dodgers the most overtly political sports team of the postwar decade.

The Cold War first brushed the team in the late 1940s, although Rickey's personal brand of red-baiting began with the
end of the Second World War. By 1949, anticommunism in America had matured into a pervasive show of Iron Curtain politics

within both the Truman administration and, increasingly, the nation at large. It stayed that way through the 1950s, helped along by the Korean War and the McCarthyism that accompanied it. The Dodgers responded to both, as did all major league teams.

Lest anyone think this an exaggeration, consider the case of the Cincinnati Reds. In 1952, the Reds were officially rechristened the Redlegs. Done at the urging of Warren Giles, the Reds' former owner and the new president of the National League, it insured that Cincinnati's foes would not mistakenly assume they were battling evil in the form of the Cincinnati Communists, thus giving the good guys in the league a leg up on the field. And this against a ballclub already handicapped by lousy pitching. A Cincinnati sportswriter noted sadly that it was a shame: "We were Reds before they were."

The Dodgers didn't have to change names, but the team's commitment to dominant American values was impressively complete. Anticommunism permeated the Dodger locker room as well as the front office. By far the largest part of the Brooklyn community was amenable, for it counted itself a bastion of patriotism. Most borough dwellers were comfortable with the knowledge that the team reflected their own political leanings. Dodger players, mostly following their own political inclinations anyway, gladly bent to the ascendant political culture. Branch Rickey, as we shall see, willingly delivered a lecture on Americanism to any who weakened.

Rickey actively espoused displays of patriotism, and he understood better than most the mystique baseball held for many Americans. He once commented, by way of example, that men universally turned to the language of the game to express themselves politically.* He told *Sports Illustrated* in 1955 about seeing a television interview with Senator William Knowland, in which the Republican majority leader answered a question offhandedly with, "Well, I think the Administration has a pretty good batting average." Rickey pointed out that responses like

---

* The absorption of the language of baseball into the language of the street is discussed in Chapter 7.

24

this were virtually automatic for many Americans. He went on to quote a *New York Times* editorial published in the aftermath of the 1954 Army-McCarthy hearings. The *Times*, Rickey recalled, remarked that the Wisconsin Senator possessed "a good fastball but no control." These colloquial analogies were too commonplace to be dismissed, Rickey concluded. The game had long since become deeply absorbed in the country's political culture.

Rickey was a political anomaly: politically sophisticated, cynically anticommunist, and altruistic enough to integrate baseball in the name of that very patriotism that drove the engine of his Cold War rhetoric. Integrating baseball was the most American thing the sport could do to help improve the superiority of the "American way of life," as he saw it. Bringing Jackie Robinson to the majors would also prove very profitable, but that was perhaps a secondary consideration to the social change Rickey engaged. He forced baseball's hand, compelled it to do the right thing.

Rickey shrewdly tied Robinson's signing to baseball's traditional role of embodying historic American values. Rickey did believe this, so it was more than either political stratagem or money-making scheme. Baseball, Rickey felt, was the keeper of the American flame in key ways. "The game is ideal" as a socializing presence in America, he said in 1949. He wasn't far off the mark, and in the wake of the war, Rickey cannily exploited the game's classic mystique. Many writers have explained that mystique very well.

Baseball, we have been frequently reminded, evokes a nostalgia for a mythic vanished America. Ironically, major league ball has always been entirely an urban game, even as its wellsprings, both amateur and minor league, are largely small-town and rural. As a result, baseball, even in the cities, retains a familiar pre-industrial, agrarian hint of the past. The green playing field is only part of the story. The sport also delivers egalitarian opportunity (fair play, in baseball terms) that drew American men back to an earlier, better era. The vision is purely neo-Jeffersonian, a vision that worked better fifty years ago, "When It Was a Game," as a recent popular cable television presentation put it. This mythic agrarian vision has been perpetuated as well in the recent "Baseball" series produced for PBS by Ken Burns. The fact that the belief in a better, simpler era was built on popular hype and little substance doesn't matter. White men thought it mattered.

That idyllic agrarian tie to baseball may be astounding in its misrepresentation, but few who have reflected on the game doubt its impact even as they deny the validity of the myth. The notion that the sport is an "echo of our pastoral past," George Will has written, is "agreeable nonsense," but very influential. Fans, Thomas Boswell has said, "prefer that myth, prefer pastoral, slyly anecdotal . . . slightly-dated things over those which are urban."

A. Bartlett Giamatti, both a Commissioner of Baseball and an academic who in his primary career became Yale University president, thought about these things. Baseball conjures up an image of "the people's paradise of the field" and is "the most strenuously nostalgic" American sport. The game "simulates and stimulates the condition of Freedom. Americans identify the game with the country." Rickey knew something about this, and would have agreed with Giamatti that the game is "the story of our national life," a part of "the tale America tells the world." Giamatti offers up an applicable insight in terms of Jackie Robinson's story, although nowhere does he relate the perception to the Rickey-Robinson saga. Baseball, Giamatti has said in *Take Time for Paradise*, "restates a version of America's promises every time it is played. The playing of the game is a restatement of the promises that we can all be free, that we can all succeed." Think of the Robinson-Rickey mindset as Giamatti articulates the opportunities the game offers in general terms for the American public: "It sends its players out in order to return again, allowing all the freedom to accomplish great things in a dangerous world." More than forty years before the late commissioner wrote those words, Robinson was baseball's classic wanderer.

During the decade he played in the National League, Jackie Robinson incarnated that baseball ethic more than any other player who played the game before or since. It was an ethic Robinson grasped in terms of the times in which he and his mentor lived; that is, both understood baseball's greater role in the context of a "free world" defined by the Cold War. Baseball then was seen as speaking to the nation. As Red Smith put it (he didn't change his nickname) in writing about Robinson's trials, the game "was the last place" one should face race prejudice. For this reason, Jackie's success in integrating the game, Smith concluded at the end of the Robinson era in 1956, "was a turning point in the history of the country."

While Robinson would eventually see things far more cynically after he retired, as a player he saw them much as Rickey did, and as Giamatti would later articulate. In his first effort at autobiography in 1949, Robinson explained his belief in America in hopeful terms, and stated that creed in the lingua franca of the Cold War: "Can you sit down in Russia," he asked, "and say the head man is a louse?" No, Robinson answered his own rhetorical query, "not unless you want to play center field in the Siberian League."

Robinson was only restating what most Americans thought, and to an audience for whom the game was more a metaphor for American values than it would ever be again. The *Brooklyn Eagle* summoned up these images often and well. It did so on its editorial pages, for example, after the tough 1952 World Series loss to the Yankees. The Dodgers, the *Eagle* reminded, did "not need to apologize to a soul. In the midst of much cynicism in politics and the world scene generally, baseball does a great job for the people." Both teams "gave everything they had," put on a great show, "in the best American tradition." Baseball, as the "national pastime," thus reached its zenith in postwar America. It emerged a forceful symbol of America as the great hope of the free world in the eyes of a significant portion of the male American public. Robinson both extended and incarnated the promise of expanding freedom implicit in the American post-1945 mindset. That theme turned up often in Jackie's mail.

The first black major leaguer was the recipient of lots of mail, offering encouragement and not a little advice, as well as the better-known hate mail he encountered. Some conventional wisdom imparted by a Jersey City lawyer was representative. "Don't—please don't—look for assistance among the very radical thinkers," Harold McDowell wrote. "Pick a conservative. . . . Enthusiastically endorse our country, our churches, our generosity, our mothers, our youngsters, our schools—and all the rest."

McDowell's shopping list mirrored exactly the majority view in Brooklyn. Advertising exec Jerry Della Femina remembered ethnic Brooklyn in the '50s as "people who . . . go with the union, vote for the right thing, and believe in the American way of life." No question that May 1 was the high-water mark for public expressions of patriotism, at least in Brooklyn. Touted as Loyalty Day in that era, it was intended to exorcise the memory of crowded left-wing May Day parades of the Depression years. Brooklyn excelled beyond all other communities in America in getting out the faithful. An astounding 250,000 marched in 1952, swinging past the reviewing stand at Borough Hall, parading before perhaps a million more fellow Brooklynites. Catholic schools in "the borough of churches" typically contributed legions of youngsters and their schools' marching bands, but so did the public schools and the yeshivas (sans marching bands). *Eagle* columnist Robert Grannis said triumphantly about the parade, "We ain't got enough Commies to stage a parade in Brooklyn. They march in Manhattan. . . ."

The Dodger presence was visible, as team cars carried the players if they were in town. The "Alert America Convoy," as part of the 1952 parade dedicated to civil defense requirements for bomb shelters, was led by Happy Felton, host of the pre-game "Knot-Hole Gang" television show; and he was in a Dodger uniform, bursting at the seams though it was.

Many Brooklyn citizens were perfect fans for Branch Rickey. Their politics were his. In turn, he actively set the political tone of the team, a tone that Walter O'Malley, despite his loathing for his predecessor, gladly perpetuated from 1951 on. Rickey was a patriot of the old school. Speaking at Cooperstown at the groundbreaking for the new Hall of Fame museum in 1949, he reminded listeners that America's heroes "invariably have been military men" who defended flag and country. Rickey longed for peace, he said, and maybe baseball can "furnish the virtues of war" in combat's stead. His own political hero was Herbert Hoover. As "a Dodger and Republican," according to John Lardner, Rickey believed it fitting that Harry Truman of Missouri, of whom the Mahatma "coldly disapproved," was a Cardinals' fan. ("Mahatma" was a nickname the press used to convey Rickey's authoritarian demeanor.) After columnist Jimmy Powers of the *Daily News* executed a journalistic vendetta against Rickey in the late 1940s, it was characteristic of the Dodger president that he branded Powers a "ghastly unAmerican" in retribution.

Rickey was never reluctant about imposing his views on his team (his "boys," as he so often referred to them). He had two versions of his "Americanism" lecture: the long one was delivered at intervals to the Dodgers as a unit, usually at spring training camp at Vero Beach. The short version was saved for individual players in need. Most accepted it as part of Rickey's universal right to influence their lives in a paternal way. The telescoped rendition, for example, was communicated individually to the Dodger petitioners protesting the arrival of Jackie Robinson in 1947. It was used again to convince a reluctant Roy Campanella a year later that St. Paul was a good assignment, for he would be "the first Negro to play in the American Association." Campy privately felt he could do without the "pep talk," but never passed on his reservations about integrating anything to Rickey. Robinson himself was one of those who got the full Americanism lecture at his signing in 1946.

The Dodger front office believed, or professed to believe, as Rickey did. Public relations man Irving Rudd, for example, developed a canned speech touting the Americanism of the Dodgers, position by position. It didn't always succeed as planned. He described Gil Hodges as "Jack Armstrong, the All-American Boy," someone one would be glad to have marry his daughter. But when he delivered his line to a group of Jewish War Veterans, he was reminded that Hodges, whatever his virtues, would not be a welcome groom because he was a "goy."

Given the management's political outlook, it should be no surprise that as the police action in Korea began in 1950, the Dodgers renewed its practice of welcoming servicemen to Ebbets Field. Korean War vets, those disabled in the war, and, eventually, returning prisoners of war, were in turn paid special and very public attention at Ebbets Field. Veterans' organizations of all stripes had their days, including local chapters of the American Legion, Veterans of Foreign Wars, Disabled American Veterans, and Catholic and Jewish veterans' organizations. The team thus showed its fans it supported its men overseas; usually, but not always, it worked out well, both producing good public relations copy and increasing ticket sales via blocs of seats going to participating chapters for sale. Once, however, public relations plans went awry. In 1954, the First Army quartered at Fort Dix designated eight soldiers with the best conduct records to be honored at Ebbets Field. Only five turned up. Three had been arrested the night before for starting a brawl in a Times Square bar. The front-page news story in Brooklyn went heavy on the irony.

In 1951 and for several years after, the Dodgers found a way to do more. After April 1951, when Harry Truman fired him, the Dodgers snared Douglas MacArthur, that colossus of veterans. One of the places the old soldier faded away to was Ebbets Field. Taking up residence at the Waldorf-Astoria Hotel, he quickly became a favorite of Walter O'Malley, who had taken over management of the Dodgers after the 1950 season. MacArthur's hopes for the presidency were dashed by the political tide that swept another military hero, Dwight Eisenhower, into the White House. O'Malley nevertheless saw the visible and glamorous Mac-Arthur as useful in two ways, first as a continuing symbol at Ebbets Field of the Dodger organization's commitment to correct patri-otic values, and second as perhaps the next Commissioner of Baseball. A longtime fan from a distance while serving in the Philippines and later Australia and Japan, MacArthur had also played varsity baseball at West Point in his student years. The Dodger president awarded him permanent free access to an Ebbets Field box.

MacArthur returned to the United States a hero, welcomed in New York by a ticker-tape parade before an enormous crowd in April 1951. O'Malley wasted no time in capitalizing on the general's politics and popularity. Usually, according to Dick Young, Brooklynites "live in their own wonderful little orbit," and would have been more concerned with who played left field, letting "the rest of the world argue about MacArthur." Not this time. The general won over the borough the first time out. Accepting O'Malley's invitation to honor Brooklyn's war veterans, he wowed the crowd and the television audience by using a line provided by Irving Rudd: "Somebody said if you want to see a *real* game of baseball, go over to Ebbets Field, so here I am."

The Old Soldier was "prepared to die with the Dodgers" that day, the *Eagle* reported, and he nearly did. That Dodger serendipity was at work again. The team trailed 12–5 with two outs in the ninth against the Braves, only to score five runs on six straight hits, ending the game short two runs when a wicked line drive was caught. Both Snider and Campanella homered in that rally. Dick Young noted that MacArthur "probably came to the conclusion that old managers never die, they just grow an ulcer." After MacArthur's presidential balloon burst, O'Malley floated the possibility of making the general baseball commissioner. MacArthur briefly allowed the idea to hang in the air before deflating it. "If he isn't making a pitch for the baseball commissionership," the *Daily News* reported, then "he certainly loves baseball."

As it turned out, MacArthur did love baseball. He became a fixture at Ebbets Field over the next several years, helping to forward the team's patriotic agenda. At O'Malley's urging, the soldier marched in Brooklyn's Anniversary Day parade, serving as its "chief reviewing officer." He made a short, jingoistic speech and listened as Brooklyn pols praised the patriotism of a press-exaggerated "100,000" Protestant Sunday school children gathered in the vicinity of the Borough Hall reviewing stand. The general also heard the publisher of the *Eagle* denounce "godless and lawless countries behind the Iron Curtain." Lest anyone think it was all chocolate cake and icing for the dignified chieftain, on at least one occasion he visibly cringed as the Dodger Sym-phony (an amateur band, often described as dissonant, that haunted the park) serenaded him at Ebbets Field with its remarkable rendition of "The Caissons Go Rolling Along." Even taking that hazard into account, MacArthur came away less tarnished by the Ebbets Field experience than did Richard Nixon.

In accord with his own anticommunist political agenda, Walter O'Malley over the years also gave Nixon access to the team. Trying to put his "Checkers" speech behind him, he turned up for a World Series game. Nixon, who had built his career as an anticommunist politician, had had to defend his honesty on national television as a candidate for Vice President in 1952. He did so with his dog "Checkers" sitting nearby. At Ebbets Field weeks later, he posed with Carl Erskine, Jackie Robinson, and Roy Campanella. Even though the players were impressed, some cynical journalists were not. "When I saw Dick Nixon shaking hands with Erskine," a columnist wrote, "I said to myself Carl is paying him a compliment. Nixon isn't in the same league." As if to punctuate that point, the candidate was roundly booed by many fans present. But that was at Yankee Stadium, at a World Series game, where so much of the crowd came from Manhattan. Nixon never encountered that kind of hostility in Brooklyn. A few years later even the circumspect *New York Times* took a swipe at Nixon's perceived insincerity. Still exploiting his relationship with the Dodgers, he accepted an invitation to speak at an on-the-field celebration of Pee Wee Reese's birthday. The Vice President "praised Pee Wee Reese inordinately," the *Times* reported. For the 1955 *Times*, the word "inordinately" in connection with a sitting Vice President was akin to an undeleted expletive today.

Even though the public relations mileage picked up from his invited attentions to the Dodgers may have been tainted on occasion, he did pick up one long-term gain. Nixon made Jackie Robinson a believer who would support Nixon's 1960 presidential bid; the retired Dodger remained a staunch Republican until his death in 1972. Robinson was convinced of Nixon's commitment to civil rights, and at least in his playing days shared his anticommunism. Robinson's politics were, by his own admission later, influenced by two factors. First, he believed deeply during his years on the Dodgers (he would develop reservations later) that the path to black equality lay wholly within the existing political system, not outside it. A religious man, Robinson was also influenced by Branch Rickey's intense rejection of godless communism. Robinson was a political product of his time, one who separated out his passion for integration and social justice from his views on the Cold War.

Robinson shared Rickey's views on the left. Branch Rickey's active hostility to what he saw as the Communist menace reflected not only a more generalized American attitude after World War II but one common to the baseball establishment as well. American anticommunism dated back to the Bolshevik Revolution of 1917. Prewar hard-line domestic antipathy was evident in the "Red Scare" of the 1920s and visceral domestic reaction to the Nazi-Soviet Pact of 1938, to name just two domestic episodes exemplifying deeply felt American animosity to perceived support for the Soviet Union in America. An uneasy alliance with Russia during World War II imposed only a temporary lull in a generalized American rejection of communist ideology. The Cold War went on to make anticommunism a continuing domestic political issue. Robinson, more politically active than his teammates, thought about these things. By 1949, homegrown resistance to the "communist menace" was a life force in Brooklyn, as it was in the rest of America.

Brooklyn first: the borough consciously fought the Cold War. According to the *Eagle,* Brooklyn was shamed in 1950 by its native daughter Judith Coplon, a government employee convicted of attempted espionage for the Soviets. The community's longstanding abhorrence of communism was expressed again by its embarrassment that Julius and Ethel Rosenberg were to be buried in Brooklyn after their execution for espionage in 1953. The *Eagle*'s outraged front-page headline announced, "A-Spies Bodies Here." The funeral took place in Flatbush as 250 policemen, fearing a local riot, kept the peace. Brooklyn saw itself in the trenches in the Cold War, and with the revival of the House Un-American Activities Committee (HUAC), the Dodgers were enlisted, too.

In the late 1940s, even before Senator Joseph R. McCarthy brought political anticommunism to a high art, the House of Representatives Committee did a good job of stirring up a kind of political paranoia in the United States. Both Branch Rickey and Jack Robinson were caught up in the politics of militant anticommunism.

People who opposed or blackened the Mahatma were described as "communist-inspired" or "un-American," as was, for example, *New York Daily News* columnist Jimmy Powers, after he tagged Rickey "El Cheapo." In 1946, as the Cold War deepened, Rickey publicly denounced two St. Louis Cardinal players for their "avowed Communist tendencies" in jumping the club to play for more money in the Mexican League. In 1945–46, Robert Murphy of the CIO successfully organized a baseball local that included most of the Pittsburgh Pirates and small minorities of several other major league clubs. It failed after briefly threatening the reserve clause that bound players to teams as virtual chattel. Rickey helped the failure along by denouncing both Murphy and the offending players as communist-inspired. So by 1949 Rickey was both a doctrinaire and opportunistic foe of the communist menace. He deftly harnessed generalized fears of the day to the interests of organized baseball.

In a speech before the Advertising Club of Baltimore in April 1949, the Dodger president again declared that only those of "avowed communist tendencies" didn't like the reserve clause. Communists, he added, "deeply resent the continuance of our national pastime." Baseball, he concluded, "is a profound sport," and that is why communists hate baseball. To Rickey, by way of explaining the source of his red-baiting, baseball was "a civil religion which acted out in public functions that which organized religion was unable to perform." And for the parochial, Bible-thumping head Dodger, in the political currency of postwar America, communism was nothing less than baseball's godless antithesis. His protégé Larry MacPhail, after their falling out, caught the essence of Rickey's arrogant certitude about all things when he said of Rickey, "There but for the grace of God goes God."

But neither Rickey's brand of conservative politics, nor Rickey himself, can be dismissed so simply, for he also believed in integration and social justice. He was singlehandedly responsible for moving African Americans into organized white ball a full decade earlier than it might otherwise have occurred had he not forced the issue with both wisdom and political acuity.

At the same time, he specifically denied he was a "liberal." "No, no, no," he told an interviewer, "there was no element of liberalism" in bringing Robinson to the majors. Revealingly, he saw himself instead as a moral purist, perhaps a "Sunday School mollycoddle," he said, concurring in another's description of himself. But he heatedly rejected the liberal label. Bringing Robinson to the big leagues was simply the right thing to do, Rickey felt, although he never denied it was also profitable. It was this mindset that caused Rickey to see the HUAC invitation to Jackie as a means of both supporting anticommunist ideology and delivering a blow for black civil rights.

The appearance before the House Un-American Activities Committee on July 18, 1949, met Robinson's goals entirely, at least he thought so initially. He nursed a life-long black anger at second-class citizenship and saw his major league baseball celebrity as providing a stage to help erase race prejudice. Robinson's actions made that clear, and others confirmed it. Rachel Robinson pointed out that an important part of Robinson's difficulties with some sportswriters was simply that "they wanted to talk about the score; he wanted to talk about social issues." Nearly a decade after Robbie's death, Rachel told Robert Curvin that "she would prefer that people would understand that baseball was an arena for Jackie Robinson's fight for racial and social justice." Walter O'Malley, whom Robinson neither liked nor trusted, backhandedly confirmed this. He told an interviewer in 1960, "Jackie has a purpose in life and he is trying to accomplish that purpose in the most effective way possible." O'Malley added sourly, "a great way to attract attention is to get the Dodgers involved somehow. Jackie is an expert in the field of publicity."

Robinson the ballplayer did not see the political left as the friend of African Americans, so his anticommunism was the obverse side of his strong, consistent, and early espousal of civil rights reform. The left could also slap at Robinson. The *Daily Worker* denounced *The Jackie Robinson Story* as "patronizing and offensive," in particular because Robinson, playing himself, allowed others to refer to him as "boy" in the course of the movie.

In the '50s, Robinson believed that America could change, that the political system would work, that whites were educable in matters of race. He did not die believing these things. But in 1949, Robinson denounced communism before HUAC, and that wasn't an isolated instance. He did so at about the same time in a brief life story published under his byline that appeared in the *Brooklyn Eagle.* Later, his response to a critical telegram from the Young Progressives of America was to tear it up in public."I knew they were Communists," he explained afterward to the press, "so I paid no attention." Whatever his reservations about denouncing Paul Robeson before HUAC, Robinson confirmed as late as 1955, "I feel the same way about Communism" as he had in 1949. "Negroes in America were stirred up long before there ever was a

Communist party and . . . they will be stirred up long after the Communist party has disappeared. . . . The Negroes can win their fight against racial discrimination without Communists . . . we don't want their help."

This was borne out in *The Jackie Robinson Story*. A trailer at the end of the film made clear that the Robinson story was one battle in a long war for justice in the free world. The movie, seen four decades later, really goes heavy on "the American way." Baseball as a repository of American virtue, sportsmanship, and fair play forms another theme. "America the Beautiful" is played in the background throughout the movie. *The Jackie Robinson Story*, finally, plays a little havoc with the facts by moving Robinson's HUAC testimony back from 1949 to the end of Jackie's 1947 rookie season.

That movie in fact is a key to Robinson's political mindset in his playing days. That's why he took on Paul Robeson in 1949. Robeson had been an All-American football player at Rutgers. He was in the 1930s and early '40s a nationally known operatic bass vocalist and a budding African American movie star. But by the late 1930s Robeson had also become an outspoken American communist who hoped to use generalized racism, exemplified most graphically in America by lynchings and segregation, as a means of building communist sympathies in the African American community.

Robinson in 1949 feared that Robeson's effort to drive a wedge between white and black America would undermine postwar efforts to challenge segregation and racism. He believed he was a symbol of those efforts, but he was also acutely aware that the Truman administration was attempting to ameliorate segregation in both the military and private industry. Before turning to the Robinson-Robeson contretemps, a word is in order about Robinson's politics in 1949. If Robeson didn't believe America would someday cease to be racist, Robinson did. *The Jackie Robinson Story* stresses that Jackie's breakthrough could happen only in America. But in its anticommunist fervor, it selectively overlooks the conditions over which he triumphed. Since Robinson played himself, I can only assume he understood it to be both potentially useful to African American efforts to end segregation and, at the same time, unapologetic positive propaganda. If Robinson knew the latter—that the movie was a fable—then he was used in the making of it, just as he was manipulated (by his own later admission in this instance) into appearing before HUAC. At least, in the case of the movie, it provided the Robinsons with a good deal of much-needed income.

It was before the House Committee that Robinson's anticommunism was placed in a national spotlight. That was not what Jackie wanted; he longed for a countrywide visible forum to express his resistance to racism while he was at the height of his baseball skills and influence as a symbol of integration. What he got was the national focus on his anticommunism, a much smaller component of his political mindset. Far from muzzling his second baseman (there was no way Robinson would have been muzzled anyway), Rickey, to the consternation of his fellow clubowners, encouraged him to speak out, to employ his fame in the political marketplace. Rickey arranged for Robinson to be invited to testify in order to answer Paul Robeson's allegation that African Americans would never fight for, or shed their blood, in a war against the Soviet Union. According to Rickey's alter-ego Arthur Mann, Rickey even helped draft Robinson's statement, but Robinson later downplayed Rickey's influence. It was written mainly by Jackie, his wife Rachel, and their friend Leslie Granger, black executive secretary of the Urban League.

Robbie admired Robeson, but did not defend him. Instead, after perfunctory reference to Robeson, Robinson used the high-visibility platform to assault racism and push hard for integration. He was doing so, remember, a full decade before any real mainstream public thrust in that direction. In testifying, the ballplayer was militant, articulate, and well ahead of his time. Strip away HUAC auspices, strip away Robbie's lip-service denunciation of communism, strip away his tepid criticism of Robeson, and what remains is an impassioned demand for social justice that was pure Robinson. This was an expression of his life-long commitment to racial equality that never wavered.

In 1988, Hall of Fame player and pioneering Baltimore Orioles manager Frank Robinson dedicated his autobiography to Jackie, noting that long after retirement the ex-Dodger urged

Frank Robinson "to speak out on civil rights issues." It was "particularly important that established players speak out," Jackie Robinson urged. It was advice the Baltimore skipper regretted not taking. Hank Aaron in 1991 echoed much of what Frank Robinson said. In talking about his future, Aaron said, "I'll still be trying to carry on the job that Jackie Robinson started." He may lack Jackie's "vision," Jackie's "voice," but, he said, "I feel it's my task to carry on where Jackie Robinson left off." Both acknowledged that the Dodger pioneer had urged emerging black players to remember who they were, to remember that "the job was never done," that their obligation to remain both politically aware and active never ended.

It is that perspective, the way the next generation of black ballplayers saw Jackie, that made the HUAC public relations failure so poignant. Jackie never intended Robeson to be his target. The expatriate actor only provided Robinson with an excuse for the Dodger to grab the national spotlight. That is why Robinson in time came to regret even his mild assault on Robeson. What he intended, and what he remained proud of to the end of his life, was that he spoke out for "those anguished Negroes still groping for even the smallest place in the sun." His incidental use of the term "silly" in describing Robeson's statement about black Americans not fighting against Russia was taken out of context by the press, marring the moment. It grabbed the headlines, and so "silly" undermined the effectiveness of Robbie's real message, misleading the American public (who were listening) as to the real thrust of the HUAC statement. Robinson, in baseball Brooklynese, wuz robbed. If Jackie differentiated between the issues of segregation and anticommunism, the press chose not to honor his distinctions.

Shortchanging by the press aside, what Robinson had to say about race relations in the U.S. stirred black Americans. It aroused less awareness among American whites than it might have had he not provided an anticommunist handle for the press to grab. His statement, read now in perspective, stands on its own as an early and articulate assault on denial of opportunity and social justice in America by reason of race bias. The statement deserved to see the light of day untainted.

The Dodger second baseman started out his July 18, 1949, appearance by reminding the committee that many Americans who opposed communism also opposed the existence of the committee itself. There were not many Americans in 1949 who could have gotten away with that direct challenge to HUAC's legitimacy, but Robinson was leading the National League in hitting and was on his way to a Most Valuable Player year, so he possessed certain immunities. Jack went on to say that while he was no expert on politics, "you can put me down as an expert on being a colored American with thirty years of experience. . . . I'm not fooled because I've had a chance open to very few Negro Americans." "It's true that I've been a laboratory specimen," but the time has come "to make progress in other American fields besides baseball." Every "single Negro who is worth his salt is going to resent any kind of slurs and discrimination because of his race, and he's going . . . to stop it." This last point was prophetic, and it was said with force. And here his real message got lost: Robinson's virtual demand for social justice, he concluded, "has got absolutely nothing to do with what Communists may or may not be trying to do."

Robinson's fury came through, though it was unreported in the white press. In an age of virulent anticommunism, he suggested, "the American public ought to understand, if we are to make progress . . . [that] because it is a Communist who denounces injustice in the courts, police brutality and lynching, when it happens, doesn't change the truth of the charges." The black star went on to affirm his own loyalty, but added, "that doesn't mean that we are going to stop fighting discrimination in this country until we've got it licked." This kind of militant public statement was unheard of from mainstream African Americans at the time; given its auspices, it was almost revolutionary. Robinson died believing correctly that his testimony had done some good in educating Americans to the realities of race prejudice.

But almost immediately after the press returns were in, he regretted (and would always continue to rue) his assault on Paul Robeson. The actor, from his exile in Paris, told reporters that HUAC would "do better to summon any of the millions of Negroes who are suffering from unemployment, privation and oppression, rather than some who, like Robinson, have no complaints." Robinson realized that he had been had. Only weeks later, when the Queens chapter of the Catholic War Veterans presented him with a plaque extolling his patriotic testimony, Robinson accepted the award *under* the stands. Ambivalence characterized his feelings about the event until his death. In his 1957 valedictory announcing his retirement, he strongly defended his HUAC appearance, as he had in 1955. Three years later, though, Carl Rowan's authorized biography, one on which Robinson had collaborated, carried Robeson's criticism and Robinson's implied concurrence in the expatriate's response. Around 1970, left-wing author Howard Fast asked Robinson at a party why he testified against Robeson. Jack responded, "If Mr. Rickey at that time had asked me to jump headfirst off the Brooklyn Bridge, I would have done it." That was regret. It may have contributed to the nearly defensive title of his final autobiography, *I Never Had It Made*, published in 1972, months before he died. Even as some were labeling Robinson a "fanatic on the issue of racial equality," Jack was kicking himself for coming down on Robeson.

In the end, Robinson felt bad. Even before testifying, Jackie acknowledged in 1972, "I knew that Robeson was striking out against racial inequality in the way that seemed best to him. However, in those days I had much more faith in the ultimate justice of the American white man than I have today." He apologized: "I do have an increased respect for Paul Robeson who, over the span of twenty years, sacrificed himself, his career, and the wealth and comfort he once enjoyed because, I believe, he was sincerely trying to help his people." Robinson added that if he had to do it over again, he wouldn't have come before HUAC. This sad note at the end of his life suggests the degree of frustration Robinson experienced as he attempted to use his baseball career in the interest of social justice. His triumphal tour through the national game occurred only at a public level. The private political reality was another story.

If Robinson had his doubts about the HUAC appearance, most Brooklyn denizens must have loved it. Loyalty Day parades like that of 1952 were solid demonstrations, if any were needed, of the majority's committed anticommunism. The *Eagle* routinely reinforced anticommunist militancy in the borough with its rhetoric. In particular, it often offered up the Dodger team as an example of all that was right and good in America. "When Gladyce Goodding sings The Star Spangled Banner as a curtain raiser to a baseball game at Ebbets Field," columnist Bob Grannis wrote in 1951, every spectator "is conscious of his membership in the world's greatest fraternity of freedom-loving people," Americans thankful not to be in "Stalin's Russia." As Brooklynites awaited the start of the 1952 World Series, a cartoon showed the Series crowding all the pressing problems of the world to the corner of the picture; only the forbidding visage of Joe Stalin remained prominently in caricature on a depicted horizon. Even the World Series could not prevent awareness of Uncle Joe, ever watchful, on the perimeter of the American horizon. *Eagle* sportswriter Robert Murphy laid it on the line: "If the poor saps who fall for the Commie bunk," he wrote, "could only get a peep at the way Americans go about friendly strife" on the diamond, "they would run Joe Stalin and his Yes Men off a cliff." This was routine rhetoric in what amounted to a hometown paper, the gargantuan size of the borough notwithstanding.

The left-wing reaction in Brooklyn was just as revealing. It was home to a fairly visible minority of ethnics on the left: Jews committed to socialist labor-oriented Zionism and trade unionism; radicalized Italian families militantly pro-union, many still mourning the injustice done Sacco and Vanzetti a generation before. Other pockets of left sympathizers existed here and there, but lacking the density of the above groups. Even among Jews and Italians, radical elements constituted only a small percentage of their numbers. Brownsville, for example, a largely Jewish neighborhood, offered up huge moderate Democratic majorities at each election. Only a visible and vocal minority found its way to the Workmen's Circle or Industrial Worker's Order organizations, or to left-wing CIO locals.

How did Brooklyn fans accommodate to the right-wing orientation of the Dodger club? Easily. A large majority of fans either agreed with the team's politics, or were only dimly aware of it. But Robinson was not the only Republican-in-the-making on the club. Brooklynite Chuck Connors, up for only a brief stay, was later "active in Republican and conservative causes." It was an era when, Robinson aside, players didn't at all publicize their leanings, but as in the case of Connors, a later hint turns up. Take pitcher Billy Loes, for another example. In the '60s he was disgusted that "they got guys playing today with earrings in their ear. If I was still pitching, I'd throw one in their earring." Manager Charley Dressen in 1952 more or less used the "Rosenberg analogy" in talking about any highly touted rookie who fails: "If he doesn't come through he's treated as though he sold the atomic bomb to the Russians." There is no evidence that any Dodger in that era was even mildly left of center.

As for those fans on the left, psychologist Howard Senzel offers a fairly clinical explanation as to why politically radical individuals can retain deep partisan commitment to a team they knew to be right-wing. "The resistance to either the 'frivolity' of baseball," Senzel wrote, "its being touted as the 'national pastime,' or even its presence in the American arsenal against the Soviet Union in the Cold War," would not compute for most left baseball partisans. "The evidence is that there are depths beyond which an intellectual process cannot go" in the human mind. "The evidence is that there are aspects of your own identity so strongly established that they cannot be penetrated by conviction, not to mention thought. These are things about our own identity that we cannot alter by decision. And baseball is one of these things."* Conclusion: no matter what your politics, and intellectualizing aside, if you were a kid living in Brooklyn after World War II, you were going to be a Dodger fan. Unless, that is, you were going to grow up as iconoclastically as Woodrow Allen Koenigsberg (Woody Allen), and choose to be a Yankee fan in Brooklyn.

How to test this hypothesis about baseball and politics? Interestingly, two nostalgic 1990s Brooklyn Dodger-centered novels unknowingly play off Senzel's baseball-Cold War thesis: Alan Lelchuk's *Brooklyn Boy* (1990), and Mark Lapin's *Pledge of Allegiance* (1991). "Aaron" (Lelchuk) and "Josh" (Lapin) are alle-

---

*This is the *simple* explanation. For the complex construction, see the notes.

gorical characters, Brooklyn boys from 1950s left-wing families. The integrated, virtuous Dodgers provide the basic storyline for both novels.

In Lelchuk's *Brooklyn Boy*, Aaron's father has forbidden his son from going to Ebbets Field. He has also barred Aaron from seeing Harry, a wounded war veteran who has befriended the young boy. Harry clandestinely took Aaron to see the Dodgers play anyway. "Narishkeit" (foolishness), that's what baseball was, according to the radical immigrant father. On one occasion the parent offers an alternative, taking his son to see a Soviet film screened in a Brooklyn theater. The background music "was that patriotic chanting of the Red Army Chorus." Aaron:

> I sat low in my seat, despite my father's protestations. . . . Gradually, in place of the somber Russian chorus, I began to hear the cheerier sounds of Gladys's organ, and instead of the snowy war front, to see a green baseball diamond splashed by sunlight. And sure enough, there was Jackie, in his white flannels with "Dodgers" written in blue across his chest. . . .

Baseball, as American as it gets, willfully replaced the alien Red influence in the boy's mind. In the happy ending, of course, Aaron comes to understand and assimilate both cultures.

Josh's story, in Mark Lapin's *Pledge of Allegiance*, was a much different one. But the basic theme was the same. Josh is an alienated Brooklyn boy in a family of Communist party activists in the McCarthy era. Josh's communist father is hiding from the FBI. A clandestine agent befriends the boy by helping him improve his baseball skills and, ultimately, takes him to Ebbets Field in return for the promise of information on his father's whereabouts. The temptation is great: A visit with Pee Wee Reese in the Dodger dugout, the locker room after the game, the promise of a team-autographed ball. In the end, the boy escapes through the allegorical subterranean labyrinth of Ebbets Field, no information revealed. Josh, finally, did not become an FBI informant.

Once again, the same premise manifests itself as it had in Lelchuk's novel. The Dodgers form an anchor of moderate conservative political influence in a leftist miniworld made alien by the McCarthyism of the 1950s. Baseball, the national game, comes to the rescue of a forlorn, lonely Red Diaper kid. In the end, Dale, the FBI agent, taken with Josh despite his failure to extort information on the father's hiding place, stops his car alongside the boy weeks later. Dale reaches out of the car, tosses Josh an autographed ball, calls out "Thanks for nothing, kid," and drives off into the Brooklyn sunset. Allegorically, of course, for sunsets are privileged sights in Brooklyn, even for FBI agents.

In both books everyone is a hero: the alienated kids, the leftist fathers, even the FBI agent in Lapin's book, and the wounded veteran in Lelchuk's novel. But the ultimate political heroes in both these 1950s Brooklyn morality plays are—you guessed it— "Da Bums,"—the familiar name for the Dodgers.

It is remarkable the degree to which the Dodgers absorbed, and are later seen to mirror, the politics of their time. Did other teams do so? If so, to what degree? It is not only that the politics of the Cold War permeated the team at all levels; that, perhaps, is to be expected. It might even be reasonable to assume that a baseball team like the Dodgers would find an active political place in the community, as the Dodgers certainly did. But why would two novels a generation later see the team as so central to the political lives of those male youngsters whose home-induced values were mostly the opposite of the Dodger reality? It seems that the Dodger team provided a politically defining context for the Brooklyn community.

3

The Dodgers' Male Culture:
The New York Rivalries

On a Sunday in September, 1953, Carl Furillo stepped into the batter's box. He heard, as he often did when the Dodgers played the Giants, the "sweet voice" of Leo Durocher yelling, "Stick it in his ear." Reuben Gomez came close; his pitch hit Furillo on the wrist. The Dodger right fielder trotted down to first, touched the bag, then veered right, headed for the Giants' dugout. Bowling over several surprised Giants, he reached Leo, knocked him down, and piled on. "Furillo is on top of Durocher," Duke Snider has written, "with his fingers around his throat." Another eyewitness noted, "You could see Durocher's bald head start to turn purple." Babe Pinelli, on top of the situation as an umpire should be, rushed over and, standing astride the two combatants, yelled, "Kill him, Carl, kill him." Among the mass of Giant players who finally pulled Furillo off, outfielder Monte Irvin, maybe accidentally, stepped on Furillo's hand and broke his finger. Payback signified in the world of professional baseball.

The incident revealed basic male themes common to baseball. Physical challenge and response, redemption of the male ego, attempts to intimidate, to provoke a failure of manhood. These were all parts of a self-fulfilling baseball tableau played out very close to the surface in New York City in the decade after World War II.

Consistent failure is universal in major league baseball. Everyone failed often in the long season. A team playing .600 ball, losing two for every three won, would win 92 games a season, a number that often guaranteed a pennant. In that sense, every team failed. The Dodgers failed less than any other team in the big leagues, save for the Yankees, during the postwar decade. Yet their failures were more visible and closely scrutinized than those of any other men. The team was more vulnerable than other teams for three reasons: it played in New York with its intensive media coverage and successful local rivals; it pioneered integration and was closely examined for evidence of choking on racial grounds; and, most important, the Dodgers were flawed winners, failing in full sight each October—against the Phillies in 1950, the Giants in 1951, and repeatedly, until 1955, against the Yankees. At stake, as we shall see, was Dodger manhood. That the Dodgers were in post-season play almost every October between 1946 and 1956 (except for 1948 and 1954) was in itself evidence of remarkable skill, fortitude, maturity, and success. It almost didn't matter. The myths the players lived with, fostered by the press, fans, and management alike, did matter.

Brooklyn masculinity was tested often and in many ways on the diamond, especially when the Dodgers confronted the other New York teams. Even sophisticated ballplayers succumbed. Among the most articulate and urbane Dodgers, Carl Erskine affirmed that when playing the Giants, "your manhood seemed to be on the line." Clem Labine, another smart, introspective pitcher, before shutting out the Giants in game two of the 1951 playoffs, said, "This is the day when I find out whether I'm a man or a boy." Young Don Drysdale, who joined the team at the very end of the Brooklyn era, was known as a pitcher who would, as Hank Aaron said, "test your manhood" by throwing at batters. Gil Hodges's slump in 1953 has been portrayed in fiction as a tragedy deeper than baseball: it was said that it robbed him of his manhood. The fans' sympathetic response would "restore it to him."*

---

*Hodges' slump, and the community's response, is dealt with in Chapter Seven.

Jackie Robinson's effectiveness as a player rested in part on his ability to undermine the egos of his opponents by directly challenging them as men. Casey Stengel acknowledged this in cleverly motivating the Yankees on the eve of the 1949 season. After the team dropped three straight exhibition games to the Dodgers, in part because of Robinson's base running, Casey told his team: "All you guys, when you get into the locker room I want you to check your lockers. He stole everything out there he wanted today so he might have stolen your jocks as well."

Jackie's identification with proving one's manhood was a big part of his ordeal, as his fan letters reveal. It was the single greatest theme among the letters of support he received in 1947. A white southerner wrote to say he believed the black Dodger would be "man enough to shoulder" the challenges faced. A Catholic priest in New York knew that Jackie would have to be "little short of superman" to make it through his 1947 hell, but also knew he would make it. A Jewish accountant congratulated Robinson for accepting the male challenge, "following a man's career." A black machinist ended a letter of encouragement by adding he hoped his son would be "half the man that you are." Robinson understood the symbolism, gently chiding the machinist in his response, "Don't you think your boy could be just as good a man if I don't make it?" Even Red Barber fell into the male trap, remembering later that he overcame his own southern prejudice by remembering to treat Robinson "as a man."

As we have seen, a test of Carl Furillo's manhood would likely be met by his fists. It was not an isolated reaction in the right fielder's case. When his friend and road roommate Tommy Brown wouldn't turn off a light when asked, "Furillo was on him like a gorilla" and beat the benchwarmer so badly he had to be hospitalized. Naturally, Harold Parrott was told to keep it out of the papers, so the assault was blamed on an anonymous "jealous boyfriend." Writers with the team looked at that male explanation (mostly unprintable in the '50s) with suspicion, but they ran the cover story with minimum innuendo anyway, enough of the latter so that their mostly male readers could nudge each other about the report on the subways as they went to work. Furillo was an enigma. Inarticulate and moody, he seemed intermittently to fill the male animal stereotype. No other Dodger regular did.

As the other extreme, after Bobby Thomson's home run effectively ended Ralph Branca's baseball career in the 1951 Dodgers-Giants playoff game, a priest told the troubled and sensitive pitcher, "God chose you because He knew you had faith and strength enough to bear this cross." Of Branca's handling of this humiliation, sportswriter Harold Rosenthal said: "What a man!" Macho values in all their forms permeated the baseball lives of the Dodgers, from the sensitive Branca to the crude Furillo. None knew this better than Giants' manager Leo Durocher. He saw to it that the core of the teams' rivalry in the 1950s directly involved tests of manhood.

"Have You Hoid, Moitle? It's Moider! Our Leo Has Jerned the Jints!!" Headlines like this, some in English, shocked New York's baseball fans in midsummer of 1948. The event opened a new chapter in the Dodger-Giant rivalry. Macho posturing on both sides reached new heights and focused attention on the two dominant National League teams of the '50s. Durocher was the master of baseball psychology. After the overnight move, he endeavored to undercut Dodger manhood at every turn. He had the smarts and the beanball artists to do it. The Dodgers, with an awesome array of hitters, were both the best bench jockeys in the game, unmanning the opposition with taunts, and masters of the body block at first and second bases. Brooklyn could give as good as it got.

Leo's 1991 obituary noted that the hallmark of his baseball leadership was "heavy reliance on psychological intimidation of the enemy . . . sharp spikes, beanballs and umpire-baiting." Durocher played the game with as much intensity as anyone in baseball ever did, whether on the bench managing or between the baselines playing. "Leo would cut his own mother's throat to win a ball game." Durocher himself said that each game was a "war." He recognized in Robinson a kind of hated doppelganger, one whom he would want on his side if he ever went to war. But the two despised each other in those years Durocher managed the Giants. Theirs was a "bitter relationship," Duke Snider said. "They went at each other with a vengeance."

After one riotous confrontation, Durocher called Robbie a "bush player." Robinson responded to the press that if that were so, he "learned bush play from a bush manager." "Leo hated

Jackie," Roy Campanella claimed. "It was probably not racial," the Dodger catcher concluded, "it was based on the fact that Jackie and Leo were two of the most fierce competitors I ever saw." Robinson, who played angry, would bait Durocher by taunting him about his actress-wife Laraine Day. He would sniff the air while Durocher coached at third, shouting, "Leo, I can smell Laraine's perfume." Once, when the Giant manager lost it after that routine, Durocher made a gesture and shouted, "My dick to you." Robinson barked back, "Give it to Laraine, she needs it more than I do." The Dodger infielder habitually called Durocher "pussy" to his face. The two behaved on the field, according to a reporter, "like a couple of kids." Robinson was at least Leo's equal in any macho confrontation.

Durocher was only one of several Giants Robbie hectored. He would prod Giants' catcher Sal Yvars to impotent rage by signaling him when he was going to run, then taunting him after the steal. Robinson, Duke Snider wrote, was one of the few players he ever saw who "could beat you with his mouth." On the base paths, he could take someone out with a body block, but it was his words that caused male rage to explode on the field, part of a deliberately macho style the Dodger adopted.

In a 1953 game, for example, Jack rode Tookie Gilbert, a rookie, for the entire game. In the sixth, with men on base in a close game, Robinson telegraphed from third base the first two pitches, shouting for Gilbert to watch out for the fastball. Gilbert, not believing, swung late at both pitches. Jackie yelled that one more was on the way. Gilbert finally believed, and swung at and missed the curve by a foot. Gilbert threw his bat and cap at the bench, screamed and gestured obscenely at Robinson, who just laughed. "Sure I needled him," Robbie said later. "Nothing says you can't needle a player."

No wonder Durocher told a reporter in August 1951: "I'd rather beat those guys than anything else in the world." He found the perfect instrument to do so that year in the person of Sal Maglie, whose best pitch was the beanball. He made macho intimidation of the Dodgers an art form. A misconception about beanballs (in an era before the batting helmet was much used) is that they were meant to frighten. That sometimes was true, but major leaguers knew that they could never let that happen. Anger, rabid male anger, was Maglie's goal. Speaking later of Campanella and Furillo in particular, but really of the entire "murderous lineup" the Dodgers fielded, "The Barber" boasted "down he'd go, and all the Dodgers would start screaming. They'd get so damn angry they'd try to kill me with home runs— be the big heroes—and they'd break their backs swinging at bad balls. They didn't get anything. I had their number." At the risk of being obvious, Maglie's nickname was based on his reputation for applying close shaves.

In the words of a bard:

> In Ebbets Field I'd watch
> Sal "The Barber" Maglie train
> his batter with a hard one at the head
> for the next pitch.

Over the years, Maglie played on Dodger nerves to perfection. Robinson's ability to bunt gave him pause, but it didn't stop him from throwing at Jackie. Knocked down twice by Maglie at the beginning of the 1951 season, Robinson succeeded in forcing Maglie to field a bunt near the base line; he body-blocked the pitcher into foul territory. For a brief moment, Maglie came up looking for a fight, according to witnesses, but as Robinson advanced, Sal quickly took refuge behind the umpire.

Four years later, in 1955, after being decked by Maglie, Robinson bunted and, head down, chugged into first base. Thinking Maglie was covering, Robbie threw a crushing football block. It seriously injured Giant second baseman Davey Williams, who covered first when Maglie wouldn't "put himself within range of Robinson." The latter only discovered after the play that he had gotten the wrong Giant. A few innings later, with Robinson playing third, Giant Alvin Dark, like Robinson a former college football player, stretched a double into an attempted triple in order (successfully) to pay Robinson back. A fight was quickly broken up by the umpires.

As a matter of longstanding practice, Maglie wouldn't merely throw the usual brush-back inside pitches. "His were unmistakable bean balls." They "sailed behind the batter's head," so that "the involuntary flinch backward" was likely to result in a "serious skulling." Maglie remained "contemptuous" of the Dodgers until the moment he joined them in time to help the team win the 1956 pennant. It was then that he taught rookie Don Drysdale the uses of the beanball, a lesson that helped the intimidating pitcher to reach the Hall of Fame. "It's not the first one," Maglie instructed, "it's the second one. The second one makes the hitter know you meant the first one." Forty years later, Henry Aaron vividly recalled that Drysdale had learned that lesson well, subjecting Aaron, by then widely considered a dangerous hitter, to two straight knock-down pitches.

Roy Campanella and Carl Furillo were Maglie's favorite targets. Both would lose their tempers, not only making them easier to handle at the plate, but breaking the concentration of the other Dodgers as well. Campanella's reputation as an easy-going, good-natured ballplayer is an error. He was a prime target of many Giant pitchers, including Maglie, Larry Jansen, Ruben Gomez, and, briefly, Hal Gregg. Maglie wrote that at a typical team meeting to go over the hitters, when Campanella's name came up, Maglie simply announced, "Campanella's going down on the first pitch."

Carl Furillo was hit on the head by pitched balls six times in his career, hit elsewhere many more times, and thrown at too often to count. His habit of crowding the plate and his ability to hit in the clutch were factors, but the most important reason was that Furillo "becomes murderously mad when he suspects he's being thrown at." Durocher, playing on the Dodger outfielder's temper, often shouted "stick it in his ear" from the dugout just to distract him. Giant hurlers occasionally obliged, none more so than Maglie. On one occasion in 1953, Furillo was sent down by Maglie and on the next pitch swung and missed deliberately, throwing his bat "viciously" at the mound, hitting the pitcher in the shin. Dodger pitchers Joe Black, Billy Loes, Clem Labine, and Don Newcombe regularly threw at Giant batters, but with nowhere near the killer intensity that Durocher demanded of the Giants' mound staff.

Dodger regulars learned to look after themselves. Once in 1953, after Duke Snider was knocked down, both he and Jackie

Robinson bunted in succession toward first, trying to nail the Giants' Larry Jansen. It didn't matter so much that the two didn't succeed; the message had been returned. Battles between the two teams sold tickets in part because the rivalry in the Durocher years brought male egos on the field right to the surface for the fans. For the Dodgers, that male ego was never more on the line than in 1952, the year following the two end-of-season failures to win the pennant.

Did the Dodgers choke in '50 and '51? In the dictionary "choking" means "to perform poorly because of tension"; in its baseball essence it is a failure of nerve. The connotation, according to two psychologists I consulted, basically refers to male sexuality, for example, a man "choking" in the midst of the sex act, unable to perform. The choking insult, then, perhaps the most devastating in sports, is one that strikes at the very heart (or something) of the male athlete's usually sensitive ego.

On the last day of the 1950 season, the Dodgers failed to score the winning run late in the game, when Cal Abrams was thrown out at the plate trying to score from second on a line single to center by Duke Snider. Brooklyn lost the game and the pennant in the tenth inning on a homer by Dick Sisler, a less famous hit than Bobby Thomson's, but one no less damaging. The Giants' more celebrated win in 1951 really placed the Brooklyn team on the spot in 1952. The Dodgers responded to Leo's psychological goading, the press's relentless second-guessing, and even broad hints of male gutlessness on the team by the Dodger manager by winning the pennant. Baseball in general looked for the Dodgers to fold in 1952. They didn't.

Both the 1952 and 1953 teams have been retrospectively perceived as among the great clubs of all time.* But the '52 Dodgers played under exquisite pressure and should get the edge (along with the 1955 Dodgers, of course). George Will called the '52

---

*Differences between the '52 and '53 teams were almost nominal. The pitching was virtually unchanged. Joe Black in '53 did not duplicate his 1952 achievements, but Russ Meyer picked up the slack. Among the regulars, Andy Pafko (who had a good year in 1952) was traded. To some degree new players Wayne Belardi and Don Thompson helped the Dodgers compensate for the loss of Pafko. Otherwise, the '52 and '53 teams were identical.

club "one of the great teams in history." Both manager Charley Dressen and Carl Erskine see the '53 team (with 105 wins) as the best of the Brooklyn teams. Perhaps Neil Sullivan's post-mortem said it best. The Dodgers of the 1950s generally were "a team too good to merit despair but not quite able to fulfill the aspirations of its followers. Had Tantalus received his punishment in the 1950s, he would have been sent to Brooklyn."

Even the most frustrated Dodger fans had to feel good about the 1952 pennant. The male-laden "choke" factor was right out there all season long, from all sides. The New York press knew a good story when it saw one. Dick Young of the *Daily News* started the talk, and remained a major goad all season. After the 1950 loss to the Phillies, he wrote a clever (and cruel) story around the theme that "the tree that grows in Brooklyn is an apple tree." The Dodgers "took the apple," that is, they were "a bunch of chokers." Arthur Daley of the *Times* virtually dined out on the story in 1952. He started out mildly on July 4, noting in his column that "the Dodgers have a commanding lead and can't miss. Or can they?" On August 23, he raised the possibility that the Flock once again could "blow the pennant . . . nothing is impossible." Early in September, before the anxious Dodgers turned the corner, the influential columnist reminded his readers that Dodger fans should "count no more chickens until they are not only hatched but cooked and on the table." Dodger manhood was openly on the line.

Even the partisan *Brooklyn Eagle* was not immune. After a tough early loss to the Giants, the usually sycophantic Harold Burr wrote that the Dodgers were "beginning to crack up." Tommy Holmes, a good newspaperman and, of course, uncrowned king of Brooklyn fans because he had the hometown column, felt it by August. "Do your knees knock together," he asked. "Do your feet feel icy? . . . Then you know how a hawk-harried ball club feels—and how the Dodgers looked in yesterday's matinee." In another column he queried, "What happens if the Dodgers zoom into one of their patented nervous breakdowns?" The Dodgers read these stories, and so did Leo the Lip. Durocher, smelling blood and taking every macho psychological advantage, provided an answer.

"If we can pull this one out," Leo told the press early in September, "there will be 100,000 suicides in Brooklyn." He worked the Dodgers' male egos through New York reporters as early as July. Talking often about anything being possible, even though the Dodgers led by ten games, he promoted columns like that in the *Times* headed "Can Leo Do It Again?" He arranged to have his "Day" on the occasion of a Dodger visit to the Polo Grounds in early August; the Brooks had to sit through a graphic and excruciating reminder of the '51 loss as Leo was honored. Few ever claimed major league baseball is known for its good taste. The "Day," however, was part of a smart game plan. As pressure peaked in early September, Dodger captain Pee Wee Reese intervened. Asked baldly about the possibility of another "fabulous foldup," he responded with the reserve that was his hallmark: "There's no reason for alarm, the fellows on the club feel confident of winning." But with the lead cut to six games on September 6, there was cause for alarm, and it came in the form of a Trojan Horse in the Dodger dugout.

Charley Dressen, Red Smith once observed, "has a gift for saying and doing graceless things on important occasions." In the first week of September, his article "The Dodgers Won't Blow It Again!" hit the newsstands. This judgment on the propensity for macho failure on the part of "his boys" was right out there in the *Saturday Evening Post* for the entire nation to read. In claiming to want to pump up his team for the stretch just before a crucial five-game series with the Giants, he exposed his players to renewed fan suspicions about their choke-prone qualities.

The article reflected on the Dodgers' collective manhood. The reality that this was a team with several key black players, whose fortitude (a manifestation of manhood) was suspect generically in parts of America, should not be dismissed as a motive for soliciting and ghosting the article. Dressen promised that his boys would prove they weren't "chicken-hearted bums." The press response was instantaneous. Calling Dressen "the Hemingway of the Diamond," Arthur Daley tore into the manager: "What's that Charley? Speak a little louder please. It almost sounds as though you said that your staggering heroes cannot miss this time." Tommy Holmes pointed out that it was the kind of incendiary piece to post in the Giants' locker room to pique *their* manhood. Although publicly claiming only a desire to motivate his charges, Dressen privately acknowledged that he put his name to the article ghosted by Stanley Frank for "the three grand I received." It was, he said, "found money. If the Dodgers lose this year, I'll be fired anyway." Dressen cynically played havoc with his team's collective male psyche, and initially it showed.

Still stunned on the day after the article appeared, the Dodgers dropped a doubleheader to the Giants on September 6. The team played badly at this opening of the five-game series at the Polo Grounds. But the Dodgers did believe in themselves and, whatever happened in the clubhouse after the twin losses, they rebounded and played the rest of the series as if they were starting a three-game set. The Dodgers' lead was down to four games with twenty-five to go when they took the field on the evening of September 7. They took two of the three remaining games and never looked back. Preacher Roe won 4–1 on September 7, and Joe Black pitched eight innings of shutout ball in relief on the following day. Billy Loes pitched well in the last game of the series, but lost 3–2. Still, the Brooks had pushed their lead back up to five games.

Pitching aside, it was Gil Hodges's intensity and sheer power to intimidate that provided the spark. Hodges, usually an imperturbable player, one who revealed no emotion on the field, had been thrown at by Giant pitchers from the beginning of Durocher's tenure as manager. In this, of course, he differed not at all from other Dodger regulars. Facing Maglie in the critical third game on September 7, having dropped two the previous day and watched the lead shrink to four games, a "nervous" Roe gave up a run in the first. That was the Dodgers' low point of the season—probably the low point of the postwar decade. In the second, Hodges, "pale with tension," according to witness Roger Kahn, drove a Maglie curve into the upper deck in left to tie the score. Maglie threw at Robinson the next inning, and Roe hit Monte Irvin in the fourth. By that time, however, Maglie had given up two more homers to Reese and George Shuba. Reese had the day before assured Dodger fans the "fellows" wouldn't fold; as always, he put his ability where his mouth was. Hodges, meanwhile, wasn't finished. In the eighth he sent a message to Leo and the Giants when he "took out" the ever unfortunate Davey Williams with a vicious body block on a slight ballplayer playing second. Williams was helped off the field with an injured back, out for a week.

The next day Hodges was repaid. Hoyt Wilhelm hit him with a pitch in the fifth inning. On first and murderously angry, Hodges, the physically strongest of the Dodgers, launched himself at a Giant for the second day in a row. This time he took out substitute second baseman Bill Rigney on a double play grounder, intentionally spiking him and opening a three-inch gash on his calf. Like Williams, Rigney was put out of action for a week, leaving Durocher to patch together an infield from the remains of his bench in the midst of a pennant race.

Monte Kennedy, another Giant pitcher, threw at Hodges and Joe Black in the seventh, sending them into the dirt but not hitting them. Larry Jansen did better, hitting Andy Pafko an inning later. Joe Black, meanwhile, had been sending Giants down all game, and both teams were officially warned in the eighth. When Jansen hit Billy Cox with a pitch in the ninth, both the Giant pitcher and Durocher were thrown out of the game. It was obvious by then that Leo had gone too far in his frustration in failing to put the Dodgers away. The Giants this time around had seized a tiger by the tail.

The Dodgers had long since secured the game, finally winning 10–2. In a patented display of Dodger power, for the second day in a row, Cox, Furillo, and Snider all hit home runs in a game in which the Dodgers collected thirteen hits. Brooklyn played .700 ball down the stretch and won the pennant going away. In the National League, at least, there was no more talk of choking.

A word about Gil Hodges's and baseball's male ethos. Hodges was an ex-Marine who, in his teens, fought in some of the major battles of the South Pacific. There isn't much question that his male acculturation was honed by both his Marine experience and professional baseball's macho code of honor. His anger surfaced on those two September days. Provoked, he physically hurt two Giants in twenty-four hours. In perspective, one would not have been surprised if violence-prone Carl Furillo was named here; that it was a much more thoughtful, college-educated and normally controlled Gil Hodges suggests the degree to which Dodger manhood was stung by a general expectation that the team would experience a failure of nerve. Challenged this way, the Dodgers responded as a team and achieved a partial redemption in ridding itself of the "choke" label hung on it.

It took a while longer to beat the "October choke" tag hung on the Flock by the Yankees. Objectively, the Dodger-Yankee World Series were cumulatively exciting, offering good and occasionally great baseball. Objectively, the teams usually went the limit: seven games in 1947, 1952, 1955, and 1956. In 1953, the Dodgers, down two games, made it a six-game series. Only 1949 was a disaster. Objectively, as Yankee second baseman Jerry Coleman said, the Dodgers lost simply because the team lacked enough good pitching in a short series. "They were all-stars, the Dodgers," Coleman said, at every position. "With a couple more starting pitchers—they would have been completely unbeatable." Arthur Daley and many others echoed the judgment about the pitching gap. "The Brooklyn pitching staff seems sounder for the long pull of a pennant race, but how about a short series," Daley wrote in 1953. Objective truths did not apply to Yankee-Dodger baseball.

On the one hand, the very real Yankee mystique was at work; on the other, the Dodgers were spooked. Brooklyn couldn't help but be aware of fan feeling before 1955. Don Honig (a fan and later a baseball writer) put it well, however unvarnished and painful the truth: "You rooted for this team, and every October it would die. . . . Dodger fans very well knew the sentiments of the mythical Man on the Street. He knew that it was said that the Dodgers choked every October, and what the hell were you going to say? They did lose every October." Macho vindication came only in 1955: "We had beaten the Yankees and we were better men for it." Bill Reddy (a fan) echoed both the sentiment and the male ethic. When, in an October bar room "dialogue" about the Series, a Yankee fan needled, "You Goddamn Dodgers, you lay down like dogs," Reddy "popped him in the mouth."

Inevitably, the Dodgers were vaguely defensive except for Robinson. "As far as the two teams were concerned," Clem

Labine told Peter Golenbock, "we were equal. Just the outcome was unbalanced." Carl Erskine, usually painfully honest, dissimulated a little, not admitting but not denying the Yankee jinx. "We knew we weren't playing Pittsburgh. . . . We didn't go into those Series other than with good professional confidence that we were going to do it." After losing the first two games of the '55 Series, however, Jackie Robinson laid it on the line: "We gotta win this one. If we lose again, they'll be calling us choke-up guys the rest of our lives. Do we want that?" Perhaps framing it so baldly broke the mold for the Dodgers. Anyway, they won four of the next five games, and the World Series. It was a response not dissimilar to the five-game 1952 series against the Giants.

The Yankee mystique was formidable. The *Brooklyn Eagle*'s editorial writer described it well for the faithful before the 1952 Series. "Maybe the Yankees are professional World Series players. Perhaps . . . they cast a spell over the opponents and give them the jitters before the battle gets fairly under way. But there comes a day. . . ." That day didn't come in 1952, although it was close. "The Bombers," John Drebinger claimed, always possessed "a psychological edge" in these encounters. By 1955, he added, "the pressure has never been greater." Casey Stengel subtly raised the psychological ante from time to time. With the Series tied after game four in 1953, the Dodgers claimed, picking up echoes of Leo Durocher, to have heard Stengel "order Vic Raschi to 'stick it in his ear' while pitching to Roy Campanella. After the game Stengel told the press, "I'm not interested in what the Brooklyn players say or in their opinions. . . . I'm fed up. The Dodgers have been crying all year. That's what they are—cry babies. . . . All season long I've been hearing and reading about somebody trying to kill the Brooklyn ball players. Well, they're still alive." Macho needling was also active in the Bronx. In 1955, however, even Casey may have gone too far. "Don't worry," he told reporters on the eve of the confrontation, "the Yankees always take care of the Series." That had to be posted in the Dodgers' clubhouse.

Robert Creamer officially put the "Yankee Jinx" to bed in *Sports Illustrated* after the '55 victory. The seventh game was the most important win ever for the Brooklyn team (a 2–0 shutout by Johnny Podres). "It was undeniably historic," Creamer wrote, "the culmination of a tremendously spirited comeback by the Brooklyns." The World Series win marked "the end of the current domination the New York Yankees had held for so long over the Dodgers, and destroyed the last myth of Yankee invincibility."

In truth, the win did not wholly erase the stigma that followed Brooklyn into history. Dodger failures of the early 1950s were sealed by the team's departure for Los Angeles. Both the male-based "choke" label and wide acknowledgment of the team's greatness, contradictory though the two perceptions were, became forever part of the *Brooklyn* Dodgers' mythology. Personal allusions of male failure, sometimes with devastating long-term implications, also followed several individual Dodgers into the post-Brooklyn future.

We now know from the vast literature available on American women's climb toward equality that women made significant strides toward that goal during the Great Depression and especially during World War II. But in the years immediately following the war, and until the resurgent feminist movement of the 1960s and '70s, the gains were largely compromised, some even rolled back. (See Chapter 5.) The late 1940s and '50s, then, can be seen as an era of heightened, self-conscious male posturing, evident in movies, music, television, and mating mores, among other elements of popular culture; certainly that posturing was all too evident in sports.

The Dodger experience brought that male acting-out as close to the surface of American culture as any other example one could choose to examine. The Dodgers couldn't know it, but looking back it seems they were living both the 1950s American male dream and gender nightmare at one and the same time.

4
Male Culture: Owners, Chokers, and Dumb Kids

In the aftermath of World War II several players, Dixie Walker among them, surfaced as mildly militant critics of the baseball establishment. No one openly dared to criticize the reserve clause; that kind of resistance was beyond the pale in the wake of the harsh penalties meted out to would-be unionizers and "Mexican jumping beans" (major leaguers who jumped to the Mexican League in 1946).

Dixie Walker was a classic product of time and place. He had a solid, long-lived major league career, but not quite of Hall of Fame quality. He was both from the Deep South (Alabama) and an intelligent young man of the Great Depression. The first made him hostile to Robinson, although with a mixed report card (deeply resentful at first, grudgingly accepting in the end). The second made Walker formidably sympathetic to workers' rights, and as such he emerged as one of the earliest champions behind reform of the reserve cause.

Walker, an established star, accepted the responsibility of representing National League players in negotiating with owners some minimal gains. These included establishing a pension program and some modification of the waiver rule allowing owners to farm out players to the minors for years on end at microscopic salaries. Walker may have been traded after the 1947 season largely because he couldn't live with Robinson, but his central role in questioning the tyranny of management may have had something to do with it as well. Pensions, the waiver rule, unpaid exhibition games players were required to play, and a proposed expansion of the 154-game season all weighed on players' minds as evidence of their powerlessness, as Walker indicated as one of baseball's spokesmen. The supreme control owners exerted over players' lives via the reserve clause held them in legal bondage all their playing days. Infantilization in all its forms was the primary tool management used to keep players submissive and under control.

Baseball magnates and their field managers found great advantage in perpetuating the myth that players were boys playing a game. It was a widespread and potent myth in a sport with "more myths than any of our games," as Thomas Boswell has concluded. Big-kid Babe Ruth stories, for example, always abounded, and there was no lack of examples on the Brooklyn Dodgers. Owners and sportswriters both encouraged the childish jock image, the former employing it as a means of controlling valuable properties, the latter to get easy press coverage. Typecasting ballplayers as boy-men hurt. As a management device to dominate its properties it worked fine, but its impact on players was far from innocent. Billy Loes remains firmly ensconced in baseball lore as a classic dumb jock. Duke Snider for most of his playing days carried the tag of perpetual brat. Loes and Snider survived, meagerly or well. In the cases of Erv Palica and Don Newcombe, their reputations as infantile choke artists who habitually failed in the clutch quickly drove them out of baseball, and in Newcombe's case at least, put him on the long, tortuous road to alcoholism and recovery before he could reclaim his self-respect.

Meanwhile, owners like Branch Rickey and Walter O'Malley cynically profited from the often grotesque caricatures baseball mythology invented. Before turning to the uses to management of the cynical and demeaning typecasting of players, we need first to take a closer look at that management, at least as it was exemplified on the Brooklyn Dodgers. Like all owners, Rickey and

O'Malley were businessmen, and they knew the reserve clause was crucial to profitable operation of the Dodger franchise. A component of the reserve clause was the waiver rule, permitting absolute control of the minor league players. Rickey, the inventor of the farm system, showed the way.

Reporters occasionally referred to his farm clubs as "Rickey's plantations," to Rickey as "The Old Woman in the Shoe," and to the farm teams' properties as "Mother Rickey's chickens." Maybe the metaphors suggest paternalism posing as maternalism, but the results were the same. Contemporary movies about Robinson (*The Jackie Robinson Story* in 1950) and Campanella (*It's Good to Be Alive* in 1974) both portray Rickey and O'Malley respectively as kindly and paternal faces of management. "The Mahatma"—Rickey's least favorite nickname—frequently sold young players to teams with less productive farm systems than his, taking a commission on each sale. The least fortunate players were those warehoused for possible future use, thus they were neither permanently on the parent club nor sold to major league teams they had a chance to make. Too talented to part with, they would languish for years in the minors at puny salaries.

The surviving 1916 pennant-winning Dodgers were Rickey's guests at the 1949 World Series, where they were honored at pregame ceremonies. Red Smith, looking on at the festivities, cynically observed that "it is a matter of record that Branch Rickey resisted an impulse to decorate them with a *For Sale* sign." On his treatment of players generally, Maury Allen concluded, Rickey "was a moral man who made some clearly immoral maneuvers to get ahead in the game."

When it came to business, Rickey had no edge on "The O'Malley," Walter's least favorite nickname. He took over the Dodgers just as Congressman Emmanuel Celler's Judiciary Committee was hitting high gear in its investigation of the reserve clause as a violation of federal anti-trust laws in 1951. O'Malley launched a counteroffensive in a way no other club owner could: locally, in Celler's backyard. The *Brooklyn Eagle* noted that the Dodger owner, "hot under the collar," defended the "game" and its fiat over the players. Celler responded blandly, backed off, trying to keep the issue out of local politics, for he represented half of Brooklyn in Congress, and what O'Malley thought mattered politically to the congressman. Celler fudged the investigation when he realized he faced a local public relations crisis, and he said finally that he didn't really want to change anything, he only wanted to find out "if baseball is strictly a business or really a national pastime." The *Eagle* columnist got it right: "Now Congressman, how naive can you get? Everyone's out to make a buck."

Walter O'Malley could always be depended upon to defend "the game," but when he began lobbying for a new stadium at public expense, he inadvertently acknowledged that "my business is baseball." Columnist Red Smith said of O'Malley that he "was all business—a business that he owned and could operate as he chose." Robert Moses, who did not like the Dodger president, once said that O'Malley could play the game-game as well as anybody. He had "a speech indicating he would die for dear old Brooklyn. . . . Walter has embroidered it with shamrocks, harps and wolfhounds." But, Moses concluded, the reality was that O'Malley ran a business, not a game. O'Malley, writer Melvin Durslag said in the *Saturday Evening Post,* was "a smart operator pursuing a maximum profit in the normal tradition of American business."

Sometimes the two successive owners, who quickly came to hate each other, got caught up in their own machinations, catching the same macho fever they spread so ruthlessly among their players. When O'Malley was forced to spend a million dollars to buy out Rickey's share of the club in 1950, the negotiation became a clash of stags. Not only did the buy-out cost O'Malley big money, Red Barber observed dryly, it damaged "the O'Malley *machismo,* which is male Irish ego in Spanish."

Owner paternalism never really masked the serf-like reality of the Dodgers' professional lives. It was important to Rickey and O'Malley alike that the public (the fans) thought of professional baseball as a game, one played by generally dumb, dependent juveniles. Player anger at their condition occasionally surfaced, often enough to make the point that they resented the ego-emasculating roles into which they were forced.

In a rare angry outburst of contemporary criticism, several Dodger pitchers who would speak out anonymously in 1950 complained about early spring barnstorming in cold weather. "Sure, I was in shape when I left Vero Beach," one said, "but I'm not now. My arm aches all over." If he had a "bad year," another noted, "will it have been worth it to the club to have drawn 5,000 extra fans to an exhibition game?" "It's a joke," a third Dodger pitcher said. "We're supposed to be down here to train, not make money for the management." In fact, many pitchers on the team believed, according to Roger Kahn, that Rickey's relentless spring exploitation coupled with indiscriminate use of pitchers interchangeably in starting and relief roles, resulted in the team's "best pitching prospects rapidly destroying their arms." He pointed to Rex Barney, Ralph Branca and Jack Banta as examples. Erv Palica, Billy Loes, and Don Newcombe, as we shall see, might well have charged Walter O'Malley later with the same tight-fisted, destructive exploitation, an exploitation they could resist only at great psychic cost.

Carl Furillo, moody and inarticulate, was not one of O'Malley's "good boys." After fifteen years as a Dodger star, he was released following an injury early in 1960. In violation of his contract, O'Malley refused to pay him for the season. Furillo actually had to sue the club to recover that salary, a messy public squabble. To make the point that public embarrassment of management was not tolerated, O'Malley blacklisted Furillo, making him untouchable for any job in any organization. As if to underscore that this was no isolated response, Dodger pitcher Clem Labine, asked after he retired if Furillo had gotten a raw deal from the team, responded yes. But in baseball, he added, "raw deals are a dime a dozen." Underscoring the fact this was no game, as "The Boys of Summer" grew older, The O'Malley gradually reduced his insurance coverage with Mutual of Omaha from $250,000 per player to $150,000 by 1955. As Happy Felton, long heralded as "just a kid at heart," told Irving Rudd on leaving Ebbets Field one night and seeing a church adorned with a large *Jesus Saves* sign: "They never heard of O'Malley."

Several Dodger players learned just how arrogantly tight-fisted the Dodger owners were. Roy Campanella, having won Most Valuable Player awards in 1951 and 1953, had a dismal 1954 season. The front office convinced him to have an operation to restore full use of his hand, the better to throw and to grip a bat. According to the catcher, O'Malley had promised to pay for the $9500 operation. O'Malley reneged, and when the ballclub "disclaimed responsibility," the surgeon sued Campanella. Furious, Campanella denounced management to the press, but he still had to pay the bill. During the 1955 season, he took it on the chin from opposing bench jockeys for trusting O'Malley.

Rickey had been no better. His relentlessly paternal control was wielded like a scalpel when it came to negotiating salaries. Years later, successful television actor Chuck Connors, up with the Dodgers twice, in 1949 and 1950, said of Rickey: "It was easy to figure out Rickey's thinking on contracts. He had both players and money and he didn't like to see the two of them mix." Eddie Stanky echoed the sentiment. "I got a million dollars' worth of free advice, and a very small raise," he said of The Mahatma.

Both Carl Erskine and Pee Wee Reese were team leaders in the decade after World War II. Both were thoughtful and mature individuals, and both understood the reality of their positions, a reality they rarely alluded to for public consumption. But occasional off-hand remarks reveal some anger at the opportunistic paternalism they lived with. Erskine became the Dodgers' player representative in the early 1950s, and was involved in negotiations over pensions, a matter on which owners both stalled and penny-pinched. Erskine was instrumental in 1953 in convincing the National League players to hire J. Norman Lewis as the players' counsel to pursue some grievances forcibly, the pension among them. Erskine denied the recruitment of a lawyer was the first step toward unionization, but he did not deny it very strongly. He was quoted as describing the owners as "greedy" in general. One can see Erskine's fine hand behind the Dodger team's closed meeting with Baseball Commissioner Happy Chandler in 1951. The Dodgers unanimously requested of him that *all* World Series television receipts be placed in the pension fund. That was a militant "request." "The baseball czar," the *Eagle* reported revealingly, "strongly recommended that the players don't interfere with the magnates' plan." The mixture of patronizing "advice" with a clearly implied threat was commonplace in organized baseball, and the Dodger team, despite its national reputation as the team that integrated baseball, was no exception. In fact, perhaps because of that political reputation, the unanimously agreed players may have touched a nerve. The 1951 meeting was taken as player intrusion on management turf.

Pee Wee Reese, for one, occasionally grew weary of baseball paternalism. He embodied a reputation for boyishness that dogged him all his professional life. Early in his career he was characterized as boyish because his nickname made good copy, even though it had to do with his childhood prowess at marbles, not his size. After the war, as with many Dodger veterans, it was hard to describe Reese as immature. But it wasn't as hard to denigrate intelligence. After one of Arthur Daley's patented "boys will be boys" columns, as usual featuring "Pee Wee," Reese told Daley, with a rare touch of overt anger, that he and his teammates had been made to sound simpleminded. "All ballplayers aren't dumb," he reminded Daley, turning away from yet one more inane interview.

Some players paid a higher price than others for their media-hyped, management-serving reputations for immaturity in all its forms. Billy Loes was typecast as a classic case of arrested development: dumb, impulsive, quirky. Duke Snider was pegged as a perpetual child. Most destructively, Erv Palica, briefly and fatally, and Don Newcombe, over an entire career, were both made out to be gutless wonders on a choke-prone team. In this climate, it was easy for management to encourage this manipulative stereotyping, and it happened in varying degrees to most Dodgers. Columnist Tom Meany once quoted an unnamed National League owner as saying, "The Dodgers may win the pennant, but they'll never win the World Series. It's that kind of club."

All stereotyping was possible in a world in which paternal control equaled good business, and where media stereotypes were weapons in that effort to control, and in an era when all professional athletes were considered to be in a perpetual state of arrested development. That male myth was imposed commonly even on superior players in an era when ballplayers were habitually underpaid and victimized by their servitude under the reserve clause. Those were the years before professional athletes proved their adulthood to the public by their undeniable success in making grotesquely big bucks. Americans respect nothing more than that, regret though they may its impact on the "national game."

Billy Loes's problems with the Dodgers ironically derived from just that—making good money with only average talent. He was a good journeyman pitcher who infuriated the Dodger front office and was thus fair game for "inside" press revelations about how dumb and flaky he was. In fact, both in terms of his contributions to the team and his outspoken shrewdness in confronting the Dodger establishment, the reality was much different. The "dugout savant," as Daley bitingly satirized him, won 50 and lost 25 in the four years he pitched for the Dodgers (1952–55), winning 10 to 14 games each year. Loes was also an able financial negotiator, one of the best on the club, and this was apparent even at age eighteen. He even bested Branch Rickey. With a little help from a high-school coach, he personally drummed up the interest of several scouts and arranged a tryout at Ebbets Field. Loes then manipulated Rickey into paying him a huge (for 1949) bonus of $21,000. Nobody had offered him more than $6000 to that point. Rickey went into the meeting determined to sign Loes for no more than $10,000. Gus Loes, Billy's Greek immigrant father, was at the meeting because his son was a minor, but he shrewdly let Billy do all the talking. The father, who had fought at Belleau Wood in World War I, had been in America a long time. After the signing he said, tongue-in-cheek, "On that day, I was no talk English and no understand beizbol."

Rickey signed Loes for too much money because Loes stampeded him, perhaps the only time this ever was to happen. Rickey incorrectly believed, from what Loes communicated, that the young pitcher had several other viable offers. Loes, father and son, immediately bought property in Queens with the bonus money, and did the same with Billy's '52 and '53 Series shares. Afterward Loes let no one push him around. Dressen told Billy Loes to take good care of himself, and if he did, he could stay in the majors for fifteen years. Loes responded, "I'll have enough money in five." That was exactly how long his career lasted. And the entire five years he spent in the majors he spent on his terms.

Dodger management understandably considered Loes odd and unpredictable. In truth, he was superstitious to a fault, and this made him vulnerable. He also spoke with an unrelieved New

York accent. But his main failing was that he had a dangerously big mouth. In this he was a kindred spirit to Jackie Robinson, who was a close team friend. Roger Kahn seemed not to understand how Jack could be Loes's buddy: "I guess he felt he was a misfit and felt sorry for him." That wasn't it. Both were openly contemptuous of O'Malley, vice president Emil "Buzzy" Bavasi and manager Walter Alston, and both openly despised the controlling system management imposed on the team. Both Bavasi and Alston were widely and knowingly seen as O'Malley's men in all things. Each understood that to act independently of O'Malley's will was to face instant dismissal. Neither, so far as I know, ever did.

On a pre-game "Knothole Gang" show, Loes told a promising youngster that if he ever signed, "get a lot of money off these clubs." That was not considered on-the-air talk in 1953. At mid-season that year, Loes facetiously told Buzzy Bavasi that he was going home: "You said you expect me to win twelve games and you paid me accordingly. Well, I've won twelve, so I'm going home." If this seems capricious, it wasn't. Before the beginning of the 1954 season, he told a reporter he felt "like a white slave, shackled . . . to President Walter O'Malley." No wonder Robinson liked him, and no wonder Dodger brass went out of its way to demean and infantilize him. Loes's acerbic directness gave voice to what many major leaguers (and most Dodgers) were thinking. Charley Dressen indulged Loes's big mouth and superstitions, but when Walter Alston took over in 1954, he felt threatened by the pitcher's independence and quickly found reason to get rid of him, Loes's consistency on the mound notwithstanding. Loes never allowed himself to be overworked, and when he complained of a sore arm in 1954, Alston was asked where it hurt. "In his shoulder," the Dodger manager told reporters, "in his head, too."

Loes was a great example of how *juvenile* translated into *stupid*. Most of the permanent damage was done in a nationally circulated article in the *Saturday Evening Post* in 1953. Jimmy Breslin, who knew better and said so if one reads between the lines, nevertheless followed Dodger management's take on Loes. He got all the anecdotes he wanted for the piece. It was titled "The Dodgers' New Daffiness Boy," and Loes was clearly and colorfully portrayed as being in a dead heat with Carl Furillo for the honor of being the dumbest of several dumb Dodgers. Colorful stories that fed athletic stereotypes sold papers and magazines, and Breslin deliberately confused uneducated with stupid. According to *Eagle* columnist Tommy Holmes, Breslin unfairly made Loes look like "Simple Simon." That kind of characterization of Loes was so firmly fixed in the '50s that it has stuck and Loes's reputation as a mindless flake remains intact. One anecdotal baseball book recently concluded that Loes's "successes could not be attributed to brain power." In Alan Lelchuk's 1990 novel, Loes comes up "disturbed."

This typecasting had little to do with reality. Loes and Robinson were the best bridge players on a club that generally loved the game and indulged in it often. There also exists a picture of Loes bent over a chessboard with Don Drysdale. These takes, his successful and thoroughly disciplined real estate investments from the beginning of his career, his plan to need no more than five years in the big leagues to make his stake—all these seem much at odds with press characterizations of the immature, dumb pitcher. Superstitious? Outspoken? His own person? Hostile to management? Yes. Stupid? By no means.

Loes was no more a dumb-bell than Duke Snider was a spoiled brat. Nobody ever said Snider was dumb. But he was widely regarded during his playing days as "Peck's Bad Boy" on a Dodger team of boys. The label was pinned on a Hall of Fame class player who, for a fact, generally exerted a mature and steadying influence on the team. In particular, he was at the center of efforts to ameliorate persistent race tensions on the Dodgers. Snider was a team leader in the ways that counted most. He occasionally acted out as a young, high-strung player under stress (there was, as with Loes, a germ of truth to early allegations of immaturity, but no more than a germ). But management encouraged badmouthing of his alleged puerility, always good copy for the press, and it put him in a weaker position to negotiate much-deserved raises in salary. News stories and features painted Snider early on as a shallow prima donna.

At the beginning of the 1951 season, for example, Jimmy Powers resurrected an apocryphal tale dating to Snider's rookie season to remind fans of what a kid he was. Put down by a veteran, Snider was supposed to have flung down his bat, "growling . . . 'It must be great to be a star!'" "You'll be one too," the avuncular senior was supposed to have retorted, "when you grow up!" These stories kept repeating themselves in different venues all through Snider's career.

This color could be sold for cash, lots of it, as Arthur Mann proved in 1954. Branch Rickey's former man Friday wove together tales of Snider's "tantrums" to produce a feature in the *Saturday Evening Post* entitled "The Dodgers' Problem Child." This was 1954. Snider was already a star, fruitlessly seeking to be paid some pale approximation of his real worth to the team. He woke up one morning to read in a national magazine that he moronically acknowledged his perpetual immaturity by saying, "My parents are to blame. I'm an only child." That was Mann's above-the-line title lead. The leaden label of "immature kid" followed Snider through his playing days. During the '50s he was never able to close the gap between his infantile reputation and the mature reality.

In the cases of Erv Palica and Don Newcombe, the label of "immature kid" was just for openers. It provided classic explanations for their supposed propensities for failing in the clutch.

At twenty-two years old, Palica won thirteen games in 1950, including two critical games in the Dodgers' September run on the Phillies. Despite Palica's gutsy contributions, the Dodgers fell short on the last day of the season. Early in the 1951 season, Palica twisted his ankle and, continuing to pitch, favored it, losing his timing and ultimately hurting his arm. Management didn't believe him, and Dodger vice president Buzzy Bavasi crucified Palica in the press as an immature, gutless kid. Manager Charley Dressen, usually considered shrewd but not bright, took it one step further. Asked by reporters to comment, he "made a significant gesture across his neck, the ball players' pantomime for saying a fellow chokes up." Asked about this verbal mugging, Palica said, "I can't sleep nights." His pregnant wife was upset, he added, because people on the street were telling her "your husband hasn't got any guts." He never again pitched effectively in the major leagues.

Palica's side of the story, probably fueled by his reference to his pregnant wife and recent fan memories of his clutch pitching in 1950, caused Bavasi's story to backfire in two ways. First, it was a public relations disaster for the Dodgers, for it "brought down thousands of letters" upon 210 Montague Street, the team front office. Even if it was only hundreds of letters, the damage was irreparable. Second, the *Eagle* claimed, at the end of that disastrous season, that the Dodger "destruction" began with the Palica episode because it effectively deprived the team of a much-needed experienced pitcher who could have been the margin of difference between winning and losing the 1951 pennant. The front office actors, the *Eagle* claimed, "planned that story as a needle for Palica, and were shocked when it boomeranged." It was a revealing moment in that it acknowledged overtly Dodger management's policy of using the press to reinforce negative stereotypes of its players to make them more tractable.

That cynical policy also misfired badly in the case of Don Newcombe. Newcombe became the first African American pitching star in the major leagues, an important distinction because even the greatest pitchers occasionally failed in ways much more visible than lapses suffered by position players. That Jackie Robinson and Roy Campanella were money players who did as well in clutch situations as any who played in the game did not convince major league bigots born into a biased belief system that all blacks would fail in the clutch. When Newk occasionally failed, it simply reinforced common southern wisdom about black Americans. That perception was expressed by many, but Dixie Walker, who later regretted having said it, put it succinctly in 1946 when he heard about Robinson's signing: blacks simply didn't have "ice water in their veins." That is, they were choke-prone and could never stomach "big league pressure."

Even before he was brought up, Newcombe carried a reputation as a hothead who lost his temper when needled. His would-be manager Burt Shotton, usually placid, refused to put him on the Dodger roster after spring training in 1949, despite the fact that he was more than equipped to help the team. After reacting angrily to a racist incident at Vero Beach, Shotton branded the pitcher a fire-eater who "couldn't keep his mouth shut." Shotton patronizingly added that he didn't want Newcombe "spoiling it for the other two [black] fellows." By May 1949, however, the

Dodgers were floundering, and Shotton had no choice but to promote Newcombe, who went on to win seventeen games, the single biggest reason the Dodgers recovered and went on to win the pennant. But because he was black, a pitcher, and an instant star, Newcombe was put under the microscope of those looking for even the appearance of failure.

Three such early "failures" underpin the choke label Newk carried with him for the rest of his playing days. The label defied both logic and Newcombe's record in the majors. The rookie pitched brilliantly in the opening game of the 1949 World Series, only to lose 1–0 on a ninth-inning home run. On the last day of the 1950 season, with the Dodgers and Phils tied for first, Newcombe went nine innings, giving up only one run, only to lose the game in the tenth, again on a home run. In the last playoff game of 1951 against the Giants, an exhausted Newcombe (he had pitched with two days' rest for the last three weeks of the season) held the Giants to one run in eight innings and left the game with the pennant seemingly won. These three games established the myth that "Big Newk" had no guts.

An examination of his record suggests the allegation was palpably not true. The Dodgers were in tight pennant races in 1949, 1950, 1951, and 1956 (the team won going away in 1955, and Newcombe was a twenty-game winner). He was in the army during the 1952 and 1953 seasons. In August and September 1949, Newcombe was 9–5, pitching always with fewer than three games separating the Dodgers and the Cardinals. Four of his wins were shutouts, two of his losses were by 2–1 and 1–0 scores. Newcombe was named Rookie of the Year. In 1950, the Dodgers were eight games behind the Phillies on September 18, when they made a great run for the pennant. The black pitcher had already pitched both ends of a doubleheader that month, winning a 2–0 shutout in the first game, and pitching six innings in the second in a game Brooklyn finally won. After that, Newcombe won complete game starts on September 19 and 23, only to lose that last game of the season.

In 1951, with the Dodgers and Giants separated by no more than two games in the last week of the season, Newcombe won on both September 26 and 29, the last a shutout. He pitched eight great innings in the last playoff game. In 1956, by which time his reputation in baseball and even among a few of his teammates as a choke artist was fixed, the Dodgers and the Braves were neck-and-neck from the beginning of September. Newcombe was already 21–6 on August 31. In that last month, he was 5–1 down the stretch, never pitching with more than three days' rest, always going the distance, and with never more than two games separating the teams. On the last day of the season, he won his 27th game and clinched the pennant by beating the Pirates with a complete game. There was, in short, no substance to the "choke" charge. Yet much of baseball—a large number of fans, some Dodgers, and the front office—all openly bought into the myth.

Through his entire career Newcombe was singled out as no other Dodger (except Palica, briefly) ever was. It should be noted that the belief that African Americans lacked fortitude was an important component of the psychology of race prejudice. It was this deeply rooted bias that Dixie Walker reflected in his 1946 statement that blacks didn't have what it took to play major league ball. This was a view prevalent among a large number of major leaguers, especially those who were southerners, in that post-World War II era. It was already obvious by 1951 that neither Robinson nor Campanella would ever qualify as race-tainted gutless wonders, but as is always the case with deeply embedded prejudice, the arrival of one possible victim would erase for many all other evidence.

Whatever the realities of Newcombe's contributions in his first three years in the majors, and despite his magnificent years in 1955 and 1956, his reputation was fixed forever by the combination of Giants' jockeying, racist stereotyping, and even the Dodgers' misguided efforts to provoke him into baseball's version of manhood.

Both Dodger managers in Newcombe's early years said publicly at various times that Newk was both lazy and gutless, unconsciously or not perpetuating longstanding racist stereotypes. From the beginning of Newcombe's career, Burt Shotton believed that the pitcher lacked both self-control and maturity. During the 1950 season, Shotton said that Newcombe was "jaking it" in order to protect himself from an illusory sore arm ("imagi-nitis"). That was the year that, in the September run against the Phillies, Newcombe started no less than every fourth day, some-times every third day, and was the only pitcher since 1930 to start both ends of a doubleheader. In 1951 Dressen claimed New-combe was "lazy and too prone to ask out," a racial parody that was made overt that year when the pitcher was portrayed in the *Eagle*, quoting unnamed Dodger sources, as ungrateful for the chance given him. He was, the *Eagle* reported, just a "big Negro kid" when the Dodgers found him and transformed him, via smart management, into a major league pitcher.

Durocher and the Giants quickly picked up on and ex-panded the scope of Newcombe's supposed weaknesses. In 1951 he was "taunted into a rage by Giant jockeys" who repeatedly shouted from the bench that he was gutless ("lacked moxie," in newspaper doublespeak). That taunting hardened into common wisdom. Some Giants passed on to reporters the Newcombe jokes making the rounds, such as, "What has two arms, two legs, and no guts?" Sal Maglie put it to reporters even more crudely: What did Newcombe and a homosexual have in common? "They both choked on the big one."

What sealed Newcombe's fate was that some Dodger players and probably the entire Dodger management bought into the al-legations. As early as 1949, even his Dodger teammates didn't take "too seriously" Newcombe's complaints about being over-worked. Newcombe's fear of a sore arm was widely considered suspect on the team and was "getting under the skin of the top brass." His "fellow players don't like it either," Tommy Holmes re-ported in the *Eagle*. In 1954, after Newcombe came back from two years in the army, Charley Dressen revived and expanded the allegations. In a bittersweet post-mortem article published after he was fired by O'Malley in 1953, Dressen wrote for *Look* maga-zine that Don Newcombe "missed repeatedly in the crucial low-run games." Newcombe went on to pitch consistent, brilliant baseball, winning twenty in 1955 and twenty-seven in 1956, but he never shook the choke charge. He knew, of course, what was being said. After getting shelled in a 1956 Series game, he heard a fan call him "a yellow-bellied slob." People say "I choke up," he told *New York Post* columnist Milton Gross, adding forlornly, "I think it's rubbed off in the clubhouse."

It also rubbed off on the public. If the Dodgers "took the apple," as Dick Young first wrote in 1950, it was Newcombe who came to personify that image publicly. So said Ray Robinson in his recent book on the 1951 pennant race. Unfair as it was, Newcombe was the goat, the embodiment of male failure of nerve, and it was so fixed in the minds of the New York baseball public. A couple of takes suggest how deeply: two decades after Newcombe left baseball, Brooklyn native Jerry Della Femina remembered that "Newcombe choked." "In the end," Della Femina concluded, Newcombe would "fold under pressure." "The rap, to put it simply," writes Robinson of the fans' reaction, "said that Newk was incapable of winning the big games. He choked up," and the fans knew it. Clancy Sigal, in his memoir of the late '50s, remembered sitting in a bar in Manhattan "chatting with the man next to me about whether Don Newcombe was really a choke-up guy in the late innings of a game."

Newcombe the player never came back from his realization that he carried that grossly unfair rap. He hung on in the majors for a few years, but he was already drinking. He left baseball an alcoholic, and it took him years to pull himself together and make it back to a real post-game life. All along the line, the allegations were touched with both race and crude macho baseball values. It wasn't the Giants who hurt the most; they did what was expected in that male baseball culture. It was the Dodger management and a few players who really did Newcombe in, for they should have known better.

Keeping the players in line was essential to extending the life of the reserve clause in the 1950s. Manipulating the male egos of the players and extending the myth of boys playing a game were ways to attend to business, if Dodger management was a representative example. Because playing off the theme of men confronting failure helped fill ball parks and controlled player properties, the Dodger front office and its field managers both subtly and overtly played havoc with the male egos of all the Dodgers, regardless of the hurt inflicted. Because these stories were grist for the newspapers' baseball mill, and were avidly followed on the sports pages, the press was complicit. The result was that the Dodger team, in dealing with the public fruits of its own shortcomings, was forced to confront the entire baseball establishment, as well as their own fans, to demonstrate their manhood, collectively and, for several, individually.

Choking was a male athlete's worst nightmare, and it was very much a part of baseball mythology. The truth is that if those "jocks" on the Dodgers were as dumb and juvenile, as gutless and choke-prone as they were made out to be, there was no way they could have persevered so consistently as a team. That the Dodgers had always to redeem their manhood before the public was a travesty, a game within a cynical business.

5
The Baseball Culture
of Brooklyn's Women

In June 1952 the Harrisburg Senators of the New York-Penn League signed infielder Eleanor Engle to a contract. A veteran of the All-American Girls Baseball League (the subject of the 1992 movie *A League of Their Own*), the infielder had several years of professional experience behind her. Nevertheless, the *Brooklyn Eagle* had a field day at her expense. "The threatened bulwark" of the national game, the *Eagle* remarked, "comes under the heading of good old fashioned manhood." But "letting the babes into baseball," reporter Oscar Fraley added, "has a certain attraction." Just think of the lucky scout assigned to the Miss America pageant in Atlantic City, for example. This kind of baseball boys-will-be-boys humor was typical of the '50s. The national pastime was a male preserve, both on the field and in the stands.

Gender attitudes were more sharply focused in the interior world of professional baseball than in other areas of life, but still, baseball did mirror a broad American male cultural norm as well. Michael Kimmel has concluded that baseball-induced displays of masculinity helped "maintain the social hierarchies . . . between men and women." Drawing on Robert Lipsyte's *Sportsworld*, Donald Sabo identified "the unholy triad of sports, politics, and journalism" as having "created a dangerous ethical value system that distorts the fans' experience of sport itself." Within this context, sport "provides an ideology for maintaining the existing system of sex stratification in America, and it reinforces traditional masculine value systems." Brooklyn men and their Dodger team were no more strident in their attitudes toward women than were other '50s males or teams. With that in mind, the Brooklyn experience is worth looking at. Athletes in general remain baseline chauvinists within current gender mores. That's why the '50s Dodgers form such a fascinating laboratory.

Baseball-bred contempt for women took many forms, none more virulent than that found in the collectively arrogant Dodger attitude toward "Baseball Annies" (groupies). It was very much in evidence in both the Dodger organization's and the press's treatment of female Dodger fans, women who ran the gamut from working stiff Hilda Chester to Pulitzer Prize poet Marianne Moore. This arrogance persisted in the front office via its permissive policy regarding press coverage, this despite the Dodger management's paradoxical pioneering economic reliance on Ladies' Day promotions to boost female attendance. Players' wives and women fans alike found that their involvement with the game could be very demeaning indeed.

It is a part of baseball lore that the road trips common to organized ball at all levels had its attractions. The shooting of Phillies' first baseman Eddie Waitkus by a woman fan who was fixated on him briefly brought Annies to the headlines in 1949. Generally, however, writers either passed on the matter of players' sexual propensities or referred to such things only obliquely. Bernard Malamud's *The Natural* (and the movie starring Robert Redford), the first popular book to take on the existence of Annies, got its original inspiration from the Waitkus incident. The Dodger players, it should be noted, took up a collection for Waitkus.

W. P. Kinsella more recently wrote openly about baseball groupies. In his short story "Barefoot and Pregnant in Des Moines," he explains that the descriptive title is the usual baseball lingo for explaining why it's okay to cheat on your wife on the road. One's wife is barefoot . . . and so on. In his effort to reveal the cultural depths of baseball to readers of the *American Scholar*, Roger Kahn alludes to the road-trip phenomenon more subtly. "A major league baseball team is a collection of twenty-five youngish men who have made the major leagues and discovered that in spite of it, life remains distressingly short of ideal." Among the realities that players confront, Kahn noted, is that "girls still insist on tiresome preliminaries."

The 1950s, in fact, may be getting a bad rap on this subject. When three New York Mets were arrested on rape charges in 1992, former teammate Darryl Strawberry came to their defense: "As disgusting as these women are, man, that's bad. It's not like these are some classy ladies. They're a bunch of pigs."

Ballplayers generally do not acknowledge in public their relationships with Baseball Annies. A few Dodgers did, but only after their careers were over, and often in indistinct context. In talking about black Dodgers' long-delayed right to stay at St. Louis's Chase Hotel, Don Newcombe said that even after they were allowed to stay there, they were denied pool-side rooms. The hotel "didn't want us looking at those pretty women in their bikinis. But what they didn't know was that I had women in my room all the time. Black women, white women, all kinds."

Both Johnny Podres and Dick Williams were young and single. Podres, who shut out the Yankees to clinch the 1955 World Series, "loved girls . . . loved to drink." The taciturn, puritanical Walt Alston threatened once to pull Podres from the pitching rotation because he picked up a woman from a groupie hangout that Alston had made off-limits to the Dodgers, an affirmation by itself that the pursuit of sex was part of some Dodgers' road life. Podres brought the woman back to his hotel room. Alston knew because he watched Podres closely on the road by establishing himself in the room next door. Duke Snider, himself a straight arrow, nevertheless put the incident in perspective for the rookie manager in 1954 when he reminded Alston that he was overreacting: "Geez, Walt, a lot of guys get laid." That comment by itself suggests that relationships between Annies and at least some Dodgers were commonplace.

Dick Williams, a bench-warming outfielder (and later a successful big-league manager), was a "free spirit" who also liked to drink and womanize. He told Roger Kahn that on a single road trip he had had an array of women, black, white, Hispanic, Jewish. Realizing belatedly that Kahn was Jewish, Williams hastily made amends. He assured Kahn that "the Jewish girl was the best lay."

Part of the risk of the Dodgers sexual activities was the paternity suit. Journeyman pitcher Hank Behrman "ran around too much" anyway, and when he was hit with a suit in 1947, he was quickly traded into baseball exile in Pittsburgh. Before the trade, he was given a "day." Expecting at least a car, he received only a hundred-dollar savings bond, all that could be scrounged up from his bar friends in Brooklyn. He stalked off the field in a fury. Tom Meany commented in the press box, "I don't know why he's so upset. He's lucky it wasn't a [paternity] summons." In 1952 a Newark woman sued Billy Loes for paternity, and when the train carrying the Dodgers from Philadelphia passed through New Jersey during the 1953 season, he had to hide in the lavatory to avoid service. Although he was a consistently winning pitcher, the paternity suit contributed to the Dodgers' eagerness to trade him.

The saddest and best publicized case of paternity involved a third pitcher, Hugh Casey. The suit lodged against Casey unleashed a painful chain of events that led to his suicide in 1951. The story reveals a great deal about baseball's general propensity to diminish women in that era. The Dodger relief pitcher owned a bar in Brooklyn. It was there, Hilda Weissman said, that Casey "seduced" her, assuring Weissman that he would divorce his wife and marry her. She declared in an affidavit that "she had been a Dodger fan for many years." The story broke in 1950, after Casey had departed the Dodgers (traded, as usual, with a suit in the offing). Probably some of the most otherwise inexplicable trades of the era could have been explained publicly as the product of paternity suits. But those explanations never made it to the sports pages. The Hugh Casey story did, and beyond. The *Eagle* treated Hilda Weissman's filing as front-page news.

Dodger reserve outfielder Al Gionfriddo, with the same classic contempt shown by Strawberry two generations later, described Weissman as "crazy for ballplayers. Shit, she screwed just about every ballplayer in the country. . . . It could have been anybody's baby." The case went to trial, Hugh Casey lost, and his wife left him. On July 2, 1951, he committed suicide in an Atlanta hotel room. Obviously, it wasn't the paternity suit alone that caused Casey to take his own life, but it was clearly a factor. The episode offered a major league insight into the shadow world of ballplayers and Annies. It also reflected cogently on the generalized abhorrence of the 1950s mass culture toward unwed pregnancy. "In the postwar prescriptive literature," Joanne Meyerowitz said, "women who defied sexual convention were vilified as deviants." No wonder players hit with paternity suits were shuffled around, the stories, Casey's excepted, buried.

Male athletes' relationships with women have become a subject for open discussion only in the 1980s and '90s. Organized baseball, however, has a long history of trivializing women. Females formed only a small minority of spectators in the stands in the early years of the century. When one of her editors took her to a Giants game before World War I, Marianne Moore shocked him by commenting on the quality of "Mr. Mathewson's" curveball. Asked how she could possibly know something about that, Moore answered, "I've read his instructive book on the art of pitching." But she was a rarity in those early years. A ballpark was not a "respectable" place for a lady. According to Kimmel, early organized ball filled the psychic role of bolstering "white middle-class masculinity." And Allen Guttmann writes that "given the folklore of the game, which associated the players with tobacco juice, beer . . . and Ruthian dalliance with baseball Annies, it is small wonder that middle class women" gave baseball a wide berth.

The Dodger organization was the first to see the problem with that. By the late 1930s, Dodger president Larry MacPhail, Branch Rickey's predecessor, saw women anew, specifically as needed sources of new revenue. It was McPhail who introduced baseball's first Ladies' Day promotions in Brooklyn. These days were run with the ambitious hope of recruiting new fans who could fill seats, especially at weekday day games. This aggressive initiative was at odds with the traditional contempt male fans felt for women boosters.

By the 1950s, baseball economics had won out over male fan sensibilities. Women were increasingly present in the stands, an economic force that helped make the Dodger club, despite its bandbox stadium, the best-drawing team in the league. "That baseball was no longer strictly a man's game," the *Eagle* concluded at the opening of the 1952 World Series, "was evident from the large number of feminine fans in the stands, from the bobby soxers to those clad in high style originals."

It was the bobby-soxers who most interested the Dodgers. Beginning in 1949, the team ran a contest in the Brooklyn high schools to choose a Brooklyn "Sandlot Queen" to encourage young female identification with the team. A cash prize of upwards of $500 would go to the winner, who would also be introduced at Ebbets Field from time to time and at Dodger promotions at local stores as well. Despite efforts like these, there remained a general contempt for unaccompanied women in the ball park: to many men, women had no business anywhere in the game.

Both the Dodgers' potent place in the life of Brooklyn and the generalized contempt to which women were subjected were symbolized in the persons of two Brooklyn members of the U.S. House of Representatives. Congresswoman Edna Kelly, before a hard-fought primary election, made sure she appeared on "the Knothole Gang" pre-game television show in complete Dodger uniform, to show Brooklyn what a regular guy she was. On the other hand, another Brooklyn representative, Louis Heller, entered a long pre-election paean in praise of the Dodgers into the *Congressional Record*. Franked home (mailed free) at significant public expense, it likened the sound of "a Japanese banzai charge" to "Ladies Day at Ebbets Field." Arthur Daley described Ebbets Field on Ladies' Day as "filled with roaring and screeching humanity—the Ladies' Day element provided the screechers." Observations like these were everywhere professional baseball was played.

This 1950s baseball norm of infantilizing women was brought sharply into focus by Abraham & Strauss department store. Brooklyn's largest retail business capitalized on the growing popularity of Ladies' Day promotions in 1952 by running a sales promotion of its own. "Gals! You may not be allowed to play organized baseball," its ad said, "but you can learn about it." The store brought in Jackie Robinson, Pee Wee Reese, and their wives, Vin Scully, Happy Felton, Chuck Dressen, and The O'Malley himself to teach "the lingo of baseball." "Drop the mop . . . it's time for the women of Brooklyn to become grandstand managers. . . . Surprise the husband or boyfriend with your new baseball banter." A whole new line of Dodger accessories for women were for sale to would-be fans. Women were potential economic assets to both the team and the retailers, but like the ballplayers they were drawn to watch, these women were treated as adult adolescents.

Dodger wives were not spared that patronizing secondary status. The press, especially at World Series time, had a field day with them. After pitching his no-hitter in 1952, the *Eagle* put a quote in Carl Erskine's mouth (that he later half-denied) saying that he had pitched it for "the little woman." Betty Erskine in no way fit that stereotype. Nor did Beverly Snider, who was described by the Brooklyn paper as "the Dutchess of Snider." Rachel Robinson, Jackie's "missus," is shown in supplicating mode in the stands in the 1952 Series, something far from Mrs. Robinson's style. Five Dodger wives were posed like simpletons with fingers crossed in a 1951 cheesecake-like team publicity shot, but one of many of that genre. This kind of posed picture probably contributed to the unpleasantness Dodger wives often experienced in the stands. Dodger players publicly objected to the harassment their wives endured. In talking about this problem to the press, Branch Rickey once said he would back up players "if they act ferociously toward any heckler who steps out of bounds." There was always an Ebbets Field security guard hovering near the section where Dodger wives were seated.

Managers' wives were also fair game. Lela Alston was described in a *New York Times* feature as always serving her "hubby" a home-baked cake or pie at midnight when Walter returned to their Brooklyn apartment after a night game. Only Charley Dressen's usually absent wife puzzled the press. When she arrived from her Los Angeles home for the 1952 World Series, she came "complete with her well-manicured French poodle, Ronnie." This was one Dodger wife not to be passed off as a hausfrau; she was Hollywood all the way.

The press relentlessly pursued two tried-and-true themes in characterizing Brooklyn's female fans: the first depicted them as either dumb or hysterical; the second exploited cheesecake photos to portray them as sex objects. "Wide-eyed, simpleminded, naive and uninformed" would describe Lil Lewis, who attended her first Dodger game in 1952; it turned out to be a rain-out. "Why are those men advertising some make of carpets rushing out on the field," she was made to ask as she watched the ground crew cover the infield. Dumb would be the description of "a lady fan in the right field stands" who was smoking and "accidentally set afire her skirt, fainted and had to be carried to the first aid room." (One should bear in mind that a falling-down alcoholic male who stumbled and injured himself on the steps would be too commonplace to report.) *Eagle* sportswriter Sid Frigand even victimized his wife for the sake of a story: "She doesn't know beans about baseball" but insisted on asking him dumb questions when he came home after a hard day in the Ebbets Field press box.

"Cheesecake" was popular in the '50s. The prize for the most tasteless snap in the *Eagle* must go to that of eighteen-year-old Alice Hall, whose boyfriend convinced her to walk down Bedford Avenue to the ballpark in a bathing suit and on a leash, carrying a *Bums* sign. A *New York Star* inquiring photographer asked dance instructor Deborah Lounsbery how she felt about Durocher's switch to the Giants in 1948. Under her picture, she offered an informed answer that the re-write promptly undermined with a last sentence reading, "What? . . . Will I give you a rhumba lesson sometime?" Newspapermen continuously exploited the "Dodger Co-Ettes," a social club of teenage female fans. They wore Dodger jackets and caps to Ebbets Field and cheered in well-rehearsed unison. When other copy was scarce, they would be posed for leg shots and, after Bobby Thomson's 1951 homer, in the stands "crying their hearts out."

Over the years, Jeff Keate's period Dodger cartoons in the *Eagle* consistently ridiculed women at Dodger games. They followed several 1950s themes that, in a different era, seem both crass and degrading. "What a dull game," one woman says to another. "Eight innings and neither side's got a hit." "Now yesterday," one "battle-axe type" says about a close play at home in another cartoon, "there was exactly the same kind of play and he called him *safe*." These were his "dumb" stereotypes. Another Keate theme was the "ballplayers are cute" focus. "What I like about this pitcher is that he nearly always gets knocked out, and then they bring in that darling relief pitcher." Or the indignant woman looking through her binoculars saying to another: "I don't understand it; always before, we've had cute shortstops." That these bubbleheads were the rule was underscored by the occasional caricature of an informed female fan, who reels off a spate of statistics about the batter while the hats of several men surrounding her lift off into space.

But in a baseball town like Brooklyn, savvy, sophisticated women fans were commonplace. (My mother and several Brooklyn aunts could have buried anyone in Dodger stats.) Two of the best examples are Marianne Moore and Hilda Chester. Moore was described in the '50s as "America's greatest poetess" and was the recipient of the Pulitzer Prize for Poetry, National Book Award, Bollingen Prize, and more. Chester was the fan supreme, who for twenty years made a fair living off her status as Dodger fan number one.

Marianne Moore moved to Brooklyn in 1929, after leaving the literary magazine *The Dial*, which she had edited for five years. Moore lived for the next thirty years in a floor-through flat in a brownstone on Cumberland Street in Clinton Hill. She followed the Dodgers out of Brooklyn, staying on for only a few years after they left in 1957. A life-long baseball fan, she came to love the Flock. She was often in Ebbets Field, and as her literary celebrity increased, she became something of an ornament in the borough and for the team. Only pitcher Carl Erskine had a real sense of how eminent Moore really was. Erskine was an aficionado of poetry who could recite from memory much of Robert Service. His appreciation was enough; Erskine apparently communicated her eminence in a different world to several teammates, and she was welcomed at the park.

In a valedictory essay in *Vogue*, Moore wrote that "Brooklyn has always given me pleasure, has helped educate me; has afforded me, in fact, the kind of tame excitement on which I thrive." When Moore wasn't at the park, she followed the team via Red Barber on the radio. People who knew her well said "her main feature is that she is talkative." Outgoing and informed, she made a good, visible Dodger fan to the end of the team's tenure in Brooklyn. With her signature tricorn "George Washington" hat and "impish sense of humor," it is possible to visualize Ebbets Field as one of her natural habitats.

Charles Molesworth, her biographer, concluded that "Brooklyn and baseball would be linked with her name every time her audience extended beyond those who read her primarily as a modern poet." Seen as one of the great literary figures of her time, one of the few "unknockables" in the literary world of New York in the '50s, Moore was as far from the Keate stereotype of the vapid female Dodger fan as one could be, yet there she was, boosting the Dodgers, often from the confines of Ebbets Field.

And in defiance of a female stereotype common to the borough and the nation, Marianne Moore knew her stuff. Her 1956 poem "Hometown Piece for Messrs. Alston and Reese" turned out unwittingly to be an appropriate valedictory eulogy for the departing Bums. She managed to work seventeen Dodgers into the narrative, and adds that "Willie Mays should be a Dodger. He should—a lad for Roger Craig and Clem Labine to elude." The sophistication of the poet should not mask her insight into the game:

> As for Gil Hodges, in custody of first—
> He'll do it by himself. Now a specialist—versed
> In an extension reach far into the box seats—
> he lengthens up, leans and gloves the ball. He defeats
> expectations by a whisker. The modest star.

This poem contained in a few lines one of the best insights into the work and professional motivation of Roy Campanella. With a poet's grace, Moore described him as a far more enigmatic and complex individual than the man the sportswriters wrote about:

> A-squat in double headers four hundred times a day,
> he says that in a measure the pleasure is the pay.

Hilda Chester was a whole different kind of fan-sophisticate. The real differences, though, cloaked some real similarities. Both Moore and Chester loved Brooklyn and loved the Dodgers.

Both knew what they were talking about when they talked baseball. For both, that last borough generation's team filled an important social and psychic place in their lives. But Chester, unlike Moore, was a Brooklyn-born working-class woman who made of the Dodgers a cottage industry in order to survive as a strapped single mother. There is no question that Moore was far more aware of Hilda Chester than Chester was of the internationally famous poet.

Born in the same generation as Moore (Chester in 1897, Moore ten years earlier), Hilda Chester did not become a baseball fan until she was past forty. For her, the Dodgers filled an economic function in the midst of the Great Depression. The team did that for many. Her story is also a sketch of how some Brooklynites were able to make a living off the Bums.

Brooklyn fans will remember Chester swinging her cowbell when Duke Snider hit one off or over the celebrated right field wall at Ebbets Field. They will recall her famous hula in the aisles when Robinson stole second, went to third when the catcher's panicked throw sailed into center field, and scored on a grounder to short. Others will conjure up the *Hilda Is Here* placard she sported at most games. She was, after all, maybe the ultimate baseball fan, the best in Brooklyn. That was the image. Chester's reality was that she was painfully poor, a mother with a daughter to raise by herself. By the end of World War II that work was done, but the poverty remained. And she was never healthy.

A compleat Brooklynite, Chester got her start as a fan in the late 1930s, drawn, as Larry MacPhail hoped, to the first Ladies' Day game he scheduled. Her instant love for the setting, the game, and her "boys" soon metamorphosed into a vocation, as it did for many locals living on the economic margins. The Dodgers were a meal ticket for many: the ushers who sold empty but better seats for up to a dollar each; vendors in the stands; the bartenders, waiters, and short-order cooks in the many watering holes that dotted the Brooklyn landscape; the street salespeople; the "parking" attendants at nearby gas stations ("Back it up till you hear glass flying. Leave the keys"). The latter would then "protect" your car for a buck.

In a universe of ghetto hustlers, Chester worked the Dodger world with consummate skill.* In the late 1930s she still had not been able to take steady work, raising a young daughter alone as she did. Chester had achieved fan celebrity, though, with her ten-cent cowbell and one-dollar Hawaiian hula skirt. Trading on that, she talked Harry M. Stevens into a job. His company was concessionaire to all the sports palaces in New York (and eventually much of the nation). The Stevens brothers saw a potentially good public relations gimmick in the very visible Hilda Chester and signed her on, first to vend peanuts, later promoting her to slinging hot dogs.

Never at Ebbets Field, of course. That was a condition of her employment, for she would not then have been able to take her usual center field bleacher seat. Her beats were Aqueduct Raceway and, improbably, Yankee Stadium. Still, what better place? When the Dodgers were home, the Yankees were on the road. Eventually she even talked Stevens into letting her work a nearby track in Florida while the Dodgers were in spring training at Vero Beach. In return, to each of the several journalists who saw her as colorful copy on a slow day, she would insist: "Tell the paper to give 'em a plug," and she would reel off by name the six Stevens brothers and their multiple offspring. Writers obliged her often enough to establish her rough public relations quid pro quo with the company that employed her.

In the early 1940s, she also established a relationship of sorts with Leo Durocher. He was genuinely fond of her, and he cajoled Branch Rickey into allowing her into the park free. In 1941, after she suffered a second heart attack, Durocher visited her in the hospital. And Hilda reciprocated. When Leo had a park policeman forcibly bring John Christian, a persistent heckler, under the stands in 1946, Leo beat him with brass knuckles. Hilda came to his rescue. At the subsequent assault trial, a mockery before Judge Samuel Liebowitz, a diehard Dodger fan, Chester "perjured herself," according to one writer. She said on the stand that Leo's actions were justified: "This man called me a cocksucker, your honor," she told Liebowitz and the jury, "and Leo came to

* The ethnic character of Brooklyn's 1950s ghettos is discussed in Chapter 7.

88

my defense." The Lip, needless to say, was acquitted on Liebowitz's probably unnecessary instructions to the jury.

When Durocher jumped ship to the Giants in 1948, Chester was thrown into crisis. "He's the man who made me," she told the *Times*, and she briefly tried to become a Giants fan. Not possible, she learned, "so I don't root either way when the Dodgers play the Giants." Even that didn't work for her. Chester, knowing who filled her rice bowl, quickly returned to the Ebbets Field bleachers full time.

Life at the edge was not easy. Hilda Chester scraped by, made her way with the work ethic of Rosie the Riveter, the street smarts of a ghetto pack-rat, and a mouth the equal of any man's. Jean Evans, a reporter of the left-liberal daily *P.M.*, interviewed Hilda Chester at Aqueduct Raceway in September of 1946, as the long-shot Dodgers made a nearly successful run on the favored Cardinals for the pennant. Evans caught Chester, "blowsy and turbulent, with wild gray hair," at her hot dog stand. The reporter described her "gnarled hands," veins "swollen and blue." But Evans concentrated on her mouth: "Don't rush me mister, the day is young, but you ain't," she told one impatient customer. To another, who artfully reminded her the Dodgers were losing in Boston: "Go freeze yer teat, an' give your tongue a sleigh ride," accompanying the words with the finger. And to a third, a Giants fan, "Like Mae West sez, to hell wit yez an' a boost for meself."

Hilda Chester played every angle as she plied her trade. She told her stories often to reporters, who saw her as a good sidebar. Of the Stevens clan she skillfully affirmed: "They're all so good to Hilda. When you got no mother, no father, it's nice to have a boss that treats you nice." As she worked the Stevens clan (to its public relations benefit), so did she finesse the Dodgers' press contingent. When *New York Post* columnist Leonard Cohen visited Chester at her Raceway hot dog stand, she reminded him that he had picked the Dodgers to finish seventh. "Ye Gods," he wrote afterward, "she could have dropped a Mickey Finn in our java. After all, a rabid Dodger fan (and Hilda heads the list by acclamation) might go to any end when aroused." As an afterthought, she told Cohen, "There's something about the Bums that gets me."

Hilda Chester thus developed a following among local sports fans by a mixture of calculated geniality, studied crudeness, and colorfully styled outrageousness. "Every place I go I know people. On Flatbush Extension, on Dekalb, the Dodger rooters always look for me. They made a nice collection once when I came out of the hospital." First Durocher and later Dixie Walker visited her, the latter catching her "crying and fearful." "He comes to see Hilda. An hour he spent wit me. He called Hilda pretty." Chester then stopped playing Jean Evans for a moment. "If I wasn't a Dodger fan, where would I be, ask me. It ain't that I'm famous, but I wouldn't be back on my feet. I wouldn't have so many friends. Win or lose, I got friends."

These stories were honed in the retelling, as Chester made her way. In the confined world of Brooklyn, she worked the angles by getting her plugs in print. "I go to Lefferts Steak House. They treat me swell there. I go to La Palina. That's a nice place on Navy Street. When I go there I don't have to worry about no bill. It isn't nice to be a freeloader, but Hilda's got friends."

An old antagonist stalked Chester at her "Big A" stand, letting her have it because the Dodgers had just lost to the Braves. "See what happens to yer Brooklyns now," he said, waving a hand in her face. "Hit the road," she retorted, "go climb a flagpole." "All I can say," her adversary added as he walked away, unknowingly summing things up neatly, "be glad you're a woman."

This story is important in two ways. First, because sports in general and baseball in particular was so completely male-oriented, it offers a crystalline insight into the harshly discriminatory gender world of the postwar decade. Second, the Dodgers were already pioneering in race relations, often in spite of themselves, so the team might reasonably have been expected to behave in a more socially appropriate manner generally. It didn't. Nearly two decades before the next feminist wave in American history, the Dodgers' story is almost certainly representative of society's tension-ridden gender relationships.

Objectively there had to be more difficult eras of gender hostility in America, but comparatively, I can't think of any. The thoughtless '50s followed hard on the quickly opened/quickly shut economic opportunities for women in World War II. But the decade also preceded the start of the gender revolution in the radical 1960s. So the gender gap between the stereotype and reality that the Dodger experience encapsulates seems larger than it might have been in another era. The sports context only underscored the existing culture norms of the times. It was in the nature of *Sportsworld*, however, that through all the gender density that surrounded the Dodgers, it was possible for Marianne Moore to find extended fulfillment in Dodger baseball, and it was possible for Hilda Chester to earn a smart livelihood from that world.

Brooklyn's women were tied to the Dodgers no less than their husbands, fathers, brothers, and sons. Woman fans were neither less knowledgeable and dedicated nor less enterprising. They were only less visible.

6
The Dodgers and Male Bar Culture

Hilda Chester and Marianne Moore aside, Brooklyn's baseball culture remained predominently male, as it did almost everywhere else in America. No institution better underscored that fact of life, in Brooklyn at least, than the neighborhood tavern. I use the male culture of Brooklyn's bars here as a symbol of both the depth of the symbiotic relationship between Brooklyn and the Dodgers as well as the male working-class world of Brooklyn that characterized a slice of the broader culture of this isolated borough. I have no doubt that there was an articulated women's culture in Brooklyn, and an upper-middle-class ethos as well, both with strong ties to the Dodgers and the larger community, and each awaiting its chronicler.* Brooklyn's bars, though, were peculiarly Dodger-oriented, characterized by two dominant life forces: they were aggressively male working-class preserves that offered cultural refuge to their denizens, and they reeked of baseball and beer. The bars, then, deserve a short chapter of their own in this context, for they provide a revealing glimpse into the importance of the Dodgers to the generalized culture of the community.

* Chapter 8 deals with religious and fraternal oganizational ties to the Dodgers.

When the Brooklyn Amateur Baseball Foundation sought to publicize its 1951 annual Sandlot Classic game, it resorted to borough taprooms to develop its publicity. The group that year decided to place Dodger memorabilia as window displays in Brooklyn stores. The Dodger artifacts and pictures were almost entirely borrowed from borough bars. These included, according to *Daily News* columnist Jimmy Powers, some wonderful murals that were vintage tavern decorations in Brooklyn. Bars, more than other Brooklyn institutions, were collectively the keepers of the Dodger past, even as they helped define Brooklyn fans for the rest of the nation.*

Man-in-the-street opinion on the Bums, so far as newsmen were concerned, was largely a euphemism for man-in-the-bar. Taverns formed a male-only world, at least for a significant part of the male working class of the borough, and the common denominators were radio (and later television), tap beer, and fellowship. Sometimes the bars were havens for the lonely; they were universally refuges for the baseball fans. Taprooms were where reporters went for sports stories on a slow day, or for human interest on a big one. When the Dodger front office raised ticket prices after winning the 1947 pennant, the public opinion that counted was found in the neighborhood pub. "The fans who lounge in taverns over small beers and listen to Red Barber and Connie Desmond," Tom Meany wrote, "complain bitterly . . . holler loudly over the price boost." 1950s male chauvinism aside, these guys knew their baseball. "It is a proved fact," Meany wrote ironically another time, "that the majority of Dodger fans prefer to listen to a Dodger broadcast within the cozy confines of a bar and grill. Quite possibly this is because the chances of a friendly debate are enhanced in the many oases which dot that fair borough."

Debate was usually the order of the day. "If the Dodgers win one of the three games they're all set," claimed a customer in Sullivan's in July 1947. The Dodgers were in a tight race for the pennant with the Cardinals that year. A stranger responded

---

*For a partial list of 1940s and '50s tavern haunts for Dodger fans, see Appendix A. I have no doubt that readers can extend that list.

strongly. He was in Sullivan's, according to Meany, "because he hadn't been able to make Henderson's by post-time." There were ten games left to play with St. Louis, the intruder reminded. "Well, leave them win three of the ten and they'll breeze in," said the first. "Why only three of ten, not seven of ten," the outsider responded (he was obviously used to a more logical confrontation at Henderson's). With the indisputable reasoning of a regular and a true baseball savant, the Sullivan's patron ended the discussion by telling the interloper: "Well, they ain't been winning from the Cards, that's why."

Backseat managing of the Dodgers was an art form in Brooklyn bars. A *New York Times* article provides a colorful example: "Barstool strategists," watching the first Dodger-Giant playoff game in the disastrous 1951 season, commented as Charley Dressen sent up Jim Russell to pinch-hit for Ralph Branca. "Oh, no, no, no!" a television-bound patron shouted. "This guy hasn't hit a ball in eleven times as a pinch-hitter!" Russell, naturally, made it twelve when he hit into a double play. "They shoulda got rid of Dressen weeks ago," the indignant fan concluded in triumphant misery.

Big events in the lives of the Dodgers were played out most deeply in bars. Durocher's treasonous departure to the Giants (the Brooklyn equivalent of Benedict Arnold's departure to the British) remained a raw wound a year later. When Leo was arrested for assaulting a fan in 1949, Dodger fans at McKeever's Bar could not muster a lot of sympathy. In the confines of this "exclusive men's club," opinion ran one way. "That monkey," mechanic Ted Griffiths said, "had a bigger batting average with his fists than he ever had with a baseball bat. He's getting what he deserves." Salesman Sam Moyer agreed. "Durocher has been begging for trouble for years. He goes out of his way to look for it. I say give it to him, and give it to him good."

When the Dodgers looked about to choke on September 6, 1952, after dropping a doubleheader to the Giants, "tavern customers were grim, and spoke about what would have happened if a ball went a foot or so the other way." Fear of a "repeat miracle" ran high in the bars that night. Usually, though, baseball talk revolved around ageless questions. At the Web Cafe in Bay Ridge in

1954, for instance, "many a beer drawn fueled the debate over who was better—the "Duke of Flatbush" (Snider) or the "Say Hey Kid" (Willie Mays). "My vote went for the Duke," Damon Rice remembered. "Most of my fellow beer drinkers were with me, but there were a few guys around the Web—men whose knowledge of baseball could not be taken lightly—who told me I was nuts."

By the early 1950s, television had largely replaced radio in the bars. But not all games were televised, and radio remained a perfectly acceptable medium; after all, Dodger bar culture antedated television by at least a generation. In the 1940s, radio still dominated the working-class atmosphere of the Brooklyn bar. Barber and Desmond formed the basis of conversation. A reporter bearing witness to a rain delay in a local inn wrote, "Tavern patrons had to put up with what one of them called 'Hill-William music.'" The customers, he concluded, looked like "they were trapped like a runner between third and home, not knowing which way to go."

Working-class Dodger fans in Brooklyn bars were a staple of feature writers in the city at large. The repeated stereotyping took its toll on this blue-collar component of the Dodger constituency. "Dodger fans are vulgar," one Manhattan denizen concluded, a common enough perception around greater New York, though obviously a superficial one. It is doubtful that the baseball culture of Brooklyn's bars was any deeper than that of Boston, say, or Chicago. As in other towns, Brooklyn's bars catered to both blue-collar workers and those who labored as salesmen or low-level civil servants. Baseball and beer were common male denominators as a way to escape urban isolation, parade expertise, and share good Dodger moments and bad. "The lonely men in Brooklyn bars/They hear the wind between the stars." Thus read one effort at newspaper doggerel in 1947.

In this habitat, the bartender presided, usually the fount of sports wisdom and the arbiter of all things baseball. Patrons deferred to the barman at least when a newspaperman was present. At Neil Sweeney's Tavern on Classon Avenue, for example, bartender Pete Carroll surveyed the scene as the Dodgers closed the gap on the Cardinals late in the 1946 season. (The regular season would end in a tie; the Cards won the playoff.) When the usual argument arose over the quality of the manager's decision, Carroll told the reporter to ignore the dispute. "About 99 percent of the boys are behind Durocher." As we have seen, that was not the case after Leo jumped ship to the Giants. But bartender Walter Gibbons provided his own sampling after the fact, noting "most of the customers I have talked it over with seem to think it is a good thing that Shotton is back. Myself, I would rather see Durocher handling the Dodgers."

When arguments threatened to erupt, it was the bartender's primary task to step in; his arbitration was usually final, a face-saving way of life in the confines of a bar. Describing one denouement, Heywood Broun noted: "Out in one of Flatbush's centers of culture . . . the other night, a couple of men at the counter just back from a night game at Ebbets Field, were sipping daintily at concoctions from frosted glasses, with white crests which might have been whipped cream." An argument broke out over a balk call, "a decorous debate, audible not more than six blocks distant." As mayhem threatened, Broun concluded, "the bartender, in an aloof way, chipped in with his version," ending the possibility of "a subdued sort of riot."

Not all barmen were olympian in their detachment. Alex Rice presided over the bar at the Web Cafe. In a close game, a pitcher's battle between Don Newcombe and Max Lanier of the Cards, Alex "had taken to pouring shots of whisky around the sixth inning," and "was getting throroughly skunked." When the Cardinals finally won the tight game, Alex grunted, "'Oh, shit' . . . slumping to the floor behind the bar." His son Damon "threw a glass of water in pop's face, pulled him to his feet, dragged him home," and came back to tend bar, underage though he was. On the night the Dodgers clinched the 1949 pennant, Alex and Damon took a busman's holiday and "hit at least a dozen saloons in Brooklyn, ending up at the Dodgers' Cafe on DeKalb."

P.M., the daily for the thinking working person, regularly ran features on Brooklyn's baseball/bar culture, sometimes with accompanying photographic essays. In one sequence, the photographer caught a patron unconsciously using his beer glass and fedora in a choreographed companion piece to events on the air. At a tense moment, the patron sucks foam off the beer, eyes on the bartender, as Ralph Branca pitches with men on base. "De won't touch ya, Ralph," reads the caption. Later, a Dodger home run, beer glass raised in a toast: "Yeow! An Old Goldie!" reads the caption. (An Old Goldie was a homer, for which the hitter received a carton of Old Gold cigarettes slid down the screen behind home plate.) A final photo of the customer as the game goes down the drain: hat pulled sideways over forehead, à la Red Skelton's character Crazy Guggenheim. Caption: "Dem double plays—moider!"

Bad Dodger moments were nowhere more poignantly observed than in Brooklyn bars, and few moments were as bad as those in September and early October, 1951. When the Dodgers lost a double-header to the Boston Braves on September 25, the front page of the *Eagle* ran its lead by noting that "bar mirrors throughout the borough reflected faces slack with disbelief. . . . Some regulars were heard to mutter that the Dodgers couldn't beat even Erasmus Hall" high school.

A week later, in the wake of Bobby Thomson's homer, Pete Hamill "went to Rattigan's Bar, where big, grown men were in tears, getting wrecked, drunk. You'd have thought the roof had just blown off their house." Leslie Slote, later Governor Nelson Rockefeller's press secretary, wrote that he was watching the game in his favorite Brooklyn bar "when Thomson lowered the boom. I aggravated in my heart," he noted in his finest Brooklynese. As the set went dark in another watering hole, the *Eagle* reported, one old man told another: "Baseball isn't everything." His aging friend responded, "What else is there?" After the two ruled out basketball and women in that order, the first concluded, "Well, there's always beer."

An even worse moment, if that were possible, was the day in 1957 when Walter O'Malley announced the Dodgers were leaving Brooklyn. "The day it was announced," fan Bobby McCarthy told Peter Golenbock, "if you were in Behan's Bar and Grill, you'd have thought it was a wake." McCarthy described one regular, Willie Grange, "a sick Dodger fan. . . . Willie wanted to go find Walter O'Malley and kill him. He wanted to kidnap him. He wanted to get him and shoot him. He figured if he shot him, the Dodgers wouldn't move." Years later, Jack Newfield told

Golenbock, he and Pete Hamill were joking in a bar about writing an article on "The Ten Worst Human Beings Who Ever Lived." As an experiment, each of the two wrote on separate napkins the names of the first three on the list. They had the same names, the same order: Hitler, Stalin, Walter O'Malley.

Dodger fans could be hospitable to outsiders, but not if they were Yankee or Giant fans. For example, when a Red Sox scout turned up in Ebbets Field and made himself known, some Dodger faithful took him on a tour of Dodger bars after the game, hitting several high spots. They were less than gracious to fans of local rivals. Archie Wolf, a Yankee fan from New Jersey (double jeopardy here), tried to watch a 1952 World Series game in Brooklyn, where he was visiting relatives. He reported that he was tossed out of several bars when he made his sympathies known, and finally gave up. In the same World Series, another Yankee fan was told, "Why don't you go back where you belong, Yankee lover?" "I got a right to cheer my team," the intruder responded, "this is a free country." "This ain't no free country, chum," countered the Dodger fan, "this is Brooklyn."

A year later Bill Reddy was even less hospitable. "I can remember I was in the Parkside Tavern one night and a Yankee fan began taunting the regular patrons." Reddy acknowledged he "whapped the guy in the head." Bartenders tried to head off these confrontations. "We got a couple of Giants fans who are beefing," George McGuire at McCormick's Bar and Grill on Utica Avenue reported. "I had to order them out. . . . It's a wonder sometimes there isn't a murder in the place."

Dodger fans' emotions ran high in bars. Occasional violence was a fact of life, but with nowhere near the frequency that baseball lore has it. The only Brooklyn bar murder concerning the Dodgers occurred in 1938. There was also a 1955 killing, but it happened in Queens, and it was perpetrated by a disgruntled Yankee fan who "couldn't stand the thought that the Yankees had lost even once." Thus does Brooklyn take a bad rap. Michael Kimmel mentions "barroom fights" as a part of baseball culture generally, one of several things that "connects American males with each other." But there are no grounds for saying that Brooklyn was more extreme than most places.

At the Pineapple Bar on the street of the same name in Brooklyn Heights, a more cosmopolitan mix of fans gathered, as befitted the classy neighborhood. As the 1951 season wound down, and the Giants won yet another game, barman Caesar Piccollo said, "I am the most dejected person in Brooklyn tonight. Every Giant fan in Brooklyn Heights . . . shows up at my bar on a night like this." Piccollo, with the Solomon-like wisdom given only to a Brooklyn barkeep, eased the tension by posting a hand-lettered weather report on the bar mirror: *Gloom Tonight. Sunshine Tomorrow.*

Some Brooklyn watering holes became legendary, among them Jay's, the Dodgerville Room in Junior's Restaurant, and Hugh Casey's Steak and Chop House among them. The latter remained a Brooklyn fixture even after Casey had been traded away. The tavern even survived his 1951 suicide. But while he was still in town and pitching for the Dodgers, it was a favorite of die-hard fans who wanted to rub shoulders occasionally with the Dodger players who frequented the place. Located hard by Ebbets Field at 600 Flatbush Avenue, it was especially a fixture in the late 1940s. Hugh Casey's became nationally known when Hilda Weissman sued Casey for paternity. It was one of the few bars where women were welcome, and so it became a pick-up spot for Dodger groupies.

In his heyday, Casey was often there. It was said he poured a mean drink and that he could "drink till it was coming out of his ears, and then he'd bottle it and drink it again." When celebrations were in order, Red Barber said, Hugh Casey's played host to the Dodger players. Casey himself lived in an apartment over the bar during the season. "Known to his teammates as the Cork," Tom Meany ironically reported, it was a nickname he got "either because he was a great stopper coming out of the bullpen or a result of his prowess with the bottle, take your pick."

Jay's Tavern at 22 Clinton Street in the Heights was also a frequent haunt for some second-string Dodgers. It was quiet, dark, more private and middle-class than most bars, reflecting, as the Pineapple Bar did, the dominant motif of the neighborhood. Hank Behrman seems to have been a regular there (and maybe some other places as well). During one of Branch Rickey's patented self-criticism sessions conducted by the coaching staff during spring training, Behrman, an acknowledged bar-closer, rose and ingenuously suggested that his greatest weakness was hitting, and that he would work on that before the season began. "You don't need more hitting, Henry," a coach replied, "you need more sleep."

Several other Dodgers frequented Jay's during the 1950s, including George Shuba, Wayne Belardi, Rocky Bridges, and a closely knit contingent of southern utility men. It was from the latter group that criticism of Jackie Robinson's "privileged" place as a regular who couldn't cut it anymore hit the *Eagle* in 1954. That was at the point that Junior Gilliam's arrival caused a reshuffling of the Dodger infield. It pushed some of the complainers another rung down the playing ladder. Steve Carillo, the bartender, ran a tight ship and protected the privacy of his Dodger customers. He chose not to do so on this occasion. The players were reported to be loud and out of line.

Another popular watering place where some Dodgers gathered was the Dodger Cafe. But after the place was exposed as the headquarters of Harry Gross, Brooklyn's most eminent bookie, the cafe was ruled out-of-bounds for players. Hung behind the long bar was the centerpiece, a large, wall-size photograph of the 1947 pennant-winning team. When the Dodgers became world champs in 1955, owner-bartender Carl Sanders replaced the '47 photo with one of the 1955 team.

The Dodgerville Room at Junior's Restaurant was probably the classiest bar in Brooklyn. Its name notwithstanding, it welcomed Yankee fans, Giant fans, and women, in that order. It was a bar favored by City Council president Abe (*Hit Sign—Win Suit*) Stark, the haberdasherer who turned both his fanatic allegiance to the Dodgers and his famous Ebbets Field billboard into a political career. It was rumored but never proven that if no one won a suit all season, Carl Furillo got one for protecting the sign.

Many of the bars and many of their patrons were Brooklyn Irish, but probably not a majority in either instance. That Brooklyn's bar culture was an exclusively Irish one is an exaggeration. What can be said is that it was exclusively white and mostly male—all male in the working-class watering holes. Some bars were exclusively Irish working-class havens, but others were popular among Jewish and Italian men. These are educated guesses; hard data on a question like this are hard to come by, maybe impossible.

What can be said with certainty is that the bar scene was a significant part of the borough's attachment to the Dodgers. The dominant baseball milieu in these watering spots was the epitome of male working-class bonding, helped along by beer, booze, radio, and television. This was true in Brooklyn in an era before men felt threatened generally by the resurgent feminism that characterized the era beginning in the late 1960s. Still, one could not imagine in Brooklyn even in the '60s the kind of revolution carried out, for example, in integrating McSorley's in the East Village of Manhattan. The only bars identified with the Dodgers that permitted women were those few upscale places that doubled as good restaurants and catered to an upper-middle-class clientele, or that handful frequented by some Dodgers because they were hangouts for Annies. In this context I doubt that Brooklyn differed culturally from other baseball cities. But Brooklyn's bar culture, if not materially different, seemed very intense, a very internalized private world for which the Dodgers formed a central focus.

7
The Dodgers and Brooklyn's Ethnic Isolation

Isolation was no stranger to the borough of Brooklyn. In the era before bridges and subways connected Brooklyn to Manhattan, geography imposed a quarantine on what was first a village and eventually a city. After those physical links were in place, cultural segregation persisted, extending Brooklyn's inward-looking tradition. From the late nineteenth century on, immigrants and their children generally stayed with their own. For its ethnic residents, Brooklyn was a borough of marbleized ghettoes. The isolation was reflected in attitudes outside the borough. Brooklyn was not really thought to be part of New York City by "genuine" New Yorkers. There were the *New York Yankees*, and the *New York Giants* after all, but the *Bums* were the Brooklyn Dodgers. A corollary to this was the frequently confrontational nature of ethnic relationships in the borough, a hostility within that matched the sense of isolation without. The Dodgers formed an ameliorating force for unity in Brooklyn, but the team's local mystique did not miraculously bring all the people to love each other. Still, the Dodger presence helped. (This was especially true of Brooklyn's boys, the subject of Chapter 8.)

Left to right: Curt Simmons, Bob Rush, National League President Warren Giles, Hank Sauer, and Jackie Robinson at the 1952 All-Star Game. (National Baseball Library, Cooperstown, N.Y.)

Above: Left to right: Jim Gilliam, Pee Wee Reese, Duke Snider, and Jackie Robinson, 1953. Reese and Snider along with Robinson were key figures in subduing late-blooming racial unrest on the team. (National Baseball Library, Cooperstown, N.Y.)

Left: Jackie Robinson's patented body-block, this time administered to Giant second baseman Ed Stanky. (National Baseball Library, Cooperstown, N.Y.)

Brooklyn boys celebrating the Dodgers' World Series victory in 1955. (National Baseball Library, Cooperstown, N.Y.)

Walter O'Malley points to the 1955 Brooklyn Pennant. The other hand, however, points west. (National Baseball Library, Cooperstown, N.Y.)

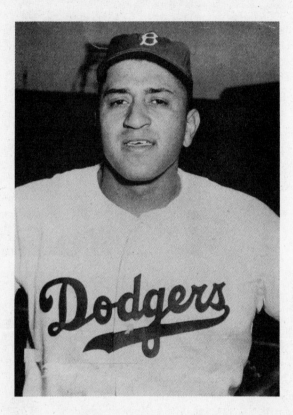

Pitcher Don Newcombe. (National Baseball Library, Cooperstown, N.Y.)

1953 "cheesecake" shot of Dodger wives. Left to right: Mrs. Bobby Morgan, Mrs. Rex Barney, Mrs. Pee Wee Reese, Mrs. Jack Banta, Mrs. Carl Erskine. (AP Wideworld)

Brooklyn fans wait anxiously in right field for a Chicago victory that would send the Dodgers into a 1946 playoff with St. Louis. (National Baseball Library, Cooperstown, N.Y.)

A talking version of the famed Brooklyn Bum. (National Baseball Library, Cooperstown, N.Y.)

A "real" Brooklyn Bum. On any given day at Ebbets Field a few fans would dress the part. (National Baseball Library, Cooperstown, N.Y.)

**Charlie DiGiovanna, right, world's oldest batboy, greets Duke
Snider at the plate.** (AP/Wideworld)

Brooklyn boys at Ebbets Field, 1955. (National Baseball Library, Cooperstown, N.Y.)

Brooklyn fans wait on Montague St. for playoff tickets, 1946. (National Baseball Library, Cooperstown, N.Y.)

As new neighborhoods rolled east from Brooklyn Heights, they reflected the realities of a ghettoization common generally to late nineteenth- and early twentieth-century American cities. While the fashionable Heights, in the shadow of Brooklyn Bridge, remained generally bedrock elite, native, and Protestant, the rest of Brooklyn was solidly ethnic: mainly Irish, Italian, and Jewish, with smaller groups of Scandinavians, Greeks, and Poles in the mix. By the end of the Second World War, a growing African American influx into what became Bedford-Stuyvesant augmented a small black community of long standing.

This was a remarkably diverse and equally tense cultural mix in a geographically contained area, and the Dodger ball club provided the major unifying focus amid this Joseph's Coat of a population. The degree to which this was true may be measured by the Dodgers' central place in the distinct language of Brooklyn. Overt class consciousness seemed to run higher in Brooklyn than elsewhere in the city, and the Dodgers' presence helped maintain an uneasy truce among ethnic groups. The comforting melting-pot notion of the American immigrant experience, with its emphasis on shared American values and a growing commonality of interests, has largely gone by the boards among American historians. The realities of immigrant differences dominated everyday life, as the Brooklyn experience yet again demonstrated. The Dodgers, in this tense setting, formed a social force for acculturation, perhaps an example of the larger role baseball has played in shaping American commonality in the twentieth century.

The borough's cultural isolation was accentuated, literally, by "Brooklynese," a dialect a shade deeper than common New York accents. It was closely identified in New York and the nation with "dem Bums." In fact the cartoon symbol of the Dodger Bum bespoke not only a scrappy and idiosyncratic baseball team but, in broader terms, the lower-middle-class origins of its ethnic fans. Because of Brooklyn's cultural isolation, both within the borough itself and as a distinct part of greater New York, the sense of class inferiority common to most first- and second-generation immigrants could only have been enhanced.

While the Dodger Bum was a visual symbol of some weight, through radio and movies in the 1930s and '40s, Brooklyn's harsh accents became even more nationally known as a signifier of the borough's apartness. That déclassé symbol was fixed deeply in the public mind during the Second World War. Because of William Bendix's starring role in *Wake Island*, a 1942 propaganda movie that hit home emotionally for many Americans after that island's capture by the Japanese, Americans related the "Brooklyn accent" to the Dodger team, and not incorrectly. After Bendix, the tough-talking Brooklyn fan became a stock character of war films.

Brooklyn became the butt of aggressive satire. When borough president John Cashmore was asked why the very name of Brooklyn would make people smile (or sometimes snicker), Cashmore replied, "It may be the whole world is pleased there is such a fine place as this." Cashmore's deft answer notwithstanding, he and many other Brooklyn denizens felt the sting of the intended ridicule. "Everyone was laughing at us," one said. "If you listened to a radio quiz program and a contestant said he came from Brooklyn, you next heard a clamor of laughter from the studio audience." And you expected the contestant to lose, he added. Yankee manager Casey Stengel said on the eve of his only World Series loss to the Dodgers, "Trouble with Brooklyn, it's been insulted too long."

"The Society for the Prevention of Disparaging Remarks Against Brooklyn" was founded during the war, to respond wherever and whenever it came upon offensive slights of the borough. This was not some tongue-in-cheek invention, but an organization driven by an educational mission. By 1946, it claimed, with a good deal of exaggeration, 40,000 members. They culled 3000 slanders in the media that year alone. If this appears to be an excessive claim, note that H. L. Mencken saw it happening. In his 1948 edition of *The American Language*, he concluded that "the vulgar speech of New York City, once known as Boweryese, [is] now generally called Brooklynese." A good part of parodied English fixed on the Dodgers, and much of that reflected outsiders' perceptions of what they took to be semi-literate lower-class

Brooklyn street talk. The language of "baseballese" (for example, Casey Stengel's popularized version), which in the borough cross-fertilized "Brooklynese," salted the latter with large doses of baseball lingo, as we shall see.

This satirical language, so widely ridiculed, coincided with the 1940s popularization of cartoonist Willard Mullins's Dodger Bum, the pictorial incarnation of the Dodgers' scrappy reputation. It was also an affirmation for many of the lower-class reputation of the borough. Leo O'Mealia, commemorating the Dodgers' 1955 World Championship, built his famous "Whose a Bum!" cartoon around Mullins's drawing. The "Bum" was never meant to denigrate the lowly. It represented at heart a lingering Depression mentality that exalted the virtue that it wasn't what you had that mattered, but how you looked at things. In this way, it was a Dodger-focused, widely understood symbol of working-class pride; the emphasis is on class here, for one of the Bum's roles was to mock perceived "upper class" pretensions.

Stephen King, a Brooklyn native, grew up a Dodger fan. In a youthful poem he remarked on "the faceless fans who cry down juicy vowels." Juicy they were. Recalling his first taste of Ebbets Field, Carl Erskine told of being spotted as he arrived at the Ebbets Field rotunda carrying his Fort Worth Cats duffel. "Hey, there's Oiskine. From Fort Woith. Hi, Oisk." "Oisk" he was forevermore, orally and all too often in print.

New York Post columnist Jimmy Cannon wrote ironically of Red Barber in 1952: "You notice they want someone to speak English on the radio they don't get no guy from Brooklyn. They get a guy from down South. It goes to prove they don't even like to hear themselves talk, don't it, when you got to get a yamer to speak for you." Was a "yamer" someone who ate yams? Someone who "yammers" for a living? Take your pick. Barber, columnist Steve Jacobson said years later, gave Brooklynites "tone and flavor and (new) expressions to mangle."

Establishment types habitually and, some might say, comically reinforced the propriety of the distinctive rules of grammar that touched Dodger-freighted Brooklynese. "The speechways of Dodger fans enriched the language," John Lardner wrote. "It was from this that philologists learned that the plural of 'ya bum, ya!' is 'yez bums, yez!'" The New York City Board of Education was asked to comment on the grammatical correctness of Charley Dressen's infamous 1953 comment that "the Giants is dead." A Brooklyn board member responded, thinking naturally of the impressionable young: "Of course," the educator explained, "if one member of the Giants were alive, like Maglie, you could not say the Giants *is* dead. But if every member of this entity is dead, hence the Giants *is* too."

The language of the Brooklyn streets brought an irresistible urge to parody even fellow Brooklynites. William Poster, in "'Twas a Dark Night in Brownsville," recounts how a suddenly self-conscious Brooklyn boy responded to an outsider's query on his turf: "Where ya from? . . . Ahah! Dat's in Brahnsvil, hah, hah, Brahnsvil. Noo? Howz Peetkin Avenue?"

Brooklynites' sensitivity to these seemingly endless satires ran deep, and language was only part of the problem. They were often defensive. Dodger fans knew they had a winner in the great team Branch Rickey put together after World War II. But continuing heart-wrenching losses to "New York" ball clubs hurt. The Yankees won the World Series with sodden regularity, and the Giants' "miracle" in 1951 was devastating, reinforcing the star-crossed feeling in Brooklyn that "we never win it all."

It was as much a class thing as it was cultural isolation. "It ties up with a sort of social neurosis," sportswriter Joe Williams said, "an elegant, smug New York versus a plain, provincial Brooklyn." Compared with mainland baseball fans, "Dodger fans are vulgar," one Manhattanite characteristically commented. Arthur Daley of the *New York Times* put the stereotype succinctly in 1949: the Dodgers had become a great team, he concluded, but the Brooklyn fan "has the brashness and ostentation of the nouveau riche while the Yankee fan has the conservatism and slightly disdainful superiority of the born aristocrat." This cultural isolation and its accompanying defiance of the world had another side: Brooklyn's "specialness" was also a source of pride. Both sides of that lower-class archetype that passed for a Brooklyn fan in the public prints were equally present in a patronizing poem Grantland Rice, an elder statesman among sports columnists, wrote in lieu of his usual *New York Sun* column. It was meant to be complimentary; it wasn't:

> He's a neolithic throwback to the past. . . .
> As he concentrates upon the vocal blast. . . .
> But he's hooked up with an outfit
> that can feed him daily thrills,
> Which is something millionaires can never buy.

The *Times*'s sportswriters in particular repeatedly exploited the perception of class gulf that separated Brooklyn from Manhattan. They rarely visited Ebbets Field, as if they felt uncomfortable there. But a descriptive, class-based column deliberately blurring the line between the borough and the team was apparently accepted as insightful. For example, Arthur Daley wrote in 1953 that "because of Brooklyn's raffish past a Yankee fan automatically assumes an air of aristocratic superiority on the eve of any World Series." On another occasion he cited nameless "baseball people" for this quote: "Dodger fans were insufferable enough when they had nothing. They'll be completely unbearable now that they have everything." In another anonymous "it's been said" representation, John Lardner described the Dodger appeal as "brash, low, even buffoonish." This comment came late, in 1956, when the Dodgers were the reigning world champions. Lardner added there is a "school of thought (again anonymous) that has always associated the Brooks with déclassé phenomena like El lines, cobblestones and walk-up rooming houses." Throwaway remarks like these were bald allusions to perceived class differences that distanced Brooklyn from "New York."

Peter Golenbock, with great insight, catches this class consciousness, revealing that "The Bums" and the borough alike were interchangeable within the web of lower-middle-class outsiders' perceptions. His oral histories are laced with examples of outside-imposed class consciousness, whether referring to the team or the town. The 1955 World Series win over the Yankees meant to one representative Brooklyn native that "a whole city . . . now can raise its head, look across the river . . . and say, 'We're number one.'" The price of class ran very high, psychologically and otherwise, as it turned out.

Author Robert Caro blamed Robert Moses (the 1950s czar of New York redevelopment) more than Walter O'Malley for the Dodgers' desertion to Los Angeles. Although Moses was billed in his heyday as the classic liberal who wanted to improve the lot of the masses via vast new expanses of concrete buildings and expressways, he was in fact an elitist who seemed to dismiss Brooklyn and its residents as important priorities in his "renewal" of New York. Moses, who did not find baseball all that edifying, was the ruthless overseer of New York's physical environment for a generation, so maybe Caro is right that Moses shares the blame for the disappearance of the Dodgers. Revealingly, in 1957 Moses wrote in his own defense that it was hard to think about spending all that money on a new Brooklyn stadium for "oafs . . . hecklers and bottle-throwers, buoyed up on home cushions, chewing chocolate nuts . . . or lapping up somebody's dry beer." Although history mainly remembers only The O'Malley, there do seem to be two villains behind the Dodger move, not one.

The déclassé image of Dodger fans was deeply ingrained in the larger New York culture. Even *Psychology Today*, a later icon of the educated upper middle class, unconsciously picked up the existing stereotype of Brooklyn fans in a 1978 article on why people root for certain teams. The author noted in passing that a six-year-old became a Yankee fan because his mother bought him a Yankee cap from a street display featuring three New York teams. The mother, the author said, picked the Yankee hat because "Dodger blue was too bold." It was in fact a stylish navy blue, so memory seems quirky here, psychologist's credentials notwithstanding. But the point is his conclusion: "My mother was a woman of taste and class," so the Dodger cap was out.

Class differences were not the same as ethnic differences in Brooklyn. Ethnics in Brooklyn were largely lower-middle-class, but their sameness stopped there, as academics have recently discovered. There have been several recent studies of baseball that include general examination of fans' social roots, and two deep studies of Brooklyn's neighborhoods (Canarsie and Brownsville). These collectively make clear, as George Will affirms, that baseball in part crystallizes Americans' "yearning for community."

Gerald Sorin's study of Brownsville youth confirms locally that widely held belief. A significant part of Jewish street culture in Brownsville revolved around the Dodgers, and the team figured largely in the consciousness of the Brownsville Boys Club. In fact, its founder and patron saint, Abe Stark, made a political career out of his combined identification with the Dodgers and the Boys Club.

Ball clubs, Ray Robinson has written, "invariably duplicate the temperament of the cities in which they play," and he characterized Dodger fans as "underdog, recidivist . . . from a land of people with hard-to-pronounce names." That Brooklyn was ethnic was a fact widely perceived in the nation as one of the sources of its strangeness. No team "had more fans with foreign accents" than the Brooklyn Dodgers, said Wilfred Sheed, a Dodger fan who had one himself. Inasmuch as foreign origin and lower-class assignment by the majority native culture usually went hand-in-hand, Brooklyn was an especially obvious example of this American social judgment.

Brooklyn's experience with the Dodgers was not unique. Chicago and its Cubs and Boston and its Red Sox offer up analogous examples. The ballclubs, in these instances, seemed often to take on the character of their communities even as they provided deep unifying forces within those cities. Is it possible to see this phenomenon as sport-related social symbiosis at work? If so, then Brooklyn was one city that needed any unifying force a baseball team could provide.

The borough was ethnically atomized. Almost all its neighborhoods were ghettoes, immigrant and racial enclaves of largely homogeneous groups. The neighborhood was as much the base point of residents' loyalty as the borough. Where local identity was concerned, greater New York City was not even in the contest. Yet in an isolated environment, Brooklynites shared common bonds: Brooklyn's children and their first- and second-generation parents spoke a common and unique street language; all felt detached from the greater city of which they were a political part; most felt ill-judged by outsiders who looked down on them (a pretty good defining component of class awareness, if not of class difference, all by itself); and locals were defensive about the misconceptions the rest of the world seemed to hold about them.

Linguists in particular in the generation after World War II seemed mesmerized by the hidden meanings of Brooklyn's language and culture, especially the latter's relationship to the Dodgers. "To the world," philologist B. A. Botkin concluded in 1954, "'Dem Bums' spells out not only the Dodgers but much-maligned Brooklyn." Francis Griffiths, in a 1972 essay, said that "these linguistic confusions in Brooklyn were the reflections of deeper confusions. They mirrored the inverted psychology of natives who called their heroes 'Bums.'" Borough dwellers in general, Griffiths concluded, possessed a very poor self-image. Academic insights like these, linguist Geoffrey Needler concluded, together formed "fearful evidence of Brooklyn's dark, sidereal pathology." As if to bear all this theory out, the borough never seemed more star-crossed than it did when it responded so explosively to sportswriter Jimmy Cannon's infamous *New York Post* column satirizing its Dodger-centered provincialism. Led by their cheerleaders at the *Brooklyn Eagle*, many Brooklynites responded in much the same way as hornets do when their hive is threatened.

Writing a tongue-in-cheek column in pseudo-Brooklynese describing the implications of recent Dodger success, Cannon deftly pushed all of Brooklyn's buttons. "The way they holler about the Dodgers," Cannon wrote in the summer of 1952, "you think they had a choice. . . . Over in Brooklyn you got to root for the Dodgers or root for the Bushwicks." This essay mauled the borough by parading the stereotypes by which it was known. "All they got in Brooklyn is to go to a ball game or stay at home and get loaded. If you don't, you got to come to New York any time you want to have a little fun." And still, Cannon continued, Dodger fans have delusions of grandeur. "Brooklyn, Brooklyn, Brooklyn, I'm sick of hearing it. The way they talk you think it was a whole country with an army and a king or something. All they got is a ball club."

The "borough of churches" took a pasting, and the word "bum" was sprinkled liberally through the narrative: "Lots of

Brooklyn bums I know would never go inside a church unless they could rob the poor box. But churches, churches, churches is all you hear from them. Let's face it, Brooklyn is out of town." The cemeteries also came in for a few caresses: "It groums me because I got to get buried in that lousy place," Cannon wrote, but what choice did he have? If you lived in Manhattan, you either got buried in the boroughs or, God forbid, Jersey.

The *Brooklyn Eagle* was furious. An editorial called Cannon's satire "coarse, even obscene," a "filthy attack upon [our] hometown . . . upon its churches . . . upon its cemeteries where our loved ones are buried." The *Eagle* deliberately fanned the embers of local outrage into a red-hot blaze. Columnist Robert Grannis, calling Cannon "Mr. Screwball," used the event to lash out at Manhattan's perpetual seizure of the lion's share of the city's resources, long a Brooklyn complaint. "The only mistake we ever made, sweetheart, was when we merged with the other boroughs."

It was, all in all, a vituperative and very defensive response, one that put an exclamation point to an almost institutionalized self-consciousness that personified Brooklyn's frustration with its inferior political and social station in greater New York City. Judging from the popular response, the borough felt itself almost pathologically isolated from the world around it.

Predictably, the *Eagle*'s aggressive retort uncorked a ton of letters. A few pointed out that Cannon's essay was genuinely funny, in both dialect and content, and no big deal. But the vast majority were pained outpourings of individuals who gave voice to long pent-up chagrin over the perceived disrespect accorded Brooklyn. Cannon touched a nerve. Residents by the hundreds expressed outrage at yet again suffering disrespect. The *Post* sportswriter's reference to "a bum from Brooklyn" who never "said a prayer in his life" in particular drew angry responses. James Kelly, Deputy County Clerk for Brooklyn and a well-connected local pol, in one of the more pompous rejoinders reminded Cannon that if he "had taken time out to see the thousands of God-fearing, God-loving people turning out to attend divine services . . . his filthy pen might have been stayed."

A gold-star mother, on the other hand, wrote poignantly that her son was "a bum from Brooklyn who now lies in a Brooklyn cemetery, a 'bum' who dared to die for the likes of James Cannon."

The allusions to Cannon's references to "bum" rang the bell in Brooklyn. Many tied their responses to perceptions of elitist Giants fans from Manhattan and the suburbs. Mary Nockowitz and others wrote that they wished the response to the *Eagle* could have been printed in the *New York Post,* "where those Giant fans could have read it and hang their heads in shame." Still smarting from the 1951 Giant "miracle" and its associated history of a long, deeply personalized rivalry, one large group of responses to Cannon was linked to newly reopened wounds caused by the eternal Giant-Dodger enmity. Cannon only wrote the column, one Dodger partisan said, "because the Giants' fans must rationalize the fact" that the Dodgers were leading the league. The Bum, many said, would triumph in the end.

In essence, the Dodger Bum, the sense of inferiority many Brooklynites felt within the context of the greater city, and the longstanding rivalry with the Giants were all wrapped up in the widespread overreaction. "Don't worry," Grace Ward reminded her townspeople, "it's the slams that made Brooklyn famous."

So if any place needed the face a winning major league team could provide, it was Brooklyn. The Dodgers were really part of the soul of the community, and the team's eventual departure must be understood in that light. Not until just before its move to Los Angeles, when the team became world champions at last, one writer has said, "would Brooklyn expunge its image as Sad Sack of the Globe." Roger Kahn caught well the nearly spiritual role the Dodgers played in Brooklyn in the face of this siege mentality. In a short retrospective piece he quoted this poetic excerpt: "Lives rooted in weary brownstones . . . /were lit up by the gods at play nearby."

Meat-handed humor was inescapable. Brooklyn was a distant place, a different place, Brooklynites a species apart. "It was rumored," *P.M.* reported, that "Professor Ernest A. Hooton, head of Howard [University's] Department of Anthropology, was in the stands for the purpose of studying the Brooklyn rooters, but this couldn't be verified." The Dodgers provided a singular and critical source of positive, even aggressive, response, a validation of the class-grittiness that white natives embraced in the borough. The ball club's newly reinforced image, though, despite the presence of black ballplayers, did not build a bridge to African Americans in Brooklyn.

A 1954 *Brooklyn Eagle* serialized survey of neighborhoods identified the changing character of what was for the first time being "loosely" called Bedford-Stuyvesant. It was an emerging ghetto increasingly inhabited by Hispanic and African Americans. Irish, Italians, and Jews were often hostile to them. Jackie Robinson's visibility mattered at one level of consciousness; but at another level, an increasing black presence in the population sent out shock waves, a reaction seemingly divorced from the example of Brooklyn's almost uniquely integrated ball club.

Jews, feeling the pain of discrimination themselves, were nevertheless often fearfully anti-black. Their exodus to New Jersey and, in particular, Westchester and Long Island, began in earnest in the early 1950s. "Ninety-five percent of them have been mugged and moved away." Then, as now, that was code for race prejudice. "With blacks moving in came great fear," one Jewish observer noted. "There was blockbusting. There was panic selling . . . parasites and vultures [real estate agents] who circle any changing or transitional neighborhood." One African American angrily told Jonathan Rieder that "people forget one thing: I didn't destroy *their* Brownsville."

Another uncomfortable truth was that Irish and Italians fully shared Jewish attitudes toward blacks and felt aggrieved in general at the threat to neighborhood seemingly posed by African American and Hispanic encroachment. "Blacks moved in and whites fled" was a common Italian perception, as they followed Jews to Long Island, according to Jonathan Rieder. "Respect" is a freighted word among Italian Americans, embracing a sociological concept involving definable conscious feelings of honor and deference due. As African Americans moved in, one Italian worker said, "Respect, it's been lost."

White groups were no better with each other. Alan Lelchuk, a novelist, indulged a common stereotype applied by Jews to

Italians by characterizing Carl Furillo's "patrolling the right field pasture" as the rightful work of "an Italian gardener." Peter Golenbock reported that as Thomson's home run carried into the left-field stands at the Polo Grounds in 1951, an Irish grandfather "bent over, called Branca a 'dago bastard,' spit at the screen, and keeled over dead."

Eagle columnist Tommy Holmes ran a story in 1951 featuring the complaints that fans had sent to him about perceived changes at Ebbets Field. The perpetual presence of "drunks" in the park figured prominently among the laments and was an encoded reference to the Irish regulars who attended many games. Allen Guttmann, an academic, fell into the same trap, unconsciously stereotyping Irish fans in talking about baseball as the sport of choice for "blue collar" Irish, and relating it to the saloons around ball parks generally run by "Irish political bosses." Even the liberal daily *P.M.* unthinkingly bought into the characterization of Irish fans as universally hard-drinking. The "majority" of Irish Dodger partisans, *P.M.* reported in 1947, "listen to a Dodger broadcast within the cozy confines of a bar and grill."

The Irish were no better in the aggregate than Jews and Italians in firing off prejudicial broadsides. One Irish correspondent wrote Tommy Holmes denouncing "the increasing presence of foreign-language speaking families" (Puerto Ricanos) in Ebbets Field as the 1950s dawned. Roger Kahn reminded readers that in Brooklyn, "on Sundays the Irish of St. Theresa's Parish worshipped a gentle Christ. Other days some of them distributed the fascist newspaper *Social Justice*," a product of the anti-Semite priest Charles Coughlin, which "warned of a revolution being organized by Jews."

Although Brooklyn was a metropolis, with three million people, it lacked even the limited political autonomy of a city, and thus any real political control over its own destiny. Large as it was, it was only a minority component of an even more mammoth urban entity. The problem was compounded because by far the largest part of the population felt itself marginalized for ethnic, racial, or economic reasons. The difficulty was magnified in the 1950s, as many of those with the means moved out. The white immigrant minorities, especially, felt a deepening sense of ethnic and racial embattlement. Each Brooklyn immigrant group had always stereotyped the others as it competed for space, political access, and work. After World War II the social transition that took place took the form of the suburbanization of American life, and that only magnified Brooklyn's urban problems.

Few escaped the sting of a prejudice newly reinvigorated by the departures. The decamping of the Dodger franchise in its turn needs to be understood in the context of these other 1950s exoduses from Brooklyn. African Americans and Puerto Ricanos who replaced the departing whites were routinely made invisible when they were not otherwise disparaged. Jews felt the pressures imposed by a widespread feeling that they were largely left-liberal in a politically conservative borough; had they not spawned Judith Coplon (convicted of espionage) and buried the Rosenbergs in their midst? Italians, both Jonathan Rieder and Jerry Della Femina made clear, felt a generalized lack of respect from outsiders who lived alongside them. When newspapers wrote engagingly about colorful Brooklyn watering holes devoted to their Bums, the subtext was that they were Irish bars where some serious drinking took place.

Peter Levine suggests that this harsh view of ethnic division may be exaggerated. In *From Ellis Island to Ebbets Field* he makes the point that sports played such a large part in Brooklyn's Jewish life that it softened the rough edges of immigrant confrontation.* This was especially true in the development of a fellow feeling between Irish and Jews in Brooklyn and elsewhere, particularly when boxing was the sport. Deborah Dash Moore, on the other hand, suggests in *At Home in America* a New York tapestry of separation of Jewish ethnics from other immigrant groups. A strong inner sense of Jewish community prevented much bonding with other immigrant groups who shared Jewish outsider status.

The other side of this story, then, deserves mention. The study of history is in part the study of social paradox, and Brook-

* The Dodgers' role on the Parade Grounds, and the adolescent ethnics' common response, suggest that, so far as Brooklyn's boys were concerned, Levine may be right. This is dealt with in Chapter 8.

lyn formed no exception in embodying historic inconsistency. People got along in Brooklyn's insular environment because there were things that brought them together as well as things that divided them. It wasn't only the Dodgers. There was as well a shared sense of embattlement, a common and much-maligned language, a pervasive male youth culture (discussed in the next chapter), and a shared role as outsiders.

The Dodgers, however, proved to be much-needed catalysts, so the team's presence was central to the sense of community. While the Dodgers did not make tensions go away, the team's universality in the borough, both real and psychic, helped ease social stress. It provided the single largest common center of local identification in a complex urban society, and rounded off the roughest edges of social pressure by periodically bringing Brooklyn together. As I said before, this is not a unique baseball phenomenon. It happened the same way, I suspect, in other immigrant-laden communities, Boston and Chicago providing possibly the most visible examples.

"The city's soul" is the phrase that Alan Lelchuk used in *Brooklyn Boy* to describe the depths of loss the Dodgers' departure inflicted on Brooklyn. "Forget the sweatshops," Lelchuk wrote, "forget the class wars, forget the family squabbles, forget the racial antagonisms . . . forget the anger and quiet despair." The Dodgers offered many inhabitants a national face and more: "All the subtle art of baseball was put on display by the Dodgers." And that came with real life off-the-field "nuance and drama." Such was the stuff of Gil Hodges's 1952–53 slump. It provides a good case study in how the Dodger presence would periodically unite the "soul" of the city.

Hodges grew up in Indiana, but when he married Brooklyn native Joan Lombardi in 1948, he settled in Flatbush and never left. Brooklyn, he told reporters, "is my home town. I'm proud to say so." His troubles at bat started in the 1952 World Series, when he set a new major league record by going 0 for 21. His difficulties continued into the following spring. His mechanics broke down, his confidence went. Hodges couldn't buy a hit, and, finally, in May 1953 Charley Dressen benched him. Dodger fans generally could be pitiless and cruel, even to their own. At points in their careers, sometimes for extended stretches, Robinson, Reese, Snider, Furillo, and, of course, Newcombe were all booed at Ebbets Field. But in overt acknowledgment of shared community, by 1953 Brooklyn's citizens had come to see Gil Hodges as one of their own. He lived in town and went to mass every Sunday during the off-season and when the Dodgers were home during the summer. Hodges was, said Tom Meany, "obligingly available during the winter for athletic dinners of all faiths."

Both during the 1952 World Series and the tough spring of 1953, Dodger fans were unusually reluctant to get on Hodges. That uncharacteristic absence of negative reaction was transformed into borough-wide support, started in this instance by divine intervention. A local priest ended a mass with a throwaway line: "Go home, keep the commandments, and say a prayer for Gil Hodges." The sermonette made the papers. Hodges was of course inundated with the usual letters of advice; but this time there was more. Talismans arrived by the score; crucifixes, rosary beads, rabbits' feet, miniature horseshoes (and a few of the real thing), and mezuzahs all deluged the Dodger mail room on Montague Street as a part of a "save Hodges crusade."

As happened periodically when the Dodgers were concerned, the borough was brought together. When they ate out, Joan Hodges recalled later, "people stopped by our table . . . to sympathize." This went on for weeks, through June 1953. Neighbors and store clerks stopped her to wish them both well. Later Hodges would say that "the way Brooklyn fans backed me when I couldn't buy a hit is my biggest baseball thrill. Their support helped me recover as much as anything else." The first baseman went on to have one of his best seasons, batting over .300 and hitting 31 home runs.

Public relations exaggeration aside, what is clear from the incident is that the Dodger presence was very close to the spiritual core of the community in an otherwise racially, religiously, and ethnically divided city. Neil Sullivan, in *The Dodgers Move West*, has amplified the immediate meaning of the loss of the Dodgers to the borough. He wrote of the anguish, pain, and loss of focus for the retired, the working-class parents and their kids. The erosion of community in Brooklyn in the years following 1957 cannot fully be laid at the door of the Dodgers, for that erosion was part of a larger urban malaise present in most American cities. But the Dodgers' departure contributed. The degree to which that was true can be gauged in part by the impact the team had on Brooklyn's boys.

8
Kids' Ball: The Dodgers and Brooklyn's Boys

"The Great Connors" of Bay Ridge, Brooklyn, USA augmented his pitiful minor league salary in the Dodger organization by hiring out in the off-season to entertain at fraternal organizations, confirmations, and bar mitzvahs. To a Brooklyn kid, the Dodger card, if it could be played, was the world. Chuck Connors lived the Brooklyn boy's Dodger dream from age eleven. He embodied the youthful white ethnic male culture of the borough, and the fact he wasn't Jewish was more than offset by his Dodger connection when it came to picking up even bar mitzvah jobs.

Among the borough's boys, baseball was the great equalizer, a way of easing ethnic conflict. Inevitably, the Dodgers were at the core of male youth culture. The team assiduously cultivated the young; admitted them to the stands for nothing, and in numbers; and supplied the many youth leagues with equipment, field maintenance, umpires, and instruction. The organization, finally, signed the best Brooklyn boys to minor league contracts. The Dodger organization, in other words, built its fan base from the bottom up, by having potential fans identify actively with the team from an early age. The story of the Dodgers' youthful following mixes class, ethnicity, and maleness into the sources of Brooklyn's isolated ethnic culture.

The Parade Grounds, at the southern end of Prospect Park, was the focus of that ethnic culture. Whatever the ethnic or religious background, baseball was a great common denominator here. (Race mattered, however, as it did among the adults; there was not much race-mixing on the Grounds.) But for first- and second-generation immigrants, if neither insular Brooklyn nor America as a whole formed a melting pot, the Parade Grounds did. The Grounds was the major league of a scattered network of neighborhood parks, elementary school playgrounds, and tiny high school sports fields. It was on the Parade Grounds that the best white ballplayers in the borough performed and where they got noticed.

The Grounds comprised forty acres, the largest portion of which was given over to twenty-six baseball diamonds, which became football fields in the fall. There was also a soccer field, a cricket field, and a bocce green as well. The complex dated from early in the century. By 1945, Dodger-raised money added grandstands on some fields, sixty-five dressing rooms with showers, all necessary baseball equipment including balls, and all the maintenance amenities one could want. The Dodger organization funneled the money it raised through the Brooklyn Amateur Baseball Foundation (more about BABF below).

In 1951, more than a thousand baseball *teams*, comprising more than 15,000 boys and young men, played there that spring and summer. They ranged downward from the crackerjack semipro Bushwicks to amateur and youth organizations, including the Bay Ridge League, the Brooklyn Boys Club League, the Ice Cream League, and leagues sponsored by the American Legion, Kiwanis, the YMCA, and many others. Virtually all Brooklyn public and parochial high school teams played their games on the Grounds as well.

Dodger scouts Al Campanis and Arthur Dede patrolled the Grounds, Dede haunting its diamonds virtually full-time, seven days a week in season. Dede, a Brooklyn native, had exactly one at-bat with the Dodgers, in 1916, as a twenty-year-old catcher. But he was a prized scout. Other major league teams also sent scouts to this mecca, but only the Boston/Milwaukee Braves came remotely close to Dodger coverage. The Braves' scout was Brooklyn's Joe Torre, Sr., who was a fine "bird dog," if for no other reason than that he signed his three sons to contracts. Two of them, Frank and Joe Jr., would go on to the majors. But it was largely a Dodger game at the Grounds. The boys dreamed Dodgers from earliest memory—how could it be otherwise?

The Dodgers shrewdly fed the dream. By the late 1940s the Brooklyn organization signed some ten or so local boys a year, helping to fill the rosters of Branch Rickey's burgeoning farm system. These professional contracts cost next to nothing, occasionally a small signing bonus and salaries that ranged from $200 to $400 a month during the season.

It mattered little, in terms of the Dodgers' financial investment, whether or not these kids made it very far, but the signings paid the Dodgers enormous dividends in lending reality to the Brooklyn boys' dreams of playing, finally, major league ball in Ebbets Field. More than any other team, the Dodgers tied that everykid's dream to perceived possibility. It was at the root of the incredible fan loyalty Brooklynites bestowed on their Bums. For Italian, Irish, and Jewish youngsters especially, it held out the promise of local nobility in the eyes of peers, family, and neighborhood. It held, too, the promise of an exotic and scary change of location: maybe to Hornell, New York; Nashua, New Hampshire; Newport News, Virginia; or Santa Barbara, California, all low in the ranks of the Dodger farm system.

Some of Brooklyn's young men were signed by other major league organizations, but probably a majority were picked up by the Dodgers. Irish, Italians, and Jews dominated the white ethnic groups whose kids regularly patrolled the Parade Grounds diamonds. In addition, a few Greek American boys and even one Scandinavian were signed, representatives of small but tightly knit Brooklyn immigrant communities in the borough. Contemporary records show that only one African American from Brooklyn, John Rucker, was signed by the Dodgers in this era. The Parade Grounds diamonds in the '40s and early '50s seem to have been virtually all-white, even if the borough and the Dodgers were not.

The Parade Grounds as professional showcase had existed for years. By the 1950s at least twenty Brooklynites signed off the

Grounds in the 1930s and 1940s were already in the majors, all of them offspring of the borough's immigrant neighborhoods. In the late '40s and early '50s, the Grounds continued to serve as a profitable baseball spawning ground, especially for the Dodgers. In 1952, at least six players were signed, three of them Italian, two Jewish, and one Irish. All were signed by the Dodgers, none made it to the majors. In 1954, seven were signed: two Irish, three Jewish, one Italian, one Greek. The Dodgers signed five of these, hitting the jackpot with Sandy Koufax. Joe Torre, Sr., signed the other two to Milwaukee contracts. Only Koufax made it from the Parade Grounds class of '54 to the big leagues.

Few of those signed would even get to class A ball, but even for these the dream lived for a while, and the lives of all those signed were touched forever. The Dodger organization, by selling that dream and making it come true once in a blue moon, got what it wanted, too.

Although Pat Jordan was not from Brooklyn and was never a Dodger farmhand, his experience seems typical of many minor leaguers who never made it to the majors. Signed out of Fairfield, Connecticut, to a Milwaukee Braves contract in 1959, he played in the minors in McCook, Nebraska; Waycross, Georgia; and the Florida Rookie League; that was it. A writer in the long run, he perhaps articulated what the chance meant for all those who signed but never made it out of the low minors:

> Baseball was such an experience in my life that, 10 years later, I still have not shaken it, will probably never shake it. I still think of myself not as a writer who once pitched, but as a pitcher who happens to be writing just now. It's as if I decided at some point in my life, or possibly it was decided, that of all the things in my life only that one experience would most accurately define me. It hardly matters whether that is a fact or a private delusion. It matters only that I devoted so great a chunk of my life to baseball that I believe it's true. I believe that the experience affected the design of my life to a degree nothing else ever will.

Those ethnic alumni of the Parade Grounds who were signed shared Jordan's experience. Only a few would make it to the majors, and usually only for the proverbial "cup of coffee" (a brief look). All of those from Brooklyn who even came close were ethnic products of the dominant immigrant groups in the borough: Italian, Irish, or Jewish (see Appendix B). Several Italian Americans did go on to major league careers; Frank and Joe Torre and Ken and Bob Aspromonte would play out distinguished careers, but not with the Dodgers.

Most of the Italian players, like most of the Irish and Jewish Parade Grounds stars, would end their careers after a year or two of D or C ball. A handful would come tantalizingly close to big league nirvana, even play a few major league games on the sacred grass of Ebbets Field. The four Italians who did were Bill Antonello, Joe Pignatano, Steve Lembo, and Jim Romano. Pignatano would put together a six-year career as a player and many more as a coach, mostly with the Los Angeles Dodgers and the Mets.

Antonello's was the most frustrating story, for he had the tools to play in the majors, or so it seemed when he was signed. He was recruited by Art Dede in 1946, a nineteen-year-old out of Fort Hamilton High in Bay Ridge. If he were like Bart Giamatti, who grew up in Massachusetts, Antonello would have seen his Dodgers as Giamatti saw his Red Sox, in his mind's eye listening to the radio, or watching the Dodgers play at Ebbets Field, most often via the Knothole Club. Like Giamatti, he might have put together his all-Italian all-star team, dreaming of cracking it himself some day. For Antonello, unlike Giamatti, there was a possibility in the vision. It wasn't yet clear in 1946, but Antonello signed with the deepest, most talent-laden farm system ever put together.

Bill Antonello was signed because he had all of Branch Rickey's unteachable prerequisites for a major leaguer: hit, hit with power, speed, a good arm. After his 1946 signing, Antonello adjusted well to life in strange minor league towns. That was an important first step; many Brooklyn boys did not. He starred in the lowest minors at Newport News, Virginia, and Greenville, North Carolina. He got his first invitation to Dodger spring training at Vero Beach in 1949 and was assigned to Mobile, Alabama, in the Southern Association, double A ball, threshold to the big leagues. Antonello expressed at the time a "consuming ambition to play with the Dodgers."

This Brooklyn kid seemed on his way. In 1952 he led the Southern Association in runs batted in, hit 22 home runs, and batted .271. His fielding was suspect, and with Furillo and Snider as fixtures in right and center fields, only left field remained a possibility. There he had to beat out, first, Gene Hermanski and Cal Abrams and later Andy Pafko, George Shuba, Dick Williams, and Don Thompson. Antonello finally got his chance in 1953, when he edged out several other wannabes for the sixth and last outfield slot a week before opening day. But in forty games he didn't hit major league pitching (he didn't get much of a chance, either) and went back to the minors, never again to live his dream.

Charlie DiGiovanna was one Italian kid who did see his dream come true, although he probably never played much baseball on the Parade Grounds. He was the aging Dodger "batboy." DiGiovanna was hired in 1951 at age twenty, and he remained the batboy till the Dodgers left for Los Angeles in 1958. That made him, I suppose, at least a contender for the oldest active batboy ever in the majors. By 1958, he was married with three children. The term *batboy* took on a whole new world of meaning when it came to DiGiovanna. But the Dodger organization had its reasons. He was hired initially because his uncle Peter DiGiovanna was a Brooklyn representative on the New York City Council, a clubhouse pol with considerable clout in the Italian community. Charlie stayed on because he could cannily and credibly forge any Dodger regular's signature on a baseball.

Charlie's most visible duty involved passing bats to the players on the on-deck circle. The most important function of "The Penman" (the players' nickname for him), however, was carried out in the privacy of the clubhouse. There, he would autograph balls by the hour, to meet the myriad requests for them, one-signature balls and in pre-ordered groupings. He saved the Dodger stars hours of tedium. Those original autographed balls that go for upwards of $300 (team-signed balls for $2500, at last count) may have been signed by Dodger players, but the odds are against it.

When The O'Malley announced the Dodgers were leaving, DiGiovanna, then almost twenty-eight, plaintively told the press,

"I've got a lot of friends here, and I'm all set with a nice little house, but I'll be glad to go if they ask me." They didn't.

The Jewish experience was remarkably similar to the Italian, except that one player, Sandy Koufax, made it all the way to the Hall of Fame. Cal Abrams, who had an eight-year major league career, also played with the Dodgers over parts of four seasons. The Great Jewish Hope to many Brooklyn Jews in the late 1940s and early '50s, he never quite made it in his hometown. He did have his moments in the Ebbets Field sun, though. Oddly, Koufax had fewer of those moments than did Abrams, for the pitcher came into his own only long after the move to Los Angeles.

A great deal has been written about Koufax's career, but not much about his Parade Grounds origins. Jimmy Murphy, the Brooklyn schools' sports columnist for the *Eagle*, was the first person to call public attention to Koufax. Given his partisan devotion to the team and the fact that he prowled the Grounds looking for local youth sports stories, Murphy was inevitably a de facto Dodger scout. He saw Koufax pitch there often and from an early age.

Others missed the left-hander because he did not pitch for Lafayette High; he played first base, and concentrated on basketball. But Koufax always pitched on the Parade Grounds, starting as a pre-teen with the Tomahawks in the Ice Cream League, the youngest league allowed on the Grounds. And one had to be good to play on an Ice Cream League team. As a teenager he moved up to the Parkviews, a Coney Island League team sponsored by Nathan's Hot Dogs. With Koufax pitching, the Parkviews won the senior division Parade Grounds title in 1953. At Murphy's urging, Al Campanis signed Koufax for a $20,000 bonus, signifying both that other organizations were interested, and that under major league rules, he couldn't be farmed out. Denied minor league seasoning, he experienced years of wildness in Brooklyn and Los Angeles, coming into his own only in 1961.

Jerry Della Femina commented in his autobiography that he too attended Lafayette. In talking about the "difference" between Koufax and Italian Lafayette athletes, Della Femina unconsciously picked up on the prejudicial notion of Jewish exclusivity. "Koufax was different," Della Femina wrote. "He was

Jewish, and [he was] therefore automatically assumed to be more sensible about behavior than the Italians." The Jewish Parade Grounds experience, on the other hand, demonstrates exactly the opposite, for all ethnic groups fared about the same there. If Koufax were all that "sensible," he either would have finished the University of Cincinnati on his basketball scholarship or at least worked out a contract that would have provided him with the minor league seasoning he so clearly needed.

The Irish American experience in Brooklyn's large world of baseball was no different than that of Italian or Jewish second-generation sons of immigrants. If anyone should have pitched for the Dodgers, it was Bob Grim. He not only came up on the Parade Grounds, his father owned and presided over one of the Dodger bars near Ebbets Field. The fates dictated that instead Grim would have the supreme Brooklyn anti-experience: he pitched against the Dodgers in the 1955 World Series—for the Yankees.

Bay Ridge's Tommy Holmes, a 1930s Parade Grounds product, went on to a fine career as player, then manager, of the Boston Braves. He briefly joined the Dodgers at the end of his career in the early 1950s. But even before that, he had no trouble remembering where home was. In 1951, with the Dodgers and Giants locked in their famous race, Holmes's Braves beat the Bums three out of four late in the season. Holmes and his family received threatening letters and calls promising mayhem, accusing the Braves' manager of treason. Let no one doubt that ethnic ball in Brooklyn was serious business.

The ultimate Great Irish Hope from Brooklyn was probably Tommy Brown. He did and didn't make it with the Dodgers. Like Cal Abrams, he never quite lived up to exaggerated expectations. And like Bill Antonello, he could hit, hit with power, run, and throw. His problem was that although he could throw hard, no one could predict where his throws from third would end up: against the screen, in the stands behind first, down the right-field line. Thus his nickname: Buckshot. After it was clear he was no third baseman, he was switched to the outfield. But like Antonello, he never became a good outfielder. In 1944, as a sixteen-year-old filling a slot on the war-depleted Dodger roster, Brown went straight from the Parade Grounds to Ebbets Field. He played for the Dodgers on and off for seven years, and he could hit. He was arguably the best batting practice slugger ever to grace Ebbets Field. There was no place for him, though, on a talent-rich team that prided itself on great defense. The organization gave up reluctantly in 1951, when he was traded to Philadelphia.

In a Parade Grounds world of fine ballplayers, few were better, none more colorful, than Kevin "Chuck" Connors. Connors was up briefly with the Dodgers in 1949, after losing four years in the military and toiling long in the rich Dodger minor league chain. He played two fine years with Montreal in the AAA International League and seemed a sure major league bet. Although he didn't know it then, Connors's big break would come in 1950, when he was traded to the Chicago Cubs which, after half a season, farmed him out to its triple-A Pacific Coast League affiliate, the Los Angeles Angels. It was there he found his metier, not as a ballplayer, but as an actor. He took to hanging around studio lots, picking up assignments as an extra because of his blond, 6'5" good looks. His first break came when he played a featured role as a state trooper in the Katharine Hepburn/Spencer Tracy movie *Pat and Mike*. Like Koufax, Connors went on to a Hall of Fame career: in 1991 he was elected to the Cowboy Hall of Fame (the last of the Bay Ridge cowboys) for his long television career as "The Rifleman."

But Connors's first and best love was the Dodgers, as he himself would often say later. His ability as a comic made him stand out in those long years in the Dodger organization. As a minor leaguer, in the off-season, he circulated business cards offering up "The Great Connors" for any gathering that wanted a prospective Dodger to entertain it. His specialty was "Casey at the Bat," complete with "deep-throated growls and piercing screams."

His locker room tour de force at Vero Beach was a great imitation of Branch Rickey, "a take-off [that] had been received poorly on Mt. Olympus" by the great man. Little wonder. Tommy Lasorda, who labored long in the minors with Connors, recounts an exchange between Connors and Rickey: "'Young man, I do not want you telling anyone how much money the Dodgers are paying you this year.' 'I don't blame you, Mr. Rickey, and you don't have to worry. I'm just as embarrassed about this contract as you are.'" The "Great Connors" was also reputed to have said about Rickey and contracts: "He had both players and money and he didn't like to see the two of them mix." This last was said years later, well after Connors had made big money as a television actor. If Connors's long-running bitterness is any indication, Rickey's well-known practice of paying his minor league properties pitiful wages was an additional source of persistent frustration for good players toiling endlessly in the minors.

It was (maybe) Connors's inability to hit a major league curveball, and not his stand-up routines, that got him traded to Chicago. The Dodgers worked hard with Connors, as the team did with all its minor leaguers, no matter how poorly paid. The Brooklyn boys were, if anything, given extra attention because they were not only the usual potential cash-cow trade bait, they were potentially great draws as well should they ever reach that Elysian Field of their dreams.

In fairness, the Dodger organization was not wholly cynical in its devotion to Brooklyn boys. The front office bought into the 1950s sociological package that hard-played sports diminished urban juvenile delinquency (more about that below). Encouraging amateur baseball was the result of a peculiar mix of hard-nosed business investment and 1950s altruism. As a result of both forces at work within the organization, direct Dodger involvement in youth baseball went far beyond merely scouting and signing second-generation immigrant kids to Dodger contracts.

Dodger-inspired community baseball organization was focused, intense, and successful. It provided a clearly defined local path to Dodger nirvana that led from the Parade Grounds to the "Dodger Rookie Team," the Parade Grounds senior all-stars. Most of the "Rookies" got professional contracts, usually from Brooklyn. The Dodger Rookies were crème de la crème, but even for them, it was still a long road to a baseball career. Sandlots in Brooklyn neighborhoods sent their young standouts to organized Parade Grounds leagues, starting with the Ice Cream League. A kid progressed upward, ability allowing, to the teen leagues. They played on the best amateur facilities in the nation:

locker rooms with showers, paid umpires, groundskeepers, free access to equipment.

That competition complemented high-school baseball. The best players played both high-school and league ball simultaneously. Just as in small Midwest or upstate New York towns, the best high-school players competed as well with the local American Legion team. There was a lot of good Brooklyn amateur baseball to watch, and the best of both (overlapping) groups made the Dodger Rookie Team. The Rookies always included a few high-school stars from Long Island and New Jersey, but about fifteen of the twenty on the squad came out of Brooklyn. None came out of the other boroughs. Usually, five to seven Rookies would sign Dodger contracts, and several more would sign with other major league organizations.

The Rookies made the team after two weeks of intensive try-outs. Those competing were there by invitation only, after having been scouted either on the Grounds or in their suburban communities by Dodger bird dogs (informal scouts, usually high-school baseball coaches). The Dodger Rookies, experienced, talented, and rehearsed, would embark on a ten-game swing upstate and into New England, playing local amateur all-stars. They would invariably win all but one or two games. This pattern of upward progression to a Dodger contract was broken only in instances where a few Brooklyn boys over the years emerged as really hot prospects. These few became early objects of competitive bidding, and they signed contracts at a time and with a team they selected, thus bypassing the Rookies.

Usually though, after the Rookies' June swing, the Dodger organization would announce six or seven signings from the team. After a wonderful round of family and neighborhood celebrations, the local heroes would be dispatched to face the cold realities of the low minor leagues. There they would be closely coached and monitored—and severely tested psychologically by the experience—far from the local adulation accorded at the Parade Grounds. Few would make it even to the high minors. The Brooklyn Rookies who did not catch on, either with the Dodgers or with another major league organization, and those who signed but were cut after a year or two of professional ball would return to Brooklyn to finish their educations and take jobs. They played on, in the adult Parade Grounds leagues— aging veterans of the baseball wars who, if they were like Pat Jordan, knew they had seen the baseball elephant.

To personalize the reality, take a look at the 1954 Dodger Rookies, bearing in mind that this entire subculture would disappear along with the Dodgers in a few years. The '54 team consisted of twenty new high-school graduates, most of them from Brooklyn. Of that group, four Brooklyn teenagers—Don Kopec, Mike Weltman, Shelly Brodsky, and Joe Musachio—were signed to class C or D Dodger contracts. The Dodger organization, with all the advantages it had, was far from infallible. Three or four of the remaining Rookies were signed by other major league teams, in effect scavenging off the Dodger selection process. Ironically, one of these was Jack Lamabe of Farmingdale, Long Island, who went on to a good major league pitching career. None of the four signed by the Dodgers from that '54 Rookie team made it very far.

Maybe the Dodger organization was too focused on its own navel, scrutinizing seriously only the Brooklyn boys on the team. On the other hand, the Bums, after facing some serious competitive bidding, also signed Sandy Koufax that summer of 1954. Koufax was by then, with big money in the offing, willing to relinquish his basketball scholarship at the University of Cincinnati to accept a free pass directly to the majors. His $20,000 bonus meant that Brooklyn had to keep him on its major league roster.

The ever-present kid's hope for that jackpot bonus statistically offered worse odds than winning the (later) New York lottery. Still, there was no element of luck in being signed. You had to be an outstanding player, then you could hope.

That hope started with the Brooklyn Amateur Baseball Foundation (BABF). It was at the center of an intricate web of orchestrated local amateur baseball in Brooklyn. Founded after World War II, BABF became the moving force in institutionalizing the mid-season Mayor's Trophy Game between the Yankees and Dodgers (which was resumed when the Mets opened in New York).

Irving Rudd, Dodger P.R. man extraordinary, was the moving force behind the Mayor's Trophy Game, just as he was the club's representative in promoting its larger purpose, organized youth ball in Brooklyn. His entire salary ($5200 when he was hired in 1951) was paid by BABF, so what he did for the Dodgers directly—it was a lot—he did on the cuff. Dodger proceeds for the Trophy Game went to BABF, which in turn paid a large part of the freight for sandlot ball in Brooklyn generally and the Parade Grounds in particular.

BABF needed far more money for its many purposes than the Trophy Game provided, so it expanded its outreach, capitalizing fully on Dodger clout. It raised large amounts of additional money through the "Sandlot Classic" baseball game at Ebbets Field, and through the annual Sandlot Dinner, both sponsored through BABF by virtually every Brooklyn service and business organization and an array of local stores and banks, all glad for the extended public association with the Dodgers.

The entire youth effort in Brooklyn was buttressed by the common sociological wisdom of the '50s about juvenile delinquency. Wrapped in academic jargon, it embodied the ageless belief in keeping youngsters busy, off the streets, and tired. In Brooklyn, at least, for the boys that meant baseball. *Brooklyn Eagle* columnist Tommy Holmes (not the player-manager of the Boston Braves from Bay Ridge) summarized the ideology that fueled BABF's efforts when he concluded that the success of the 1949 Sandlot Classic "affects your kid and mine and the neighbor's kid across the street. . . . It has been shown conclusively that juvenile delinquency is in direct ratio to the number of playgrounds in a community." Amateur baseball, he added, builds "the character of our youth." The combination of virtuous concern for the youth (read boys) of the borough and association with the Bums was irresistible. A sixteen-year-old wrote one of the many 1957 letters vainly imploring the Dodgers to stay in Brooklyn. In it, the youngster noted, "please keep them here. Baseball keeps a lot of us teenagers off the streets and prevents JD."

The Classic was first played in 1946, co-sponsored by BABF, the Dodgers, and the *Eagle*. In its usual format, it pitted the *Eagle* All-Stars (all Brooklyn boys), against the Long Island All-Stars. Several of the best players on both teams, especially those from the *Eagle* team, would find their way on to the Dodger Rookie

Team. The *Eagle* would boast in 1951 that among the alumni of the Sandlot Classic games of past years were Whitey Ford and Billy Loes (both played for Long Island). Joe Torre, who played for Brooklyn but was signed by Milwaukee, would later be added to that list. This game was a Dodger amateur showcase, so something seemed amiss in its scouting concentration, because too many Long Islanders were getting away.

Every major veterans' organization, civic group, and commercial concern in Brooklyn would fall in line as sponsors of the Sandlot Classic: the Veterans of Foreign Wars, American Legion, Jewish War Veterans, Catholic War Veterans, Kiwanis, Lions Club, Elks, Rotary, Chamber of Commerce, virtually all the banks, and most major and minor small businesses, including bars. Sponsorship meant pushing enough tickets on members, friends, and relatives to fill Ebbets Field a couple of times over (if everyone turned up, which of course never happened). One can only guess at the amount the Brooklyn Amateur Baseball Foundation raked off the top, but it was a lot. It paid the bills for Parade Grounds baseball, so few Brooklynites begrudged BABF the money.

The Dodger organization for its part never let the Amateur Baseball Foundation stray far from the spotlight. In the spring, well before the Sandlot Classic contest and the Mayor's Trophy Game, the Dodgers hosted a ceremony at Ebbets Field publicizing the two events. It was an occasion to honor not only BABF, but the Dodger front office, pols from Brooklyn and Manhattan, borough kids, and everyone else in Brooklyn, in that order.

In 1952, for example, 1000 boys from twenty sandlot leagues paraded into Ebbets Field behind four high-school marching bands—this before a regular season Saturday game against the lowly Pirates. Why not boost attendance, after all, at a game that promised to be a poor draw? New York City Mayor Anthony Impellitteri was given a citation for his obligatory sponsorship of the Mayor's Trophy Game. He in turn presented a plaque to Walter O'Malley for his intrepid sponsorship of everything. The O'Malley, in his vintage circular fashion, then gave Impellitteri a lifetime pass to Ebbets Field, always good unless you tried to use it. Nobody gave Irving Rudd anything, but he only did all the work.

A Dodger god was at work that day because Tommy Holmes (definitely not the *Eagle* columnist) drove in the winning run with a pinch hit, the only important hit he would ever get as a Dodger, after his great career with the Boston Braves.

Those BABF events took care of the first half of the season. In August, the Brooklyn Amateur Baseball Foundation hosted its annual Sandlot Classic Dinner at the St. George Hotel. Several Dodger players and all the Dodger executives were on hand, for it was time to honor Frank Schroth, the publisher of the *Eagle*, and the eternal borough president of Brooklyn, John Cashmore. Taking all BABF events together, it's hard to imagine any Brooklyn notable feeling left out of the round of self-congratulatory festivities.

The money raised at the dinner was, as always, well spent. In addition to paying for equipment, umpire stipends, playground supervisory personnel and maintenance staff on the Parade Grounds and other Brooklyn sandlots, BABF also held baseball clinics and tryout camps in the New York metropolitan area. Non-Brooklyn candidates for the Dodger Rookie Team were quietly scouted at these camps. Dodger players and coaches turned up at these tryouts, usually reserve players in rotation, to show the flag. One might conclude, cynically, that all this effort was grist for the Dodger ticket mill (the Dodgers were consistently the best-drawing team in the league), but it is also very clear that the Dodger team was, to a degree unmatched in other major league cities, deeply enmeshed in the life and psyche of Brooklyn, its ethnic kids in particular.

Yet there is an anomaly worth noting here. The Dodger team pioneered baseball integration in these years. At the same time, Brooklyn's considerable African American community remained invisible to the Dodger organization, at least insofar as the press was concerned. If there was Dodger sandlot activity in Bedford-Stuyvesant, neither was it reported in the *Eagle* nor, except for John Rucker, were any local black ballplayers signed in these years.

Only a small minority of Brooklyn boys could play league ball on the Parade Grounds, but the Dodgers provided amply for thousands of boys and girls via the Knothole Club. Upwards of

100,000 free admissions would be made available each year (the number reached 200,000 in 1954) so that Brooklyn school children would more easily be converted into devoted fans. The kids would fill whole sections of Ebbets Field that would otherwise remain vacant on weekdays. They would get out of school early, pack into buses, and troop into the park in serried ranks.

The Dodger club provided up to 15,000 free admissions, paid attendance permitting. Ebbets Field security and opposing players would be sorely tested by numbers that large. On one occasion in 1954, thousands of kids engaged in "target practice with luncheon remnants, with the outfielders in left and center-field as the most inviting targets." Umpires too were targeted, and they complained that Ebbets Field was by far the worst park in the league for that kind of behavior.

When the Dodgers came north after spring training, the Knothole Club held an annual "Welcome Home Dinner" at the St. George Hotel. Knothole sponsors included the YMCA, the Salvation Army, the Police Athletic League, the Brooklyn Jewish Community Council, the Board of Education and the Catholic Youth Organization. Some 1500 tickets would be sold for $6 each, the proceeds to pay for charter buses and incidental expenses. The dinner was a gala affair. The entire team, virtually every politician and civic figure in the borough, and representatives of all the sponsors would show up. Speeches were in abundance, including those by Rickey (and later O'Malley) and Dodger captain Pee Wee Reese.

In 1949, Ralph Branca sang "Take Me Out to the Ball Game" and Chuck Connors did yet another "Casey at the Bat," on this occasion for free. Borough president John Cashmore, who was always where the Dodgers were, gave the keynote address, as usual. "The Knothole Club," he said, "does more than keep the boys off the streets—it teaches them Americanism." In that year, because of the presence on the team of Robinson, Campanella, and Newcombe, as well as Cal Abrams, who was Jewish, and Luis Olmo, who was Hispanic, Cashmore could correctly conclude that "on the Dodger team there is no question of race, religion or nationality." The Dodgers, he concluded, epitomized "real democracy."

Despite its deep support, the Knothole Club almost met its end before it fairly got started. In the winter before the start of the 1947 season, Dodger manager Leo Durocher very visibly wooed and won the heart of movie star Laraine Day. The romance resulted in a quickie Mexican divorce and (one day later) a Texas marriage. This upset former husband Ray Hendricks. Lippy was "a snake in the grass," quoted tabloids on both coasts, a "love pirate." The events also annoyed California judge George Dockweiler, who, shortly before, had granted a California divorce decree that required a one-year waiting period before it became final. Feeling his court had been demeaned, he summoned the couple back to his chambers to determine whether the California divorce should be overturned and Leo cited for contempt. "Durocher wants to have his cake and eat it, too," was how the judge, with a real flair for *le mot juste*, elegantly put it.

The scandal did not sit well with the Catholic Church. In particular, Brooklyn's CYO director, the Reverend Vincent Powell, was outraged enough to withdraw his organization from Knothole Club sponsorship. The CYO, he told the press, did not want to be "officially associated with a man who presents an example in complete contradiction to our moral teachings." In depriving his young charges free access to Ebbets Field, Father Powell added that Durocher was "not the kind of leader we want our youth to idealize and emulate."

If one possessed such a turn of mind, it might be possible to conclude that Durocher's behavior might incite a very real desire to imitate among Powell's adolescent charges. This embarrassing and very visible confrontation between church and ball club was ended abruptly when Commissioner of Baseball A. B. Chandler suspended Durocher for the 1947 season for consorting with gamblers. In any event, both the ball club and the Brooklyn diocese were on the spot: the Dodger club, for obvious reasons, given its all-encompassing community youth involvement and the public relations benefits it derived from it; the diocese, because it effectively punished tens of thousands of disgruntled school children who couldn't care less about the morality of Durocher's Hollywood-inspired love life. Leo's subsequent suspension by Chandler in April 1947 for consorting with gamblers took both the team and the church off the hook. Within a week of the suspension, in fact, Powell told the press "he would apply for readmission to the Dodger Knothole Club" because "obstacles [to membership] have been removed."

Brooklyn boys, Parade Ground stars or not, lived Dodger baseball. Mostly they lived through the "Verce of Brooklyn," Walter "Red" Barber. If the Dodgers were a religion, Peter Golenbock said, "then Red Barber was Billy Graham." "We couldn't get through a Sunday meal," Jerry Della Femina remembered, "without a game. The macaroni was served, and there's Red Barber."

Some kids made their mark on the street imitating Barber as the stickball games played out. In Brownsville, "Frenchy" Resnick did the play-by-play with that "unique 'knock' he could make with his tongue to simulate a base hit." In Canarsie, Della Femina remembers, "Frank would provide a complete play-by-play." Red Barber, Alan Lelchuk wrote, was as important to kids "as say, General Eisenhower." Barber was the "conscience" of the borough, and even of parts beyond it. Even in the Adirondacks, where Johnny Podres grew up, "[he] used to stay up at night listening to Red Barber." And in Newark, Philip Roth wrote about hearing Red Barber announcing in Alex Portnoy's dreams: "Hit out toward Portnoy . . . and Alex gathers it in for out number three."

The true fanatics among the children would play the out-outfield on Bedford Avenue, behind the high mesh right-field fence, during both batting practice and the game itself. Woody Allen remembered the fans who "line Bedford Avenue in hopes of retrieving home-run balls." Bobby McCarthy recalled that as a kid he waited on Bedford with two dozen others: "I never caught one. I was too slow. The closest I got, the ball was bouncing around loose, and I went for it, and seventeen guys jumped on top of me and almost broke my arm." One enterprising boy, "armed with a fielder's glove and a radio," knew when the ball was coming, and got three that season, which he traded to the club after the game for two Dodger tickets to a future game. Any kid who presented a batting practice ball hit over the right-field fence could turn it in at the gate for a free admission that day. Herbie Friedman "was popular because his bedroom overlooked the [right field] screen. Standing at his window, you could see the infield, some of center." Irony of ironies, Herbie didn't like baseball, but on pain of dismemberment he "had to suffer sunshine friends."

Even for the mass of boys and girls who possessed indifferent (or unaccepted, in the case of the girls) baseball skills, much of the street life in Brooklyn revolved around the Dodgers. Looked at through their eyes, the Dodger exodus was really traumatic. This was a less cynical baseball era because, although the reserve clause was abominable for the serfdom it imposed on the professionals in the game, it did preserve teams intact over time (the Dodgers most of all). Community loyalties and psychic ties ran very deep, in Brooklyn and in America generally. That's why so many recent experts, in academe and out, see the "game" as one defining element among many in explaining the unique qualities of American culture.

Many things happened to Brooklyn in the 1950s that precipitated change for the worse. None was more devastating than the Dodger desertion.

9
The Outer Edges
of Dodger Memory

The Brooklyn Dodgers live on in memory; not only in New York reminiscences but in important ways in the historic memory of the nation: the team's early and important role in the struggle for integration, the nation's quirky fascination with both Brooklyn and its team, the borough's own enthrallment with itself and its Bums. The Dodgers' cliffhanging career in the late 1940s and 1950s, abysmal losses and soaring wins alike, make the old Dodgers now appear larger than life. All these have served to keep the Brooklyn Dodgers alive in American memory. Any number of cognitive explorations suggest themselves in trying to fix that memory, give meaning to it.

To me, it makes the most sense to take a look at the two personalities who most survive symbolically for the borough, the city, and the nation: Jackie Robinson and Walter O'Malley. Robinson's reputation suffered in the wake of accelerating racial change in the 1960s, began to ascend again at his death in 1972, and soars now to the level of baseball and integration legend. O'Malley, widely condemned for his desertion of Brooklyn in 1957, remains widely condemned now, surprisingly with as much anger in 1995 as his name evoked nearly forty years ago. So much is this true that his son Peter, a very young man in 1957, has inherited a share of the O'Malley opprobrium. This chapter will examine Robinson and the O'Malleys in American memory, twin bookends of the greater historic memory evoked by the team and town they were bound up with. A Brooklyn bar controversy in 1990 only reopened an already evident door to Dodger memories.

Immortalized first by Roger Kahn as "The Boys of Summer," the Dodgers recall at once a verdant and urban past, just the kind of contradiction that characterized the team's play. Many have died young, physical giants in their time, and death invites the ultimate memory. Premature funerals, Pee Wee Reese said, were "getting to be a terrible habit." And in the matter of the decade after World War II, because a disproportionate part of the team is now gone, the Brooklyn Dodgers have a head start in generating significant postwar memory. Gil Hodges and Jackie Robinson were the first players to go, dying in the early 1970s. Then Billy Cox and Jim Gilliam passed on later in the decade. More recently, Carl Furillo, Sandy Amoros, Roy Campanella, and Brooklyn latecomer Don Drysdale all died, the last, along with Sandy Koufax, one of two key links connecting the Brooklyn and Los Angeles teams.

The only everyday regulars who survive are Pee Wee Reese and Duke Snider. The pitchers also survive, most of them: Carl Erskine, Don Newcombe, Johnny Podres, Joe Black, Preacher Roe, Clem Labine, Ralph Branca, Sandy Koufax.

In a very short time, historically speaking, Dodger memory has set its emotional base by indulging contested memory, extremes of historic recall. Changing perceptions of Jackie Robinson form a case in point. A following generation has belatedly elevated Jackie Robinson to a kind of sainthood, a good deal of it both deserved and understandable, but writ very large indeed. Jackie Robinson remained a controversial figure through all his playing days because of the political and racial visibility he sought off the playing field. This generated a decidedly mixed reception. Many who didn't like his integrationist militancy masked their hostility by complaining only that it was unseemly for a ballplayer to espouse political causes openly (National League President Warren Giles was a good example—see Chapter 1).

Paradoxically, others who didn't like Robinson's otherwise conservative views concurred. Controversy thus dogged Robinson and blurred his image until his death in 1972.

Robinson came to regret his 1949 confrontation with Paul Robeson, and eventually said so. As racial prejudice followed him into retirement, at least in small ways, he came to understand Robeson's militancy. Despite Robinson's consistent political support for Richard Nixon, he understood (yet seemed not to approve of) the militant black civil rights movement of the 1960s. Robinson, as a result, was accused by some African American radicals of turning on his own people. Even as some whites excoriated him for speaking out for black equality so forcefully in the 1940s and '50s, so did African American militants denounce him for exemplifying tokenism and deference to whites in the '60s and '70s. He was described by that worst of epithets, "Uncle Tom." Both Stokely Carmichael and H. Rap Brown rejected him as a role model, referring to him as a "period piece." In 1963, Malcolm X denounced Robinson for criticizing Black Muslims and for his earlier testimony on Robeson before the House Un-American Activities Committee. Remembered as a great player in the years before his death, he was not much remembered as the pioneering civil rights activist he in fact was.

That contest over his memory played out very clearly a month before his death. Baseball Commissioner Bowie Kuhn used the occasion of the 1972 World Series to remember the 25th anniversary of Robinson's breaking baseball's color line. He was honored in Cincinnati before the second game. The account of what happened to Robinson at that game varies depending on who you read. Red Barber later remembered the nearly blind and feeble star making a humiliating visit to the Oakland Athletics' locker room before the game, only to be ignored by the players, black and white alike. The Athletics, Barber said, "paid him no attention, were not interested in coming over to greet him, and Jackie was quietly led away."

Fixing the ambivalence of that lifetime memory, Barber commented, "It is terrible when human beings forget their blessings and fail to say thank you." Rejected by a new generation of ballplayers, Barber concluded, Robinson at least got to hear some appreciation of his contributions to the game and nation publicly aired on national television before the second game. "Done in time by nine days," Barber concluded, for Robinson died on October 24.

Yet there is a different version of that last hurrah in 1972. Maury Allen, in his 1987 biography of Robinson, recounted a different experience. Like Red Barber, he was at the Series commemoration that October day, so like Barber's, his was at least partly a first-hand account. Allen remembered the Athletics' Reggie Jackson coming over to Robinson's box before the game to tell Jackie, "You've always been my hero." Allen recalled as well that after that game (not before) Robinson visited the Cincinnati (not the Oakland) locker room, where Bobby Toland, Johnny Bench, Pete Rose, Tony Perez, and Dennis Mencke all asked him to autograph baseballs and shared memories of watching him play when they were boys. Toland, who had gone 0 for 4 in the first game, even listened respectfully to Robinson's critique of his batting stance, supposedly changed it for game two, and got three hits.

Some echoes of that contested early memory was evident at Jackie Robinson's funeral less than two weeks later. The service was an occasion for front-page coverage across America. *New York Times* columnist Dave Anderson caught the earlier mixed signals in his piece on the Dodger star's death. "For sociological impact," Anderson wrote, "Jack Roosevelt Robinson was perhaps America's most significant athlete." As both a sports figure and an African American, he was "outspoken, controversial, combative." Referring obliquely to the harsh criticism Robinson encountered, both from whites in the 1950s and black militants in the '60s, Jesse Jackson in his eulogy said, "Jackie stole home and Jackie is safe." Jackson, who presided at that funeral, set the tone for the revision of memory that followed Robinson's death: "He was the Black Knight, not a pawn in some white man's game." That was both a denial of the existing "Uncle Tom" memory and the inadvertent signal to summon a revised recollection. At his own request, Robinson was buried in Brooklyn, and the press made much of that symbolism.

As it always is with memory, the transition was uneven, indeed it had begun before Robinson's death. Some confusion was of course evident in the conflicting accounts over what happened before and after the second game of the '72 World Series, as if some people needed to see Robinson as anachronistic, while others demanded respect after the fact for the memory of his great moral and physical courage. Even before his death, some were trying to place him in historic perspective. Gerard O'Connor rode the cusp of the wave of the future in 1972 when he wrote that "historically, Jackie Robinson changed the nature of professional athletics," redirected the whole course of major league baseball, "a hero who was not only better than the white man in the white man's game, but one more intelligent than whites, and yet proud to be black."

That kind of revision—and it was a revision of the 1960s perception of Robinson, the Nixon Republican, as anachronism—was token of the canonization to come. In some ways as well, O'Connor's appraisal was one small epitaph among many for the lost militancy of the '60s.

By the mid-1980s, few remembered the conservative, "the Tom," the anticommunist critic of Paul Robeson. Robert Curvin's commemorative 1982 *New York Times Magazine* essay, published exactly ten years after Robinson's death, both venerated the player and erased the mixed memory of the man. Written by a civil rights activist, it was a nationally circulated denial, implicit though it was, of the 1960s activists' disdain for the black star. It signaled a tack in the winds of memory.

Maury Allen's biography of Robinson in 1987 likewise banished most of the ambivalence even as it placed Robinson in perspective, at least within the framework of baseball. Allen deliberately invoked the power of memory to move the transition along. He drew on Dodger pitchers Carl Erskine, Joe Black, and Don Newcombe to fix that more consistent memory, a memory of both personal courage and broad social impact. "We cannot ever let the memory of Jackie Robinson be forgotten," Newcombe wrote. "What do they say: If we do not understand the past we are doomed to repeat it. I want young blacks and whites to know what it was like forty years ago, I don't want those times to return." By the late 1980s, Jackie Robinson's untarnished memory would be a weapon in the cause of race relations.

A number of significant 1980s books, either about Robinson or featuring him as a major player, cast him in a role beyond baseball. In terms of popular culture and awakened perceptions, '80s book blurbs tell the story. The press writer's lead to Harvey Frommer's 1982 *Rickey and Robinson* described Jackie as a ballplayer who "played a major role in awakening the pride of an entire race." In 1984, Jules Tygiel's *The Great Experiment* carried a promotion that claimed that Robinson's "breaking of baseball's color barrier in the late 1940s shook American society as profoundly as the Supreme Court's decision to desegregate education a few years later." And in 1987, the jacket of Maury Allen's *Jackie Robinson* carried the claim that Robbie "changed baseball and American society forever. . . . A figure of mythological presence and momentous courage," he opened the way "for blacks and other minorities to surge into the richness of American life." Press flack people carried Robinson's significance well beyond the claims of the books for which they were writing blurbs, exaggerations in the best tradition of popular American memory-making.

In the 1990s, Jackie Robinson's name is invoked as a metaphor for human rights across a wide spectrum of the American experience. Garland Jeffreys, an African American rhythm-and-blues singer, for example, was quoted as placing Robinson at the beginning of the American civil rights movement, in his own mind, at least. That idea, he said, was nurtured in childhood as he watched Jackie play in Ebbets Field. That was a common black experience. "My favorite player was Jackie Robinson because he integrated baseball," Jules Tygiel, who is white, has written. "I was not sure what that meant," he wrote of his Brooklyn childhood recollection, "but I knew it was wonderful. I thus learned my first lesson in politics and race relations." That was a common white experience, as well, for children of the 1940s and '50s.

In assailing Clarence Thomas's nomination to the Supreme Court, a *New York Times* correspondent reminded Thomas that it was African Americans such as Robinson who made it possible for Thomas to get the chance to aspire to such eminence. There was no mention of Robinson's own political conservatism in that reminder. And television documentary producer Ken Burns, along with many other contemporaries of widely different backgrounds, thinks of Robinson as not only "one of the greatest players" baseball has produced, but "one of the greatest Americans who ever lived." Jackie by the 1990s had metamorphosed into "the classic American hero."

At the other end of the Brooklyn Dodger legend, Walter O'Malley has enjoyed no such resurrection. In the matter of "The O'Malley" the extreme of memory offers fascinating historical juxtaposition. If Robinson has become an American icon, poor O'Malley has been consigned quite literally to perdition.

For O'Malley, unlike Robinson, there has been no evolution of memory, no exculpation worth talking about. The only popular transition that has occurred, in fact, is that, with the Brooklyn Dodger Sports Bar contretemps of the early 1990s, the O'Malley curse is now visited unto the second generation. Twenty-four years old when his father deserted Flatbush, the current Dodger owner is remembered now—at least in some quarters of New York City—mainly as the dubious heir to his father's memory. But it is Walter, not Peter, who bears the brunt of the desertion of the Dodgers. Neil Sullivan, author of *The Dodgers Move West*, is virtually a lone voice when he reminds his readers that "O'Malley as villain may offer some emotional satisfaction, but it is poor history." Much more common is the 1993 sentiment of Wilfred Sheed, who dedicated *My Life as a Fan* not to but *against* "the villainous Walter O'Malley."

In 1957, when Los Angeles first surfaced as the possible new home of the Dodgers, Brooklyn comic Phil Foster, who "viewed O'Malley's intention as no laughing matter," recorded a song called "Let's Keep the Dodgers in Brooklyn." Mercifully, it never really hit the charts, but its last lines foretold the memories in the making:

> But beware my friend and let me warn ya,
> They're thinkin' of takin' the Bums to California

"They" quickly "morphed" into O'Malley.

Within months of the announced departure, Walter O'Malley was denounced as a "Gaelic Machiavelli," a "cold schemer who would cast aside any loyalties in order to make a dollar." He was "lured by the glint of gold in California, and oblivious of the loyal, broken-hearted fans they [the Dodgers] left behind them." Few seemed to blame Giants' owner Horace Stoneham, who at the same time took his team west to San Francisco as companion to O'Malley. "Poor Horace," wrote one sportswriter, catching the general drift, "he's become a patsy for O'Malley."

The only evolution of recollection since the 1950s has been a deepening of the downward spiral of Walter O'Malley's memory in New York. Even though some historians, such as Robert Caro and Neil Sullivan, both of whom looked into the causes of the move, blamed Robert Moses as much or more than O'Malley for the westward trek, the latter remains stubbornly ensconced as scapegoat. By the 1980s, in fact, memory begat morbidity. In a short story, Pete Hamill has a father ask his son just returned from California:

> You ever run into that Walter O'Malley?
> "No," the son said. "Not in my set, Dad."
> That was a terrible man. What he did to Brooklyn, they will have a special place for him in the hereafter.

Peter Golenbock's oral history *Bums* recounts Bill Reddy's claim that the best news he ever received was "when I found out he was dead." "If it's true that there's a hereafter," Reddy added, "every Dodger fan knows exactly where he is right now." Even in 1994 a fan envisioned "Walter O'Malley, amid the sulfurous fumes of the pit." Why the venom so many years later? "It wasn't just a franchise shift" for which O'Malley was responsible. "It was a total destruction of a culture," according to another of Golenbock's interviewees. A correspondent writing to the *Times* echoed that perception: the Brooklyn Dodger organization was not only "the most profitable [team] in the National League, [it was] an essential part of Brooklyn's community fabric."

O'Malley's reputation only worsens with the passage of time; there is no abatement of emotion even in the 1990s. Perpetuation of emotional loss into the next generation suggests just how strong was the symbiotic relationship between Brooklyn and the Dodgers. Gary Goldberg, the creator of the television series *Brooklyn Bridge*, said recently that as a nine-year-old in Bensonhurst, he was horrified in 1956 when Robinson was traded to the Giants. But "O'Malley's perfidy" was only a "dress rehearsal for the vaster betrayal to come." "'O'Malley-bashing,'" writer Jay

Feldman says, is fun. But since 1990 marked the 100th anniversary of the Dodgers' first season in the National League, he adds, "I'm observing the occasion by forgiving Walter O'Malley for moving the team." Until now, he writes, "my fire could still be stoked by any mention of the scoundrel who took our team from us." But he finished his piece by reminding readers he could speak only for himself: "There are ex-Brooklynites all over the United States to this day . . . who maintain an enduring enmity for Walter O'Malley."

Hatred of the O'Malleys was rekindled recently when the Goliath represented by the Los Angeles Dodgers took on the David of the Brooklyn Dodger Sports Bar. Located in Bay Ridge, the bar represented one of the few vestiges of the Dodgers still left in Brooklyn. It had gained prominence as a beleaguered symbol of the borough's past—a sad, feisty reminder of what Brooklyn and the Dodgers had once meant to the community, and what it still means today. In 1990, Peter O'Malley, Walter's son and now president of the Los Angeles Dodgers, sent a "feral pack of lawyers" after the bar. The L.A. Dodgers claimed the exclusive right to the use of the Dodger name and challenged the bar's continued use of it. Seeing a great public relations coup, Kevin Boyle, the Brooklyn Dodger Sports Bar owner, hired a lawyer and publicly fought the Dodgers. One bitter regular of the Sports Bar sent this petition to the far reaches of Chavez Ravine (home of the Los Angeles Dodgers):

> Thirty years ago, the hearts of the faithful he did crush.
> Now he's trying to give two gin mills the Bum's Rush.
> Not this time, Pete, not this time.

Thus has the memory reached out to the next generation of O'Malleys.

Times columnist George Vecsey wrote a clever allegorical piece addressed to "one Peter O'Malley." In it a fictional Los Angeles lawyer presents Peter with a copy of Dickens's *Oliver Twist*, pointing out ruefully that someone used the D word before his father inherited it. Twist, the "Artful Dodger," threatens a possible pre-emptive strike against Peter, who claimed, in Vecsey's satire, never to have heard of Dickens when he was in business school. "Al Oliver pinch hit for us in 1985. But I've never heard of Oliver Twist until today." Reminding his readers of the continuity of generation in memory, Vecsey concludes, "Walter forfeited any claim to the name Brooklyn Dodgers the day he stuffed Duke and Gil into his personal gunnysack and lit out for the coast." As for Kevin Boyle,should he lose his rights to "Brooklyn," he has another trade name at the ready: "O'Malley's Folly."

As in the case of Jackie Robinson, the O'Malley memory remains as compellingly alive in the 1990s as it did a generation ago. The difference is that for the O'Malleys, father and son, there has been no softening of the animus directed at the family. Peter, trying to soften the antipathy to the O'Malley name that persists so stubbornly in Brooklyn, in 1995 returned to the borough the original 1955 Dodger World Championship banner. Still this memory persists. While Peter mended some fences for himself, Borough President Howard Golden reminded Peter that "this act in no way mitigates the pain O'Malley caused the borough."

The memories of the two names stand like personalized bookends at the outer edges of Brooklyn remembrance. They share only the extreme of emotional place in the chronicled mystique surrounding the Brooklyn Dodgers. One now owns a legend beyond cool logic given the ambivalence of his political convictions, the other is damned through eternity, a recollection that also defies reason. Too much of anything, even if it's correct in its essentials, will become poisonous. Those memories may well achieve historical equilibrium some day, but nearly two generations later, that time has not come.

The very extremes of memory that Jackie Robinson and Walter O'Malley together offer up suggest the degree to which the town and team were one. There is no discernible charisma attached, for example, to the old Boston Braves, or the late Philadelphia Athletics, to name two examples. Yet the Brooklyn Dodgers, nearly forty years after the team ceased to exist, carry a national reputation as pioneers in worlds well beyond professional baseball.

The popular mystique of a star-crossed team afflicted by the premature deaths of great athletes is one totem of the special place the team holds in the public imagination. The extremes of emotional memory surrounding two central characters in the Brooklyn Dodger drama is another symbol of the same. These extremes represent a depth of public memory which suggests the unique and special appeal of the Brooklyn Dodger baseball culture, a crossroads of people and place that experienced in its own way a taste of the larger transition the nation would soon endure.

Maybe that is why now the Brooklyn Dodgers remain viscerally enshrined not only in the memory of the community but, in many ways, in the remembrance of the nation.

Appendix A

Brooklyn's Baseball Bars: A Partial List

Bamonte's Restaurant & Bar
Behan's Bar & Grill
Concord Inn
Deron's Tavern
Dodgers' Cafe
Dugout Tavern
Eisen's Bar
Flynn's Bar & Grill
Freddie Fitzsimmons Bowling
    Alley & Restaurant
Henderson's Bar
Hole-in-the-Wall Tavern
Hugh Casey's Steak & Chop
    House
Jay's Tavern

Johnson's Saloon
Junior's Restaurant
Left Field Bar
McCormick's Bar & Grill
McKeever's Bar
Neil Sweeney's Tavern
Old Reliable Inn
Parkside Tavern
Pat Diamond's Bar & Grill
Pineapple Bar
Rattigan's Bar
Standish Arms Inn
Sullivan's Tavern
Web Cafe
White Rose Tavern

Appendix B

Brooklyn Boys Signed Off the Parade Grounds, 1946–56
(a partial list)

Cal Abrams*
Sonny Amodio
Bill Antonello
Bob Aspromonte*
Ken Aspromonte*
Ed Banach
Joe Belcastro
Fritzie Brickell
Shelly Brodsky
Tommy Brown*
Eddie Cahill
Vince Carlesi
Herman Cohen
Frank Colosi
Chuck Connors*
John Crimi
Babe Daskalaksis

Norman Diamond
Larry DiPippo
Larry Dunn
Bob Esposito
Jerry Folkman
Irving Glaser
Bob Grim*
William Hill
Dan Kopec
Sandy Koufax*
Wally Laurie
Steve Lembo*
Richard Lupardo
John McLean
Don McMahon
Jerry Madalena
Ralph Mauriello

Tony Mele
Joe Modica
Joe Musachio
Mike Napoli
Gerry Orleman
Willie Palumbo
Joe Pepitone*
Mario Picone
Bill Pierro
Joe Pignatano*
Charlie Ready
Charles Riccio
Saul Rogovin*
Jim Romano
Herb Rossman
John Rucker
Mickey Rutner

George Ryan
Lenny Sasso
Joe Sauralion
Frank Scorny
Len Scott
Rex Shanahan
Bob Spier
Jimmy Stagnato
Bob Sundstrom
George Thomasino
Charlie Torre
Frank Torre*
Joe Torre*
Ray Tully
John Weiss
Mike Weltman
Artie West

*Established major league careers.

Source: The *Brooklyn Eagle* and the *New York Times* reported signings from time to time. See 1946–56, passim. Readers Ed Donavan and John Doria added the following signings to my list: Sonny Catalano, Jack Daskalaksis, Ralph Dragatto, Bill Saar, Paul Sasso, Frank Taylor, and Carmine Vinci.

Notes

Introduction

xi *This was true as*—Michael A. Messner and Donald F. Sabo, *Sex, Violence and Power in Sports: Rethinking Masculinity* (Freedom, Calif., 1994), 34 and passim. Recently scholars have addressed in depth the problem of the sexual mores of male athletes. See, e.g., Merrill Melnick, "Male Athletes and Sexual Assault," *Journal of Physical Education, Recreation and Dance* (May–June 1992): 32–35; Mary P. Koss and John A. Gaines, "The Prediction of Sexual Aggression by Alcohol Use, Athletic Participation, and Fraternity Affiliation," *Journal of Interdisciplinary Violence*, 8, no. 1 (1993): 94–108; Lisa Guernsey, "More Campuses Offer Rape Prevention Programs for Male Athletes," *Chronicle of Higher Education* (Feb. 10, 1993): A37. This subject, as it played out on the Dodger team, is discussed in Chapter 5.

Chapter 1. Integration: Dodgers' Dilemma, Dodgers' Response

3 *Baseball Hall of Famer*—Henry Aaron with Lonnie Wheeler, *I Had a Hammer* (New York, 1991), 87, 99.

3 *The veteran Dodger regulars*—Robinson's rookie year of 1947 is ably and exhaustively examined in Jules Tygiel, *Baseball's Great Experiment: Jackie Robinson and His Legacy* (New York, 1983). In this chapter, I have built on and extended Tygiel's study, carrying the story of the Dodgers' race relations to the end of the team's tenure in Brooklyn.

4 *Because the South's temperate*—See Gene Schoor, *The Complete Dodger Record Book* (New York, 1984), 290–92, and passim; Tygiel, *Baseball's Great Experiment*, 336–37.

4 *Opposing teams certainly never*—For Reese, see Carl Rowan, *Wait Till Next Year* (New York, 1960), 224–25. For Roe, see Roger Kahn, *The Boys of Summer* (New York, 1971), 172–76, 302. For Dixie Walker, see *New York P.M.*, Oct. 26, 1946, April 11, 1947; Arthur Mann, *Branch Rickey: An American Life* (Boston, 1957), 257. *P.M.* was a New York City left/liberal newspaper in the 1940s. The best extant run of the daily can be found in the Doe Library of the University of California, Berkeley.

5 *Robinson at the storm*—Tygiel, *Baseball's Great Experiment*. The oral histories of the Dodgers by Roger Kahn and Peter Golenbock provided together a gold mine of primary information and interpretive insight for this chapter and the entire book. See Kahn, *Boys of Summer*, and Golenbock, *Bums: An Oral History of the Brooklyn Dodgers* (New York, 1984).

5 *In the real world*—David Halberstam, "Baseball and the National Mythology," *Harper's Magazine*, Sept. 1970, p. 24; Michael S. Kimmel, "Baseball and the Reconstitution of American Masculinity, 1880–1920," in *Sport, Men and the Gender Order: Critical Feminist Perspectives*, Michael A. Messner and Don F. Sabo, eds. (Champaign, Ill., 1990); A. Bartlett Giamatti, *Take Time for Paradise* (New York, 1989), 64–65. African Americans helped foster the same myth. In a 1954 ad in *Ebony*, for instance, a Beech-Nut gum cartoon shows Roy Campanella very conspicuously surrounded (hands on shoulders) by two white teammates after hitting three home runs in a game. That's the way to win white respect, *Ebony* and Beech-Nut were saying. Robert Curvin, a ranking African American civil rights activist, in a 1982 essay perpetuated the same myth. "Jackie Robinson, too, persevered," Curvin wrote, "and by 1949 he . . . was fully accepted by his teammates, even those who had vehemently opposed him when he was brought up." See *Ebony*, May 1954; *New York Times Magazine*, April 4, 1982, p. 50.

6 *Bearing this out, Robinson's*—*New York Times*, Aug. 3, 1952, March 19, 1954; Kahn, *Boys of Summer*, 134

6 *Jackie Robinson could be*—Golenbock, *Bums*, 283–84.

7 *Robinson initiated a running*—Rowan, *Wait Till Next Year*, 244–47; Arthur Daley's column, *New York Times*, April 1, 1955. For Gene Woodling's confirmation of the allegation see David Halberstam, *Summer of '49* (New York, 1989), 255. Yankee manager Casey Stengel seemed to have also provided confirmation of a sort. Stengel, remembering that Robinson struck out three times against Native American Allie Reynolds in the 1952 World Series, commented, "before he tells us we gotta hire a jig, he outa learn how to hit an Indian." See Roger Kahn, *The ERA, 1947–1957* (New York, 1993), 305–6.

7 *Even as Robinson willingly*—*New York Times*, May 10, 14, Sept. 6, 1952; Sept. 3, 1954; *Brooklyn Eagle*, May 9, 1952; Kahn, *Boys of Summer*, 121.

8 *Estrangement between Giles and*—Ibid.

8 *Money apart, the black*—For Erskine, see Kahn, *Boys of Summer*, 178–79. For Snider, see Duke Snider with Bill Gilbert, *The Duke of Flatbush* (New York, 1988), 22, 28. For Furillo, see Maury Allen, *Jackie Robinson: A Life Remembered* (New York, 1987), 155. For Creamer's general perception, see Robert Creamer, "Twilight of the Bums," *Sports Illustrated*, April 1, 1957, pp. 9–10.

9 *At least one southerner*—Reese's role as a team leader has been widely acknowledged. See, e.g., Snider, *Duke of Flatbush*, 62; Roger Kahn, "Dodgers in the Catbird Seat," *Sports Illustrated*, Aug. 5, 1974, p. 8. Ray Robinson, *The Home Run Heard 'Round the World* (New York, 1991), describes Reese as a "social revolutionary."

9 *As team captain, others*—For Reese's support of Robinson, and Jackie's frequent public acknowledgment of same, see *New York Times*, June 19, 1950; Jackie Robinson, *I Never Had It Made* (New York, 1972), 10. For his earliest newspaper-syndicated autobiography, see "Story of His Life Told by Jackie Robinson," *Brooklyn Eagle*, Aug. 24, 1949. For a later example, see Robinson, "A Kentucky Colonel Kept Me in Baseball," *Look Magazine*, Feb. 8, 1955, p. 82. For the movie, see reviews of *The Jackie Robinson Story* in *New York Post*, May 17, 18, 1950; *New York Times*, May 17, 1950.

10 *More than any other*—For the Chase Hotel's exclusion of African Americans, see Roy Campanella, *It's Good to Be Alive* (Boston, 1959), 193–94. For Don Newcombe's experience at the Chase, see Aaron, *I Had a Hammer*, 90. For the 1953 death threats against Robinson, see *New York Times*, Sept. 18, 1953. For other death threats, see *New York Daily News*, May 21, 1951; Snider, *Duke of Flatbush*, 27; *Brooklyn Eagle*, May 21, 1951; Rowan, *Wait Till Next Year*, 219.

10 *It was no coincidence*—For the strike threat, covered well in many baseball books, see *New York P.M.*, May 9, 1947; Stanley Woodward's column, *New York Herald Tribune*, May 8, 9, 1947; Arthur Daley's column, *New York Times*, Sept. 23, 1951; Red Barber, *1947: When All Hell Broke Loose in Baseball* (New York, 1982), 193; Allen, *Jackie Robinson*, pp. 135–37. For Musial's attitude, see Jackie Robinson, "Why I'm Quitting Baseball," *Look Magazine*, Jan. 22, 1957, p. 91ff.

10 *Robinson assaulted Garagiola's pride*—For an unequivocal contemporary account of Garagiola's racism by a reputable onlooker, see Heywood Hale Broun's column, *New York P.M.*, Aug. 25, 1947. For Robinson's feeling it was deliberate, see Robinson, "A Kentucky Colonel Kept Me In Baseball," *Look Magazine*, Feb. 8, 1955, p. 86. Both Carl Furillo and Ralph Branca later described the spiking. See Golenbock, *Bums*, 197. For accounts of the Sept. 11 game, see *P.M.*, Sept. 12, 1947; *New York Post*, Sept. 12, 1947. The *P.M.* story is particularly graphic. Both Maury Allen and Roger Kahn have recently added confirmation of both Garagiola's racism and the spiking incident, and the latter's feeble denials. See Allen, *Jackie Robinson*, 138–40, and Kahn, *ERA*,. 96–98.

11 *Robinson's teammates, whatever their*—For Durocher's description of Stanky on Robinson, see Leo Durocher with Ed Linn, *Nice Guys Finish Last* (New York, 1975), 203–6. For contemporary and later descriptions of Stanky's on-the-field supportiveness in 1947, see *New York Sun*, April 12, 1947; Golenbock, *Bums*, 191. Robinson himself said of that year, "Stanky . . . accepted me as a teammate on the basis of my ability, which is all that I asked of anyone." See Jackie Robinson, "Now I Know Why They Boo Me!" *Look Magazine*, Jan. 25, 1955, p. 28. For Stanky's locker room words in 1951, see Ray Robinson, *The Home Run Heard 'Round the World*, 150.

11 *That 1953 moment was*—Brooklyn Eagle, June 10, 11, 1952; *New York Herald Tribune*, June 11, 1952.

12 *Roger Kahn broke the*—Kahn, *Boys of Summer*, 132–36.

12 *The Dodger front office*—For Dodger management's response, see *Brooklyn Eagle*, June 10, 11, 1952; *New York Times*, June 11, 1952. Cardinals owner Fred Saigh saw the incident as an attendance bonanza, and reacted accordingly. See ibid.

12 *But the reality even*—Southerners on the team (Reese and perhaps Roe apart) more or less followed the lead of Bob Morgan of Oklahoma. With Gilliam's arrival Morgan was demoted from first to second utility infielder (now behind Cox). Other southerners on the team were Russ Meyer, Bob Milliken, Don Thompson, Ben Wade, Rube Walker, and Dick Williams (from southern Illinois). See Schoor, *Complete Dodger Record Book*. Roger Kahn dubbed a handful of these the Klan Contingent. See Golenbock, *Bums*, 425.

13 *Cox was known as*—For Cox's war experience and its aftereffects, see particularly Harold Burr's story in *Brooklyn Eagle*, Sept. 14, 1951. See also *New York Times*, Aug. 14, Sept. 18, 1952, Aug. 26, 1953; Golenbock, *Bums*, 231, 234; Ray Robinson, *Home Run Heard 'Round the World*, 69. For Daley's evaluation and Dressen's comment on Robinson, see *New York Times*, March 29 and April 7, 1953, respectively.

13 *Gilliam's presence in the*—Kahn, *Boys of Summer,* 172.

13 *Rumors of racial unrest*—For press coverage of racial tensions on the team during spring training, see *New York Times,* March 18, 20, 21, 23, 1953; *Brooklyn Eagle,* April 7 and March–April 1953 passim. For Black's comment, see *Times,* March 22, 1953. For Robinson's, see Golenbock, *Bums,* 431; Jackie Robinson, "A Kentucky Colonel Kept Me in Baseball," *Look Magazine,* Feb. 8, 1955, p. 87. For Meyer's claim, see Golenbock, *Bums,* 436–37.

14 *Preacher Roe, the team's*—*New York Herald Tribune,* March 21, 1953; Kahn, *Boys of Summer,* 172–76; Tygiel, *Baseball's Great Experiment,* 307.

14 *While the baseball public*—For O'Malley's threat, see *New York Times,* May 20, 1953.

14 *During the first six*—All the New York newspapers carried stories of the Aug. 30 game, but only the *Brooklyn Eagle,* Aug. 31, 1953, had a photo sequence of Stanky imitating an ape, and Hilda Chester protesting behind him. Ape-like imitations, grunts, as well as generalized comparisons, were and remain a virtually universal symbol of derision directed at black athletes. For a current reference, see Bill Buford, "The Lads of the National Front," *New York Times Magazine,* April 26, 1992. The characterization was often used in defense of slavery. See, e.g., the antebellum writings of George Fitzhugh.

14 *One of them was*—*Brooklyn Eagle,* Aug. 31, 1953.

15 *The incident was worse*—Ibid.

15 *Twice in that inning*—Ibid. Thomas Boswell offers up Stanky as an example of a "lousy Napoleon" type in describing poor managing styles in the majors. He also generalized in a way that might apply to the Dodgers' big inning: "Marginalized hitters glow in the reflected light of larger stars. The cliche 'hitting is contagious' is a basic truth with predictable lines of causality." See Boswell, *Why Time Begins on Opening Day* (New York, 1984), 100 and 52 respectively.

15 *There can be no*—Howard Cosell with Peter Bonventre, *I Never Played the Game* (New York, 1985), 330–47, esp. 330–31.

16 *The Milwaukee Braves also*—For the ethnic makeup of Milwaukee, and its racial attitudes, see Bayrd Still, *Milwaukee* (Madison, Wis., 1952); Frank Aukofer, *A City with a Chance* (Milwaukee, Wis., 1968). As of 1991, Milwaukee was still the seventh most segregated city in America. See *U.S.A. Today,* Nov. 19, 1991.

16 *Jackie Robinson and Roy*—The Braves in Aug. 1953 were in second place, five to seven games behind the pennant-bound Dodgers. For the generalized racism of key Braves' players, see Henry Aaron, *I Had a Hammer,* passim. For Robinson's talents as a bench jockey, see Snider, *Duke of Flatbush,* 26.

16 *At the same time*—For the racism of Spahn, Burdette, and Adcock, see Aaron, *I Had a Hammer*, 100–103 and passim. For the July 26 confrontation between Robinson and Burdette, see *Brooklyn Eagle*, Aug. 4, 1953.

16 *Milwaukee fans seemed to*—For the race hostility of many in the Milwaukee stands, see *New York Times*, May 20, Aug. 7, 1953. For Tommy Holmes's comment, see his column in *Brooklyn Eagle*, Aug. 10, 1953.

17 *The Braves still had*—For the words spoken and the fight on the field, see *Brooklyn Eagle, New York Daily News*, and *New York Times*, all Aug. 4 and 5, 1953; Tygiel, *Baseball's Great Experiment*, 310.

17 *The aftermath bordered on*—For Gorman's denial, see Tommy Holmes's column in *Brooklyn Eagle*, Aug. 5, 1953. For the forced truce between Campanella and Burdette, see ibid., Aug. 4, 1953. For the intellectual/communist/fascist menace, see ibid., Aug. 12, 1953 (the Letters to the Editor column). For Robinson's summary comment, see ibid., Aug. 6, 1953.

17 *Even that did not*—For Dressen's warning to Meyer, see *Brooklyn Eagle*, Aug. 5, 1953. For a reference to Meyer's "Red Neck," a euphemism for racism, see Jimmy Powers's column, *New York Daily News*, July 1, 1951.

18 *A payback came a*—For the continuing animosity between the teams, and Labine's beaning of Adcock, see *New York Times*, March 7, Aug. 2, 1954.

18 *Much of Robinson's own*—For the Lena Horne interview, see the Sunday Supplement, *New York P.M.*, Sept. 14, 1947.

19 *Advertising mogul Jerry Della*—For Della Femina, see Jerry Della Femina and Charles Sopkin, *An Italian Grows in Brooklyn* (Boston, 1978), 99. For the Jewish boy's hero worship of Robinson, see Alan Lelchuk, *Brooklyn Boy* (New York, 1990). It forms a central motif of the novel. For Abdul-Jabbar's recollection, see George Vecsey's column, *New York Times*, June 10, 1985.

19 *Many future black major*—For Frank Robinson's feelings, see Frank Robinson and Berry Stainback, *Extra Innings* (New York, 1988), preface; Allen, *Jackie Robinson*, 245; for Winfield and Charles, see ibid., 170, 244.

19 *Other evidence exists that*—*New York P.M.*, Aug. 3, 1947. Tygiel, *Baseball's Great Experiment*, deals ably and extensively with the Dodgers' spring training experiences.

20 *Willie Morris, long-time editor*—Willie Morris, *North Toward Home*, excerpted in *Into the Temple of Baseball*, Richard Grossinger and Kevin Kerrane, eds. (Berkeley, Calif., 1990), 196.

20 *In the end, however*—For Snider's view of Robinson, see Snider, *Duke of Flatbush*, 27.

21 *Pee Wee Reese saw*—For Reese's comment, see Allen, *Jackie Robinson*, 5.

21 *Much of the respect*—Robert Creamer, "Twilight of the Bums," *Sports Illustrated*, April 1, 1957, p. 9; Tommy Holmes's column, *Brooklyn Eagle*, Sept. 14, 1949.

21 *The Dodgers knew early*—Snider, *Duke of Flatbush*, 336; Ira Berkow, *A Biography of Red Smith* (New York, 1986), 107.

Chapter 2. Political Culture: Reds and Dodger Blue

23 *Th' two gr-eat American*—Finley Peter Dunne, *Mr. Dooley*, quoted from *The Second Fireside Book of Baseball*, Charles Einstein, ed. (New York, 1958), 105.

24 *Lest anyone think this*—Charles Einstein, *Willie's Time: A Memoir*, 2nd ed. (New York, 1992), 15.

24 *The Dodgers didn't have*—Anticommunism in the decade after World War II is a topic dealt with extensively in this chapter. For the domestic politics of anticommunism, see Richard M. Freeland, *The Truman Doctrine and the Origins of McCarthyism* (New York, 1972); Alan D. Harper, *The Politics of Loyalty: The White House and the Communist Issue, 1946–1952* (New York, 1969); Stanley Kutler, *The American Inquisition: Justice and Injustice in the Cold War* (New York, 1982); Paul L. Murphy, *The Constitution in Crisis Times, 1918–1969* (New York, 1972).

24 *Rickey actively espoused displays*—Gerald Holland, "Mr. Rickey and the Game," *Sports Illustrated* (1955), excerpted in *The Baseball Reader*, Charles Epstein, ed., 4th ed. (New York, 1980), 183.

25 *Rickey was a political*—For a perceptive examination of Robinson's impact on black integration efforts generally after World War II, see Peter Levine, *From Ellis Island to Ebbets Field: Sports and the American Jewish Experience* (New York, 1992). Because it ties Jackie more closely to the Brooklyn community and its problems, Levine complements and updates the effective treatment of the same subject found in Jules Tygiel, *Baseball's Great Experiment* (New York, 1983).

25 *Rickey shrewdly tied Robinson's*—*New York Herald Tribune*, April 14, 1949.

25 *Baseball, we have been*—There is an extensive literature dealing with the relationship between agrarian virtue and egalitarian values in early America. For an important representative example, see Merrill Peterson, *The Jeffersonian Image in the American Mind* (New York, 1956).

26 *That idyllic agrarian tie*—George Will, *Men at Work* (New York, 1990), 240, 294; Thomas Boswell, *Why Time Begins on Opening Day* (New York, 1984), 288.

26 *A. Barlett Giamatti, both*—A. Bartlett Giamatti, *Take Time for Paradise*, ppr. ed. (New York, 1989), 66–71, 83, 88, 103–4.

26 *During the decade he*—There is yet no satisfactory book dealing with baseball's complex involvement in American politics. One book that touches on the subject in important ways, and examines some aspects in particular of organized baseball's antipathy for the left, is Lee Lowenfish, *The Imperfect Diamond: A History of Baseball's Labor Wars*, rev. ed. (New York, 1991). For Red Smith's comments, see Ira Berkow, *Red: A Biography of Red Smith* (New York, 1986), 111, 113. The Cold War is another subject that comes up often in this chapter. Though not as controversial historically as it once was, it still generates markedly different interpretations. A fair and balanced view can be found comprehensively in a series of books by John Lewis Gaddis: *The United States and the Origins of the Cold War, 1941–1947* (New York, 1972), *Strategies of Containment* (New York, 1982), *The Long Peace: Inquiries into the History of the Cold War* (New York, 1987), *Russia, the Soviet Union and the United States: An Interpretive History* (New York, 1990).

27 *While Robinson would eventually*—For this early autobiographical exercise, and Robinson's early comments on communism, see *Brooklyn Eagle*, Aug. 26, Sept. 27, 1949.

27 *Robinson was only restating*—*Brooklyn Eagle*, Oct. 8, 1952.

27 *The first black major*—Harold W. McDowell to Jackie Robinson, May 16, 1947, Arthur Mann Papers, Manuscript Division, Library of Congress. The Mann Collection contains several examples of "fan" letters like this one.

28 *McDowell's shopping list mirrored*—Jerry Della Femina and Charles Sopkin, *An Italian Grows in Brooklyn* (Boston, 1978), 81, 91, and passim. For the 1952 Loyalty Day parade, see *Brooklyn Eagle*, May 4, 11, 1952. For Grannis's comment, see the *Eagle*, Aug. 17, 1952. Scenes like this were repeated annually, as were smaller patriotic celebrations in the course of the decade.

28 *The Dodger presence was*—*Brooklyn Eagle*, May 4, 11, 1952. There were major protests against "Operation Alert" days elsewhere in New York, but not in Brooklyn. See Dee Garrison, "'Our Skirts Gave Them Courage': The Civil Defense Protest Movement in New York City, 1955–1961," in Joanne Meyerowitz, ed., *Not June Cleaver: Women and Gender in Postwar America, 1945–1960* (Philadelphia, 1994), 201–26.

28 *Many Brooklyn citizens were*—An account of Rickey's Cooperstown speech can be found in *New York Herald Tribune*, June 14, 1949. Reference to Rickey's admiration for Herbert Hoover can be found in Roger Kahn, *The Boys of Summer* (New York, 1971), 100. John Lardner's characterization of Rickey's politics is in Lardner, "Reese and Robinson: Team Within a Team," *New York Times Magazine*, Sept. 18, 1949, p. 17. For the description of Powers, see Arthur Mann, *Branch Rickey: An American Life* (Boston, 1957), 240. The book's title itself characterizes both Mann's overt patriotism and his idolization of Rickey.

The long relationship between baseball and patriotic values survives. In the aftermath of the Gulf War, the *New York Times*, ran on April 8, 1991, a story on opening day under the headline "Let the Bats Sing and Patriotism Ring." The story goes on to elaborate: "Opening day 1991 will be a celebration of patriotism, with virtually every team offering some sort of tribute to the troops; from flag ceremonies, to having members of the military throw out the first ball, to singing the national anthem the way Whitney Houston would."

29 *Rickey was never reluctant*—For Rickey's two versions of his "Americanism" lecture, see Mann, *Rickey*, 256. For Campanella's experience with it, see Roy Campanella, *It's Good to Be Alive* (Boston, 1959), 140. Many have written about Rickey's early injunctions to Robinson about his demeanor on and off the field, as well as the periodic pep talks Robinson heard from a man he respected. The best description of that relationship can be found in Harvey Frommer, *Rickey and Robinson* (New York, 1982), esp. 1–16.

29 *The Dodger front office*—For Rudd's refinement of the Americanism speech, see Peter Golenbock, *Bums: An Oral History of the Brooklyn Dodgers* (New York, 1984), 417. Even New York's left-wing daily could occasionally fall prey to the front office's patriotic handouts. See for example *P.M.*, May 18, 1947.

29 *Given the management's political*—For examples of the front office's public attention to veterans' organizations, see *Brooklyn Eagle*, May 16, Aug. 26, 1951, Aug. 30, 1953, May 5, 1954; *New York Times*, May 3, Aug. 26, 30, 1953, May 20, June 11, 1954. For the story on the First Army soldiers' arrest, see the *Eagle*, Aug. 8, 1954. Other teams may have followed similar practices with regard to veterans, but those stories have not yet been written.

30 *In 1951 and for*—For background on Truman's firing of MacArthur and its implications for the Cold War, see John W. Spanier, *The Truman-MacArthur Controversy and the Korean War* (Cambridge, Mass. 1959). For the general's political appeal for the American right, see William Manchester, *American Caesar: Douglas MacArthur, 1880–1964*

(Boston, 1978). For MacArthur's interest in baseball generally, and his admiration for Jackie Robinson, see 701–2.

30 *MacArthur returned to the*—For Dick Young's account of the invitation and the game, see *New York Daily News*, April 20, 1951. For local response, see *Brooklyn Eagle*, May 21, 1951. Harvey Frommer, *New York City Baseball: The Last Golden Age, 1947–1957* (New York, 1980), 105, concludes that Rudd provided MacArthur with his winning line.

31 *The Old Soldier was*—For the game, see *New York Daily News*, April 20, 1951. For speculation about MacArthur's candidacy for baseball commissioner, see ibid., July 2, 1951; *New York Times*, Aug. 10, 1951.

31 *As it turned out*—For MacArthur's appearance at the 1951 Brooklyn parade, see *Brooklyn Eagle*, June 17, 1951. For his partiality for the Dodgers, see *New York Daily News*, July 2, 1951; Roger Kahn, "In the Catbird Seat," *Sports Illustrated*, Aug. 5, 1974, p. 39; *Eagle*, Oct. 2, 1952; *New York Times*, April 16, 1954. For the general's encounter with the symphoney, see the *Eagle*, July 2, 1952. His appearance at Dodger games was often noted in the press between 1951 and 1954. Management encouraged sportswriters to mention MacArthur's attendance, probably to bolster the team's identification with political conservatism.

31 *In accord with his*—For Nixon the candidate, see *Brooklyn Eagle*, Oct. 6, 1952; *New York Times*, Oct. 6, 1952; Duke Snider with Bill Gilbert, *The Duke of Flatbush* (New York, 1988), 117. For the critical commentary of Nixon, see Robert Grannis's column, *Eagle*, Oct. 6, 1952; *Times*, July 23, 1955. For Nixon being booed, see Roger Kahn, *The ERA, 1947–1957* (New York, 1993), 306.

32 *Even though the public*—For Robinson's relationship with Nixon after his playing days, see Maury Allen, *Jackie Robinson: A Life Remembered* (New York, 1987), 218–19. At the end of his life Robinson regretted his earlier support of Nixon, just as he felt badly about criticizing Paul Robeson. See Jackie Robinson, *I Never Had It Made* (New York, 1972), 147–52.

32 *Robinson shared Rickey's views*—Cf. earlier note this chapter, headed "During the decade he."

33 *Brooklyn first: the borough*—For reaction to Judith Coplon, see *Brooklyn Eagle*, Feb.–March 1950, esp. March 8. For the Rosenbergs' funeral, see ibid., June 21, 1953; *New York Times*, June 21, 1953.

33 *People who opposed or*—There are several good studies of Rickey. The best full-length biography is Murray Polner, *Branch Rickey: A Biography* (New York, 1982). Arthur Mann's *Branch Rickey* is a period piece, and valuable insight into Rickey on that account. There is an excellent indepth two-part "Profiles" sketch of Rickey by Robert Rice in the *New Yorker*, May 27, June 3, 1950. Another good short piece is Gerald Holland's "Mr. Rickey and the Game," *Sports Illustrated* (1955), reprinted in

The Baseball Reader, Charles Einstein, ed. (New York, 1978), 180–90. For the "El Cheapo" tag, see Melvin Durslag, "A Visit with Walter O'Malley," *Saturday Evening Post*, May 14, 1960; Mann, *Rickey*, 240. For Rickey's stigmatizing Cardinal players, and Robert Murphy's unionizing effort, see Lee Lowenfish, *The Imperfect Diamond*, rev. ed. (New York, 1991), 129–68. See also Mann, *Rickey*, 3, 240; Neil J. Sullivan, *The Dodgers Move West* (New York, 1987), 30.

34 *In a speech before*—For Rickey's anticommunist rhetoric and overview of baseball's significance as expressed in his April 1949 speech, see *New York Herald Tribune*, April 14, 1949. For other evidence of Rickey's anticommunism, see Polner, *Rickey*, 216; Mann, *Rickey*, 3, 240, 256. For the McPhail quote, see Daniel Okrent and Steven Wulf, *Baseball Anecdotes* (New York, 1989), 201.

34 *At the same time*—For Rickey's rejection of the "liberal" label, see Holland, "Mr. Rickey and the Game," 180–90, esp. 181.

35 *The appearance before the*—For Rachel Robinson's comment, see Robert Curvin, "Remembering Jackie Robinson," *New York Times Magazine*, April 4, 1982, p. 54. See also Harvey Frommer, *New York City Baseball: The Last Golden Age, 1947–1957* (New York, 1980), 66. For O'Malley's reaction, see Durslag, "A Visit with Walter O'Malley."

35 *Robinson the ballplayer did*—For the *Daily Worker*'s hostility to "The Jackie Robinson Story," see *Brooklyn Eagle*, May 17, 1950. For Robinson's early expressions of anticommunism see ibid., Aug. 26, Sept. 27, 1949. The *Daily Worker* generally was sympathetic to Robinson and did see him as a force for integration. See Tygiel, *Great Experiment*.

35 *In the '50s, Robinson*—For Robinson's earliest autobiographical denunciation of communism, see *Brooklyn Eagle*, Aug. 26, Sept. 27, 1949. For his 1955 views (consistent with his 1949 position) see Jackie Robinson, "Your Temper Can Ruin Us," *Look Magazine*, Feb. 22, 1955, p. 85. Robinson usually had a ghostwriter, as did virtually all ballplayers. But unlike most others, he shaped the material initially and edited and rewrote heavily before a piece saw the light of day. Roger Kahn, in his recent book, sees Robinson as more naive on the question of communism than do I. See *ERA*, 200–207.

The conflict between Robinson and Robeson was in keeping with an historical tradition of tension between black activists on how to best advance the race and end racial discrimination in America. Since at least the 1930s, these efforts have divided between communist/radical strategies and reformist/democratic tactics—varying, of course, upon the degree of faith one had in the ability of American society to reform itself. Robinson clearly stood, at least in this period of his career, on the reformist side, with Robeson on the radical end.

Historians have written extensively about the rise of this communist/reformist schism among black activists, which emerged most clearly in the 1930s Scottsboro rape trial of nine black youths. Debates over defense strategies split the Communist party from the NAACP and compelled the latter's shift toward the mainstream. See David Levering Lewis, *When Harlem Was in Vogue* (New York, 1981), 270–73, 286. Lewis notes that NAACP president Walter White did not want the NAACP to "risk becoming confused in the public mind with the party of revolution" (273). See also Mark Naison, *Communists in Harlem During the Depression* (New York, 1983), 59, 86–88, 132.

This tendency of reformists to disassociate themselves from communism in their bid for racial equality became fully entrenched as the civil rights movement progressed. A. Philip Randolph sought to exclude "Communists and their fellow-travelers and allies" from participating in the important March on Washington Movement in 1941. See Naison, *Communists in Harlem*, 310–12.

With the Cold War red scare in full bloom, reform-minded blacks solidly distanced themselves from anything even hinting of communism. Some were merely politically expedient; others believed America could make a place for them. Robinson clearly sided with this camp. "With undue haste, the civil-rights leadership condemned the pro-Soviet remarks of Paul Robeson, a controversial black singer and actor, and disassociated themselves from the Marxist stance of W. E. B. Dubois." See Harvard Sitkoff, *The Struggle for Black Equality, 1954–1992*, rev. ed. (New York, 1993), 17.

36 *This was borne out—The Jackie Robinson Story*, filmed in 1949 with Robinson playing himself, and released in 1950, is a Hollywood product of its times. Those times included the blacklisting of alleged communists and "sympathizers." Though not easily available now, the movie is on videocassette and can be rented or bought with a little searching.

36 *That movie in fact*—Martin Duberman's *Paul Robeson* (New York, 1988) is a thoughtful and thorough biography, and it offers a view of this event from Robeson's perspective. Duberman implicitly agrees that Robinson's testimony, the high point (or low point, perhaps) of the hearing, hurt both men. Duberman's description of Robinson's testimony does briefly summarize Robinson's impassioned assault on discrimination generally and segregation in particular. See ibid., 360–62.

36 *Robinson in 1949 feared*—Ibid. For the Truman administration's pioneering attempts to confront segregation and race discrimination, see David McCullough, *Truman* (New York, 1992).

37 *It was before the*—For authorship of Robinson's HUAC statement, see Mann, *Rickey*, 278–79; Carl Rowan, *Wait Till Next Year: The Life Story of Jackie Robinson* (New York, 1960), 204–11. Ironically, many years later Hank Aaron unwittingly inferred that maybe Robeson had a point. About to be drafted, and contemplating the interruption to his baseball career, Aaron years later acknowledged, "I admit I wasn't crazy about the thought of being in the army—when you grow up as a black kid in a Jim Crow city, you somehow don't feel a great urgency to serve your country." Henry Aaron with Lonnie Wheeler, *I Had a Hammer* (New York, 1991), 95.

37 *Robbie admired Robeson, but*—For the full text of Robinson's statement, see *New York Herald Tribune*, July 19, 1949. It was the only New York City newspaper to print the statement in its entirety. It may have been the only "establishment" paper in the nation to do so; some black publications published the complete statement. The appearance did receive wide national coverage. For extended and typical comment on both the statement itself and Robinson's appearance before the committee generally, see *Brooklyn Eagle*, July 18–20, 1949.

37 *In 1988, Hall of*—For Jackie's advice and Frank Robinson's regrets, see Frank Robinson with Berry Stainback, *Extra Innings* (New York, 1988), ix. For Hank Aaron's statements, see Aaron, *I Had a Hammer*, 4, 114–15, 333.

38 *It is that perspective*—*New York Herald Tribune*, July 19, 1949.

38 *Shortchanging by the press*—Ibid. The newspapers of America, the black press excepted, emphasized the anticommunist angle, played down Robinson's call for integration. Some clues about what continued to feed Robinson's anger off the field after he became a star are enlightening. It took a long, frustrating search for he and Rachel to find a decent house to buy. See Jackie Robinson, *I Never Had It Made*, 116–20. His six-year-old son experienced at least passive discrimination in the Stamford, Connecticut, public school system. See ibid., 121. Even after 1949, if Robinson wanted to play golf (his passion), "on days when his white friends were not available, he was forced to wake before daylight to play public courses." "He could not get a membership in a private golf club, Jackie Robinson or not." See William Fugazy's letter to the editor, *New York Times*, Aug. 17, 1990.

39 *The Dodger second baseman*—*New York Herald Tribune*, July 19, 1949.

39 *Robinson's fury came through*—Ibid.

39 *But almost immediately after*—For Robeson's response, see Rowan, *Wait Till Next Year*, 202. For both Robinson's acceptance of an award under the stands, and his encounter with Howard Fast, see Peter Golenbock, *Bums*, 280, 425–26 respectively. For his 1957 defense of his HUAC testimony, see Robinson, "Why I'm Quitting Baseball," *Look Magazine*, Jan. 22, 1957, p. 92.

40 *In the end, Robinson*—For Robinson's expression of regret about his criticism of Robeson, see Jackie Robinson, *I Never Had It Made*, 95–98.

40 *If Robinson had his*—These examples of Cold War rhetoric and caricature appeared in *Brooklyn Eagle*, Sept. 30, 1951, Oct. 8, 1952. For the 1952 Loyalty Day parade, see ibid., May 4, 11, 1952.

41 *The left-wing reaction*—For Italian political culture, see Della Femina, *An Italian Grows in Brooklyn*, 81–91 and passim. For that of Brooklyn's Jews, see Gerald Sorin, *The Nurturing Neighborhood: The Brownsville Boys Club and Jewish Community in Urban America, 1940–1990* (New York, 1990), esp. 73. For both Italians and Jews, see Jonathan Rieder, *Canarsie: The Jews and the Italians of Brooklyn Against Liberalism* (Cambridge, Mass., 1985). Rieder's book makes clear that majorities of both ethnic groups, while oriented to mainstream anticommunist Brooklyn Democratic party politics, also claimed sizable left minorities as well.

41 *How did Brooklyn fans*—For Chuck Connors, see his obituary in *New York Times*, Nov. 11, 1992. For Billy Loes, see *Baseball's Greatest Insults*, Kevin Nelson, comp. (New York, 1990), 128. For Dressen, see Charley Dressen, "The Dodgers Won't Blow It Again!," *Saturday Evening Post*, Sept. 13, 1952.

42 *As for those fans*—For the reference to Woody Allen, see Allen, *Side Effects* (New York, 1975). For the psychological analysis, see Howard Senzel, "Baseball and the Cold War," reprinted in *Into the Temple of Baseball*, Richard Grossinger and Kevin Kerrane, eds. (Berkeley, Calif., 1985), 206–11, esp. 209. The more technical explanation of why "a good communist" who was not supposed to be interested in baseball but was is: "Alienation is emotional, but radicalization is an intellectual process. Proposition, conclusion, and then anger. The process of becoming a radical is not only creating but channeling anger. And as the propositions and anger increase, they begin to form a pattern. It changes the way that the world is perceived. It changes the way that you live and the things that you want from life. The illusion is that the process is one of genuine rebirth, causing a new and different human being to emerge from the same consciousness." Got that? Not so, says Senzel. One responds viscerally, emotionally to culture patterns implanted long before "political rebirth" occurs. According to Senzel, in short, you are a fan before you acquire political commitment. The commitment to baseball survives radicalization.

42 *How to test this*—Alan Lelchuk, *Brooklyn Boy* (New York, 1990); Mark Lapin, *Pledge of Allegiance* (New York, 1991).

43 *In Lelchuk's* Brooklyn Boy—Lelchuk, *Brooklyn Boy*, 122–23, 130–31, 140–41.

43 *Josh's story, in Mark*—Lapin, *Pledge of Allegiance*, 245–59.

43 *Once again, the same*—Ibid., 275. For an example in real life of children victimized in Brooklyn for their parents' communism, see Deborah A. Gerson, "Is Family Devotion Now Subversive? Familialism Against McCarthyism," in Meyerowitz, ed., *Not June Cleaver*, 151–76.

Chapter 3. The Dodgers' Male Culture: The New York Rivalries

45 *On a Sunday in*—Dick Young wrote the most graphic contemporary account. See *New York Daily News*, Sept. 7, 8, 1953. For two close-up accounts, see Duke Snider with Bill Gilbert, *The Duke of Flatbush* (New York, 1988), 69–70; Peter Golenbock, *Bums: An Oral History of the Brooklyn Dodgers* (New York, 1984), 461–62. The latter carries sportswriter Harold Rosenthal's account.

46 *Brooklyn masculinity was tested*—For Erskine's and Labine's comments, see Ray Robinson, *The Home Run Heard 'Round the World* (New York, 1991), 18, 21, respectively. For Aaron on Drysdale, see Henry Aaron with Lonnie Wheeler, *I Had a Hammer* (New York, 1991), 172. For the Hodges story, see Alan Lelchuk, *Brooklyn Boy* (New York, 1990), 111.

Macho posturing by athletes, and its antisocial or even criminal aftermath, has become big news. Witness the accusations directed at several New York Mets in spring 1992 and the arrest, trial, and conviction of heavyweight champion Mike Tyson at about the same time, to name but two prominent instances. Theories abound. Sports in general and baseball in particular "connect American males with each other . . . through generations." Michael Kimmel concludes that "the lyrical eloquence that baseball above other sports inspires derives, in part, from the sport's centrality in the effort to reconstitute American masculinity at the turn of the century." Others dwell as well on the historic links between masculinity and sports arising rejuvenated out of the industrial revolution. See Michael S. Kimmel, "Baseball and the Reconstitution of American Masculinity, 1880–1920," in *Sport, Men and the Gender Order: Critical Feminist Perspectives*, Michael A. Messner and Don Sabo, eds.

(Champaign, Ill., 1990), esp. 56. See also Allen Guttmann, *Sports Spectators* (New York, 1986), esp. 110–11; Don F. Sabo, *Jock: Sports and Male Identity* (Englewood Cliffs, N.J., 1980); Robert Lipsyte, "Sportsworld," *New York Times Magazine*, Oct. 5, 1975.

47 *Jackie Robinson's effectiveness as*—For the Stengel-Robinson story, see David Halberstam, *Summer of '49* (New York, 1989), 61.

47 *Jackie's identification with proving*—Rodney Fisher to Jackie Robinson, May 19, 1947; Rev. John F. Curran to Jackie Robinson, Oct. 7, 1947; Lew Goldenberg to Jackie Robinson, May 15, 1947; G. Gilbert Smith to Jackie Robinson, June 1, 1947; Jackie Robinson to G. Gilbert Smith, June 10, 1947, Arthur Mann Papers, Manuscript Division, Library of Congress. For Red Barber's comment, see Michael H. Ebner's letter to the editor, *New York Times*, Nov. 8, 1992.

47 *As we have seen*—Golenbock, *Bums*, 460–61.

48 *As the other extreme*—For Branca, see Robinson, *Home Run Heard 'Round the World*, 232–33.

48 *"Have You Hoid, Moitle?"*—For that headline response see *New York Star* (formerly *P.M.*), July 18, 1948.

48 *Leo's 1991 obituary noted*—*New York Times*, July 14, 1991; Snider, *Duke of Flatbush*, 69–70; Maury Allen, *Jackie Robinson: A Life Remembered* (New York, 1987), 98, 116–17.

48 *After one riotous confrontation*—For "bush" charges, see *Brooklyn Eagle*, May 2, 1951. For Campanella's observations, see Roy Campanella, *It's Good to Be Alive* (Boston, 1959), 130–41, esp. 138. For Robinson's baiting Leo with references to Laraine Day, see George F. Will, *Men at Work* (New York, 1990), 91; Allen, *Robinson*, 98–99; Golenbock, *Bums*, 435. For Harold Burr's "kids" comment, see *Brooklyn Eagle*, May 3, 1951.

49 *Durocher was only one*—Snider, *Duke of Flatbush*, 26; Kahn, *Boys of Summer*, 91; Allen, *Jackie Robinson*, 98–99; Golenbock, *Bums*, 435.

49 *In a 1953 game*—For the Gilbert incident, one of many examples to choose from, see *Brooklyn Eagle*, May 23, 1953. For another involving Robinson and the Giants, see *New York Times*, June 27, 1952. For an excellent insight into the nearly lost art of bench jockeying, see Pat Sullivan's feature story, "Baseball's Bench Jockeys—A Vanishing Breed," *San Francisco Chronicle*, July 2, 1992. For a scholarly account of how bench jockeys extend American baseball folklore, see Tristram Potter Coffin, *The Old Ball Game: Baseball in Folklore and Fiction* (New York, 1971), 62–63. The author used the Brooklyn Dodgers as a prime example of the art in action.

49 *No wonder Durocher told*—For Durocher's desire to beat the Dodgers, see *Brooklyn Eagle*, Aug. 23, 1951. For Maglie's comments, see Sal Maglie with Robert Boyle, "The Great Dodger-Giant Days," *Sports Illus-*

trated, April 22, 1968, p. 42. For defining the macho factor in baseball, this is an enlightening piece.

50 *In the words of*—The poem is Jonathan Holden's "A Personal History of the Curveball," *Kenyon Review*, reprinted in *Into the Temple of Baseball*, Richard Grossinger and Kevin Kerrane, eds. (Berkeley, Calif., 1990), 193.

50 *Over the years, Maglie*—*Brooklyn Eagle*, May 1, 1951; *New York Times*, May 1, 13, 1951.

50 *Four years later, in*—*New York Times*, April 24, 1955.

50 *As a matter of*—Contemporarily, Tommy Holmes wrote graphically about Maglie's beanballs. See *Brooklyn Eagle*, June 22, 1950, Aug. 15, 1952. For Maglie's words, and the later folklore surrounding his beanballs, see his obituaries: *New York Newsday*, Dec. 29, 1992; *New York Times*, Dec. 29, 1992. For his instruction to Drysdale, and the latter's knocking Aaron down twice, see Dave Anderson's column, ibid., Dec. 29, 1992, and Ira Berkow's column after Drysdale's death, ibid., July 5, 1993. For Hank Aaron's feelings on the matter, see Aaron, *I Had a Hammer*, 172.

51 *Roy Campanella and Carl*—For Campanella as a target, see Sal Maglie, "The Great Giant-Dodger Days," *Sports Illustrated*, April 22, 1968, p. 42 and passim; *Brooklyn Eagle*, April 23, 1951, Aug. 8, 1952; *New York Times*, April 22, 1951.

51 *Carl Furillo was hit*—For Furillo as a target, see *New York Daily News*, May 8, 16, June 26, 1951; *Brooklyn Eagle*, June 29, 30, 1950, July 9, 1952; *New York Times*, June 28, 1951, April 26, July 21, 1953, April 25, 1954. For Dodger pitchers throwing at Giants, see, e.g., *Eagle*, Aug. 19, 1953; *Times*, Sept. 5, 1953.

51 *Dodger regulars learned to*—For the Snider-Robinson incident, see *New York Times*, Sept. 5, 1953.

52 *Both the 1952 and*—For George Will's judgment, see *Men at Work* (New York, 1990), 218. For Dressen's and Erskine's appraisals, see *New York Times*, Sept. 13, 1953, and Peter Golenbock, *Bums*, 462, respectively. For Neil Sullivan's metaphor, see *The Dodgers Move West* (New York, 1987), 60.

53 *Even the most frustrated*—For the Young story, see *New York Daily News*, Oct. 1–3, 1950; Allen, *Robinson*, 186. For Daley, see *New York Times*, July 4, Aug. 23, 1952; Arthur Daley, "Wait-Til-This-Year," *New York Times Magazine*, Sept. 7, 1952.

53 *Even the partisan Brooklyn*—For Burr's and Holmes's fears, see *Brooklyn Eagle*, Aug. 5, 6, 8, 1952, respectively.

54 *"If we can pull"*—For Durocher, see *Brooklyn Eagle*, Sept. 8, 1952; *New York Times*, July 18, Aug. 7, 1952. For Reese's response, see ibid., Sept. 6, 1952.

54 *Charley Dressen, Red Smith*—Charley Dressen as told to Stanley Frank, "The Dodgers Won't Blow It Again!.," *Saturday Evening Post,* Sept. 13, 1952. The magazine actually appeared at newsstands a week earlier than the publication date, as usual. For Red Smith's comment, see "Where's Charley?," *Sports Illustrated,* Oct. 4, 1952, p. 41.

54 *The article reflected on*—Dressen, "The Dodgers Won't Blow It Again!.," 41. For Daley's cutting appraisal, see *New York Times,* Sept. 11, 1952. For Holmes's view, see *Brooklyn Eagle,* Sept. 9, 1952. For Dressen's later private admission, see Daniel Okrent and Steven Wulf, *Baseball Anecdotes* (New York, 1989), 217. Even Walter O'Malley publicly doubted the Dodgers: "We have to beat the Giants. If we don't, we don't deserve winning," he told the *New York Times* (July 27, 1952).

55 *Still stunned on the*—The most dramatic accounts of the five-game Giant series are in *New York Daily News,* Sept. 7–9, 1952.

55 *Pitching aside, it was*—For an account of the game that featured Hodges's role, see *New York Times,* Sept. 8, 1952. For Kahn's comment, see Kahn, *Boys of Summer,* 157. For a history of Hodges being thrown at by Giant pitchers, see, e.g., *Brooklyn Eagle,* June 22, 30, 1950; *New York Times,* Sept. 9, 1952.

56 *The next day Hodges*—For the Sept. 8 game, with graphic descriptions of both Hodges's role and the beanball war, see *New York Times,* Sept. 9, 1952. For adept post-mortems on the pennant race, see Tommy Holmes in *Brooklyn Eagle,* Sept. 26, 1952, and Arthur Daley in the *Times,* Sept. 29, 1952. As Daley said in that column, the key Dodger that season was Joe Black, who carried "fourteen spear carriers" on the Dodger pitching staff. An exaggeration, but Black won fifteen and saved fifteen more. Rigney was accessible as both a second baseman and a favored Dodger target. Furillo called him "no goddamn good. He tried to be like Durocher." Furillo claimed that many Dodgers, Reese in particular, felt that way about Rigney. Golenbock, *Bums,* 357.

56 *Monte Kennedy, another Giant*—*New York Times,* Sept. 9, 1952.

56 *The Dodgers had long*—Ibid.

57 *It took a while*—For the Coleman quote, see Harvey Frommer, *New York City Baseball: The Last Golden Age, 1947–1957* (New York, 1980), 125. For Daley, see *New York Times,* Sept. 30, 1953.

57 *On the one hand*—Golenbock, *Bums,* 527, 461 respectively.

57 *Inevitably, the Dodgers were*—For Labine and Erskine, see ibid., 471, 463 respectively. For Robinson, see Campanella, *It's Good to Be Alive,* 190–91.

58 *The Yankee mystique was*—For the *Eagle* quote, see *Eagle*'s editorial page, Oct. 2, 1952. A cartoon in the issue of Oct. 1 tells a different story.

One Dodger with uniform askew and jersey on backwards is telling a teammate, "Me nervous? Naw! World Series pressure doesn't bother me." For Drebinger, see *New York Times*, Sept. 25, 1955. For Stengel's words, see the *Times*, Oct. 4, 1953, Sept. 24, 1955.

58 *Robert Creamer officially put*—Robert Creamer, "When Brooklyn Won the Series," *Sports Illustrated*, Oct. 17, 1955, pp. 57–59.

59 *We now know from*—Recent revisions by women's historians suggest that the postwar era did form a feminist bridge between World War II and the 1960s, so the evidence on the '50s is mixed. See Joanne Meyerowitz, ed., *Not June Cleaver: Women and Gender in Postwar America, 1945–1960* (Philadelphia, 1994). The title of this book itself suggests, however, just how suspect the 1950s were, from a feminist point of view. (June Cleaver, to the uninitiated, was the mother on the television show "Leave It to Beaver.")

Chapter 4. Male Culture:
Owners, Chokers, and Dumb Kids

60 *In the aftermath of*—Lee Lowenfish, *The Imperfect Diamond: A History of Baseball's Labor Wars*, rev. ed. (New York, 1991), 129–70, discusses both the unionization movement and the threat posed by the Mexican League in 1946.

60 *Walker, an established star*—For Walker, see *New York P.M.*, Sept. 11, Oct. 26, 1946, April 11, 1947; Arthur Mann, *Branch Rickey: An American Life* (Boston, 1957), 287. Lowenfish, *Imperfect Diamond*, 148, 178.

61 *Baseball magnates and their*—See Thomas Boswell, *Why Time Begins on Opening Day* (New York, 1984), 177. Boswell often illustrates the ballplayer-as-kid theme in this book.

62 *Reporters occasionally referred to*—For a reference to "Rickey's Plantations," see *Brooklyn Eagle*, May 13, 1949. For references to "chickens" and "The Old Woman," see Mann, *Rickey*, 226.

62 *The surviving 1916 pennant*—For Red Smith's remark, see his column in *New York Herald Tribune*, Oct. 9, 1949. For Maury Allen's characterization of Rickey, see Allen, *Jackie Robinson: A Life Remembered* (New York, 1987), 70.

62 *When it came to*—For the Celler-O'Malley contretemps, see *Brooklyn Eagle*, June 1, 4, 1951, and passim for that year.

63 *Walter O'Malley could always*—For O'Malley's acknowledgment, in seeking a new stadium, that his business was baseball, see ibid., Oct. 1, 1952. For Red Smith's comment, see Smith, *To Absent Friends* (New York,

1982), 377. For Robert Moses's characterization of O'Malley, see "Robert Moses on the Battle of Brooklyn," *Sports Illustrated*, July 22, 1957, p. 27. For Melvin Durslag, see Durslag, "A Visit with Walter O'Malley," *Saturday Evening Post*, May 14, 1960, p. 31.

63 *Sometimes the two successive*—For Walter "Red" Barber's comment, see Barber, *The Broadcasters* (New York, 1970), 169.

63 *In a rare angry*—*Brooklyn Eagle*, April 9, 1950; Roger Kahn, *The Boys of Summer* (New York, 1972), 96–97.

64 *Carl Furillo, moody and*—For Furillo's treatment at the end of his career, see Neil Sullivan, *The Dodgers Move West* (New York, 1987), 196; Kevin Nelson, ed., *Baseball's Greatest Insults* (New York, 1989), 129. For Labine's take on the Furillo incident, see Peter Golenbock, *Bums: An Oral History of the Brooklyn Dodgers* (New York, 1984), 460. For the insurance coverage of the players, see Robert Creamer, "The Twilight of the Bums," *Sports Illustrated*, April 1, 1957, p. 10. For Happy Felton, see *Brooklyn Eagle*, May 23, 1953; Golenbock, *Bums*, 567.

64 *Several Dodger players learned*—For Campanella's operation and its aftermath, and the lawsuit that resulted, see *New York Times*, May 28, 30, 1955. Campanella early in his career borrowed money from Branch Rickey to open a liquor store in Harlem. Rickey gave him a hard time, offering fatherly religious platitudes about the evils of alcohol. The club president advised Campanella to invest in a sporting goods store instead. Rickey relented, but Campanella considered it a humiliating experience. See Roy Campanella, *It's Good to Be Alive* (Boston, 1959), 13–14.

65 *Rickey had been no*—For Connors's and Stanky's comments, see Nelson, ed., *Baseball's Greatest Insults*, 116–17.

65 *Both Carl Erskine and*—For Erskine's leadership role on the team, and his latent anger at the baseball establishment, see *Brooklyn Eagle*, Aug. 28, 1953; *New York Times*, Aug. 7, 1955. For the Dodgers' team encounter with Commissioner Happy Chandler, see the *Eagle*, June 6, 1951. For J. Norman Lewis's role on behalf of the Dodgers and the major leagues as a whole, see the *Times*, July 13, 1954, Aug. 7, 1955; Lee Lowenfish, *Imperfect Diamond*, 184–91.

66 *Pee Wee Reese, for*—See Arthur Daley's columns, *New York Times*, July 5, 1951, July 18, 1955. There were several others as well. It was those simulated on-the-field, boys-will-be-boys columns that won Daley a Pulitzer Prize.

66 *Some players paid a*—For Tom Meany's comment, see his column, *New York Star* (formerly *P.M.*), Sept. 1, 1948. Meany was quoting an unnamed bigoted baseball magnate when he wrote that column. It was a subtly racist statement on the part of the owner.

67 *Billy Loes's problems with*—Loes was often taken down in the press, at best as a colorful character, at worst as a flaky ignoramus. For Arthur Daley's public take on Loes, see his columns, *New York Times*, July 9, 1954, Sept. 30, 1955. For other examples of the same, see Tommy Holmes's and Harold Burr's columns in *Brooklyn Eagle*, Oct. 2, 1952, April 2, 1954, respectively. For the story of Loes's negotiations with Rickey, and the former's father playing the insular greenhorn for the occasion, see Jimmy Breslin, "The Dodgers' New Daffiness Boy," *Saturday Evening Post*, Aug. 22, 1953, p. 11.

67 *Rickey signed Loes for*—For Loes's investing his money from the start, see Jimmy Breslin, "The Dodgers New Daffiness Boy," *Saturday Evening Post*, Aug. 22, 1953, p. 26ff. This story was both sophisticated and, if read between the lines with the perspective that time provides, discerning about who Loes really was, for all the flaky behavior described. For Loes's comment to Dressen about his longevity in the majors and money, see Golenbock, *Bums*, 397–99.

67 *Dodger management understandably considered*—For Kahn's take on Loes's friendship with Robinson, see Golenbock, *Bums*, 399, 424.

68 *On a pre-game*—For the "Knothole Gang" story, see Breslin, "The Dodgers' New Daffiness Boy," 118. For the Bavasi story, see Arthur Daley's column, *New York Times*, Sept. 30, 1955. For Loes's characterization of O'Malley, see Harold Burr's column, *Brooklyn Eagle*, April 2, 1954. For Loes's run-ins with Alston, see the *Eagle*, April 29, Sept. 22, 1954.

68 *Loes was a great*—Breslin, "The Dodgers' New Daffiness Boy," 26ff. For Holmes on the Breslin piece, see his column, *Brooklyn Eagle*, Aug. 24, 1953. For recent perpetuation of the Loes "stupid" myth, see Daniel Okrent and Steve Wulf, *Baseball Anecdotes* (New York, 1989), 217; Alan Lelchuk, *Brooklyn Boy* (New York, 1990), 108.

69 *This typecasting had little*—For Loes and Robinson, see Golenbock, *Bums*, 424. For the picture of Loes playing chess with Don Drysdale, see Arthur Daley, "Automation on the Diamond," *New York Times Magazine*, March 18, 1956, p. 25.

69 *Loes was no more*—A good example of how Duke Snider's early reputation as a prima donna carried over for his entire career can be found in Kahn, *Boys of Summer*, 374–85. Kahn, late in Snider's career, wrote a piece in *Collier's* with Snider's collaboration describing the cynicism of the "game" via Snider's long-held view that, given the demeaning way players were dealt with by press and management, only the money mattered to a professional. Neither Kahn nor Snider could foresee the public relations disaster that followed publication, as all of the old perceptions of Snider were trotted out yet again. Kahn felt that the press had deliberately chosen to misinterpret the real meaning of the story, in order to take Snider to task yet one more time for his alleged immaturity and callowness. The real intent of the story, both felt, was its emphasis on the stereotyping the players experienced in the interest of both "the game" and its control over players.

69 *At the beginning of*—Jimmy Powers column, *New York Daily News*, April 20, 1951.

70 *This color could be*—Arthur Mann, "The Dodgers' Problem Child," *Saturday Evening Post*, Feb. 20, 1954, p. 27ff. The reality for more than a decade was that Snider was a team leader and a moderating force in the struggle to maintain team unity in the face of racism both in baseball at large and on the Dodgers. Snider, according to several accounts, knew early what he said later: "We were a symbol of baseball, and of America itself." Snider was an important element of the "sheer greatness" of the Brooklyn team, Robert Creamer wrote, among "the dozen or so athletes who were at the core of the team." They "knew they were set apart." Maury Allen, in his biography of Jackie Robinson, counted Snider among those closest to Robinson on the club, and an important and mature source of moderation. See Duke Snider with Bill Gilbert, *The Duke of Flatbush* (New York, 1989), 27, 336; Robert Creamer, "Twilight of the Bums," *Sports Illustrated*, April 1, 1957, p. 9; Allen, *Robinson*, 115–18, 187.

70 *At twenty-two years*—Brooklyn Eagle, July 19–21, 1951.

70 *Palica's side of the*—Ibid., Oct. 2, 1951. It has long been postulated in sports that there was a "causal connection between aggressiveness as a personality trait and success in competitive sports." The Palica episode is a fine case in point, because Dodger management seemed explicitly to be acting on that belief to motivate the young pitcher. For a popularized but revealing clinical discussion of the psychology of that subject, see Warren R. Johnson, "Guilt-Free Aggression for the Troubled Jock," *Psychology Today*, Oct., 1970, pp. 70–73.

71 *That cynical policy also*—For Dixie Walker's 1946 comment, and his later expression of regret, see Ira Berkow's column, *New York Times*, Oct. 28, 1992. Roger Kahn recalled an incident aboard a storm-beset plane carrying the Dodgers that reveals the same mindset among others on the Dodgers. When Jackie Robinson acknowledged he was frightened in response to some needling by Kahn, the latter found himself "the hero of the Dodger Klan contingent," including coach Billy Herman, Jim Hughes and Bobby Morgan. See Golenbock, *Bums*, 425.

71 *Even before he was*—New York Herald Tribune, March 11, 1949; Jules Tygiel, *Baseball's Great Experiment: Jackie Robinson and His Legacy* (New York, 1983), 316–17.

72 *Three such early "failures"*—All the New York papers carried lead stories of these games. See, for example, *New York Daily News*, Oct. 6, 1949, Oct. 2, 1950, and Oct. 4, 1951. All the papers make clear how well Newcombe pitched.

72 *An examination of his*—For detailed accounts of Newcombe's clutch games over a decade, see any New York City daily. For crisis games pitched in his early years see, e.g., *New York Post*, Aug. 1, 5, 9, 13, 17, 22, 25, 29, Sept. 3, 7, 11, 17, 22, 25, 30, 1949, Sept. 24, 26, 28, Oct. 2, 1950. For Newcombe's feat in pitching both ends of a critical doubleheader in 1950, see *New York Times*, Sept. 7, 1950.

72 *In 1951, with the*—*New York Post*, Sept. 18, 23, 27, 30, Oct. 4, 1951, Sept. 1, 8, 16, 20, 24, 25, 27, Oct. 2, 1956. With the possible exceptions of Yankee pitchers Whitey Ford, Eddie Lopat, Vic Raschi, and Allie Reynolds, no other pitcher in the 1950s pitched and won more clutch games than Don Newcombe.

73 *Through his entire career*—Major leaguers', especially southern players', responses to Newcombe's ups and downs were rooted in a race-biased belief system. That bias in baseball mirrored in a specific and heated context America's deeply ingrained race bias. For that long tradition and its cumulative cultural impact see, for example, Reginald Horsman, *Race and Manifest Destiny: The Origins of American Racial Anglo-Saxonism* (Cambridge, Mass., 1981); Albert K. Weinberg, *Manifest Destiny: A Study of National Expansion in American History* (Baltimore, 1935); Stanley M. Elkins, *Slavery: A Problem in American Institutional Life* (Chicago, 1976); Walter LaFeber, *The New Empire, 1860–1898* (Ithaca, N.Y., 1963). For a lively discussion of how this bias played out in immediate postwar America generally, see Eric Goldman, *The Crucial Decade and After: America, 1945–1960* (New York, 1961). For Walker's statement, see *New York P.M.*, Sept. 11, 1946.

73 *Both Dodger managers in*—For both Shotton's and Dressen's allegations that Newcombe was lazy, see Tommy Holmes's column, *Brooklyn Eagle*, Sept. 4, 1951. See ibid. for the anonymous allegation he was just a "big Negro kid." For his effort in pitching a doubleheader in 1950, see *New York Times*, Sept. 7, 1950. *Eagle* beat writer Fred Downs quickly echoed these sentiments, reinforcing the stereotype. See the *Eagle*, Sept. 16, 1951.

74 *Durocher and the Giants*—For evidence that the Giants seized on these public statements about Newcombe, and the fallout that followed, see *Brooklyn Eagle*, Sept. 14, 16, 1951; Kahn, *Boys of Summer*, 90–91; Ray Robinson, *The Home Run Heard 'Round the World* (New York, 1991), 76, 175, 191, 199, 223.

74 *What sealed Newcombe's fate*—For Tommy Holmes's summary of the feelings of some of Newcombe's teammates, see *Brooklyn Eagle*, Sept. 14, 1951. For Dressen on Newcombe, see Charley Dressen as told to Stanley Frank, "The Dodgers Won't Blow it Again," *Saturday Evening Post*, Sept. 13, 1952. For Newcombe's comments after his 1956 World Series loss, see Milton Gross's column, *New York Post*, Oct. 11, 1956. This piece was reprinted in *The Second Fireside Book of Baseball*, Charles Einstein, ed. (New York, 1958), 169–71.

75 *It also rubbed off*—Ray Robinson, *The Home Run Heard 'Round the World*, 76–78; Jerry Della Femina and Charles Sopkin, *An Italian Grows in Brooklyn* (Boston, 1978), 99. Clancy Sigal, *Going Away* (New York, 1961), 444.

Chapter 5. The Baseball Culture of Brooklyn's Women

77 *In June 1952 the*—*Brooklyn Eagle*, June 24, 1952. For a long review of *A League of Their Own* that deals with gender issues, see *San Francisco Chronicle*, July 1, 1992. An essay on the same subject that helped focus some issues I dealt with in this chapter was written as a term paper in 1993 in the History Department of New York University: Deb Steinbach, "Muscle-Molled Tomboys and Diamond Damsels: Representations of the All-American Girl's Baseball League in the National Media, 1943–1954."

77 *Gender attitudes were more*—Michael S. Kimmel, "Baseball and the Reconstitution of American Masculinity, 1880–1920," in *Sport, Men and the Gender Order: Critical Perspectives*, Michael A. Messner and Don Sabo, eds. (Champaign, Ill., 1990), 65; Don Sabo, *Jock: Sports and Male Identity* (Englewood Cliffs, N.J., 1980), 163. See also Robert Lipsyte, "Sportsworld," *New York Times Magazine*, Oct. 5, 1975.

78 *Baseball-bred contempt for*—For a recent study that discusses the roots of postwar male attitudes, the nature of gender relations in that era, and the ways in which many women sustained their sense of identity within the confines of the '50s mass culture, see Joanne Meyerowitz, ed., *Not June Cleaver: Women and Gender in Postwar America, 1945–1960* (Philadelphia, 1994). The current take on the era, Meyerowitz suggests, "flattens the history of women." Nevertheless, the essays in the book generally reflect the deep biases of the '50s dominant male culture against women outside the home. By Meyerowitz's own account in her essay in this collection, Babe Didrikson Zaharias was dismissed in mainstream culture as an "Amazon" ("boyish bob, freakish clothes"). After her marriage, in popular literature she "became a woman." See Meyerowitz's essay, "Beyond the Feminine Mystique: A Reassessment of Postwar Mass Culture, 1946–1958," ibid., 233–34. Sports culture marked the very edge of masculine misogyny in the life of America immediately after World War II.

78 *It is a part*—For the Dodgers' reaction to the Waitkus shooting, see *New York Herald Tribune,* June 20, 1949.

78 *W. P. Kinsella more recently*—For W. P. Kinsella's fictional account of "Baseball Annies," see his "Barefoot and Pregnant in Des Moines," in *The Thrill of the Grass* (Toronto, Canada, 1984), 131–40. In the same collection of short stories, Kinsella's "Driving to the Moon" also deals with baseball's groupie subculture in a different way. See ibid., 109–27. For Roger Kahn's reference, see his "Intellectuals and Ballplayers," *American Scholar* 16 (Summer 1957): 14.

79 *The 1950s, in fact*—For the Mets incident, see *New York Times,* April 10, 1992. For Strawberry's "defense" of the Mets, see *New York Newsday,* March 30, 1992. As both the Mike Tyson and New England Patriots incidents demonstrate, gender attitudes leave much to be desired in sports other than baseball.

79 *Ballplayers generally do not*—For Don Newcombe, see Henry Aaron with Lonnie Wheeler, *I Had a Hammer* (New York, 1991), 90; David Halberstam, *Summer of '49* (New York, 1989), 253.

79 *Both Johnny Podres and*—For Podres, see Peter Golenbock, *Bums: An Oral History of the Brooklyn Dodgers* (New York, 1984), 502–4, 518.

79 *Dick Williams, a bench*—For Williams, see Roger Kahn, *The Boys of Summer* (New York, 1971), 130–32.

80 *Part of the risk*—For Hank Behrman, see *Brooklyn Eagle,* July 16, 1951. Golenbock, *Bums,* 235–36. For Billy Loes, see Jimmy Breslin, "The Dodgers' New Daffiness Boy," *Saturday Evening Post,* Aug. 22, 1953, p. 118.

80 *The saddest and best*—For the lawsuit against Hugh Casey, see *Brooklyn Eagle,* April 21, 1950, July 3, 6, 1951.

80 *Dodger reserve outfielder Al*—For Gionfriddo's disdainful remark, see Golenbock, *Bums,* 46–47. For Casey's suicide, see *Brooklyn Eagle,* July 3, 6, 1951. For '50s attitudes on the subject, see Meyerowitz, ed., *Not June Cleaver,* 9.

81 *Male athletes' relationships with*—For the Marianne Moore anecdote, see Charles Molesworth, *Marianne Moore: A Literary Life* (Boston, 1991), 164–65. For Kimmel's comment, see his "Baseball and the Reconstitution of American Masculinity," in *Sport, Men and the Gender Order,*

Messner and Sabo eds., 64–65 and passim. For Allen Guttmann's conclusions, see his *Sports Spectators* (New York, 1986), 113–15.

81 *By the 1950s, baseball*—Brooklyn Eagle, Oct. 1, 1952.

82 *It was the bobby*—For the origins of the "Sandlot Queen" contest, see *Brooklyn Eagle*, June 3, 1949.

82 *Both the Dodgers' potent*—For Edna Kelly, see *Brooklyn Eagle*, June 22, 1954. For Louis Heller, see ibid., June 6, 1949. For Arthur Daley's remark, see his column, *New York Times*, Sept. 5, 1954.

82 *This 1950s baseball norm*—For the Abraham & Strauss event, see *Brooklyn Eagle*, June 25, 1952.

83 *Dodger wives were not*—Brooklyn Eagle, June 20, Sept. 28, Oct. 2, 7, 1952; *New York Times*, Sept. 13, 1955; *New York P.M.*, Sept. 21, 1947; Richard Goldstein, *Superstars and Screwballs: 100 Years of Brooklyn Baseball* (New York, 1991), 292–93. For Branch Rickey's reaction to heckling of wives, see *New York Post*, June 15, 1945.

83 *Managers' wives were also*—Brooklyn Eagle, Oct. 2, 7, 1952; *New York Times*, Sept. 13, 1955.

84 *The press relentlessly pursued*—These are a few of many such stories that make the point, and were especially abundant in the *Brooklyn Eagle*, *Daily News* and *Daily Mirror*. For these examples, see the *Eagle*, Aug. 22, Oct. 8, 1952, June 5, 1953. Even the staid *New York Herald Tribune* was not immune. See for example, Red Smith's column, June 9, 1949.

84 *"Cheesecake" was popular in*—For the Co-Ettes, see *Brooklyn Eagle*, July 29, 1951; *New York Times*, Oct. 4, 1951, Sept. 21, 1953. The use of posed "leg shots" was also a common photographic practice on the sports pages. For these illustrations, see the *Eagle*, Oct. 4, 1951; *New York Star*, July 18, 1948. The *Star* was successor to *P.M.*

84 *Over the years, Jeff*—For these representative examples of Keate's cartoons, see *Brooklyn Eagle*, June 6, 25, Sept. 5, 1951, May 1, 26, July 31, 1952.

85 *Marianne Moore moved to*—Molesworth, *Marianne Moore*, especially 164–65, 247ff, 333ff, 428–33.

85 *In a valedictory essay*—Ibid.

86 *Charles Molesworth, her biographer*—Ibid.

86 *And in defiance of*—Marianne Moore's "Hometown Piece for Messrs. Alston and Reese" has been reprinted often. For the complete text, see Golenbock, *Bums*, 584–86. Appropriately, he ends the book with it. Some people, not many, perhaps, remember Moore's connection with the Brooklyn Dodgers. In 1990, the U.S. Post Office issued a Marianne Moore commemorative stamp. When a latter-day Brooklyn fan went to buy some, the postmistress said, "Well, at least I got rid of some of them." See "Metropolitan Diary," *New York Times*, May 16, 1990.

86 *Hilda Chester was a*—Much of what I learned about Hilda Chester, including the realities of her work life, her life in Brooklyn outside Ebbets Field, and her use of language, was found in a fine interview/feature written by Jean Evans for *New York P.M. Magazine*, Sept. 22, 1946.

87 *Brooklyn fans will remember*—Ibid.

87 *A compleat Brooklynite, Chester*—Louis Effrat's sketch, *New York Times*, Sept. 3, 1955.

88 *In a universe of*—*New York P.M.*, Sept. 22, 1946.

88 *Never at Ebbets Field*—Ibid.; Golenbock, *Bums*, 58; *New York Times*, Sept. 3, 1955; *New York P.M.*, Sept. 22, 1946.

88 *In the early 1940s*—Ibid.

89 *When Durocher jumped ship*—*New York Times*, Sept. 3, 1955; *Brooklyn Eagle*, Oct. 4, 1951; *New York Star*, July 18, 1948; *New York Herald Tribune*, Oct. 10, 1949.

89 *Life at the edge*—*New York P.M.*, Sept. 22, 1946.

89 *Hilda Chester played every*—*New York P.M.*, Sept. 22, 1946, April 1, 1948; Leonard Cohen's column, *New York Post*, May 29, 1945.

90 *Hilda Chester thus developed*—*New York P.M.*, Sept. 22, 1946.

90 *These stories were honed*—Ibid.

90 *An old antagonist stalked*—Ibid.

90 *This story is important*—Meyerowitz, ed., *Not June Cleaver*, suggests that feminism was alive and present, if not well, after World War II, but the book's essays amply confirm that gender tensions and discrimination were the norms for the era.

Chapter 6. The Dodgers and Male Bar Culture

93 *When the Brooklyn Amateur*—See Jimmy Powers's column, *New York Daily News*, April 20, July 22, 1951.

93 *Man-in-the-street*—For the above sampling, see *New York P.M.*, July 30, 1947, April 29, 1948. Largely because of Brooklyn-born Meany, thoughtful sportsbeat reporter Heywood Hale Broun, and the left-wing, working-class orientation of *P.M.*, that paper caught the Brooklyn bar culture best. The last incarnation of *P.M.*, the *New York Star*, folded in 1950.

Working-class urban bar culture for an earlier era has been examined in Perry Duis, *The Saloon: Public Drinking in Chicago and Boston, 1880–1920* (Urbana, Ill., 1983); Roy Rosenzweig, *Eight Hours for What We Will: Workers and Leisure in an Industrial City, 1870–1920* (New York, 1983); Eliott J. Gorn, *The Manly Art: Bare Knuckle Prize Fighting in America* (Ithaca, N.Y., 1986).

93 *Debate was usually the*—See Tom Meany's column, *New York P.M.*, July 30, 1947.

94 *Backseat managing of the*—*New York Times*, Oct. 2, 1951.

94 *Big events in the*—*New York Herald Tribune*, April 30, 1949.

94 *When the Dodgers looked*—For the reaction to the double loss to the Giants, see *Brooklyn Eagle*, Sept. 7, 1952. For the bar debate over the comparative skills of Mays and Snider, see Damon Rice, *Seasons Past* (New York, 1976), 397.

95 *By the early 1950s*—*New York Times*, Oct. 2, 3, 1951; *Brooklyn Eagle*, Sept. 30, 1951.

95 *Working-class Dodger fans*—For the doggerel and the "vulgar" comment, see *New York P.M.*, Sept. 29, 1946, and July 29, 1947, respectively.

95 *In this habitat, the*—Ibid., Sept. 20, 1946, May 30, 1947, July 18, 1948.

96 *When arguments threatened to*—Ibid.

96 *Not all barmen were*—Rice, *Seasons Past*, 356–57.

96 *P.M., the daily for*—For the photo sequence and captions described here, and another example of the same, see *New York P.M.*, Sept. 20, Oct. 2, 1946, respectively. These were beautifully executed visual sequences of men moving hats on their heads, shifting beer glasses from hand to hand, tippling, blowing foam. So far as I know, runs of *P.M.* exist now only on microfilm, making effective reproduction here impossible. The most complete run of this paper of the 1940s is located in the Doe Library, University of California, Berkeley. A less complete run can be found in the New York Public Library.

97 *Bad Dodger moments were*—*Brooklyn Eagle*, Sept. 26, Oct. 3, 4, 1951.

97 *A week later, in*—For Hamill's and Slote's reactions, see Ray Robinson, *The Home Run Heard 'Round the World* (New York, 1991), 240–41. For the report from *Brooklyn Eagle*, see issues of Sept. 26, Oct. 3, 4, 1951.

97 *An even worse moment*—Peter Golenbock, *Bums: An Oral History of the Brooklyn Dodgers* (New York, 1984), 579, 582.

98 *Dodger fans could be*—For the Red Sox scout, see *New York Times*, Oct. 2, 1955. For the Yankee fans' encounters, see *Brooklyn Eagle*, Oct. 6, 1952, and the *Times*, Oct. 8, 1952, respectively.

98 *A year later Bill*—For Reddy's reaction, see Golenbock, *Bums*, 471. For the Giants' fans at McCormick's, see *New York P.M.*, Sept. 20, 1946.

98 *Dodger fans' emotions ran*—For the 1938 murder, see a comprehensive account in Frank Graham, "The Brooklyn Dodgers," in *A Treas-*

ury of Brooklyn, Mary Ellen Murphy, Mark Murphy, and Ralph F. Weld, eds. (New York, 1949), 227–29. For the 1955 killing in Queens, see Golenbock, *Bums,* 528. For Michael Kimmel's observation, see his "Baseball and the Reconstitution of American Masculinity, 1880–1920," in *Sport, Men and the Gender Order: Critical Perspectives,* Michael A. Messner and Don Sabo, eds. (Champaign, Ill., 1990), 56.

99 *At the Pineapple Bar—Brooklyn Eagle,* Sept. 29, 1951.

99 *Some Brooklyn watering holes*—For a general description of the Dodgers frequenting Casey's, see Red Barber, *1947: When All Hell Broke Loose in Baseball* (New York, 1982), 294.

99 *In his heyday, Casey*—For Casey's "pouring a mean drink," see Peter Williams, ed., *The Joe Williams Baseball Reader* (Chapel Hill, N.C., 1989), 183. For Tom Meany's characterization of Casey's nickname, see *New York P.M.,* Oct. 6, 1947. For other stories about Hugh Casey's Steak & Chop House, see *P.M.,* April 16, Aug. 19, Oct. 5, 1947; *Brooklyn Eagle,* April 21, 1950, July 3, 6, 1951.

99 *Jay's Tavern at 22*—For Jay's, see *Brooklyn Eagle,* Oct. 8, 1952, Sept. 13, 1954; Golenbock, *Bums,* 234; Harvey Frommer, *New York City Baseball* (New York, 1980), 45.

100 *Several other Dodgers frequented—Brooklyn Eagle,* Oct. 8, 1952.

100 *Another popular watering place—New York Times,* Sept. 9, 1955.

100 *The Dodgerville room at*—Ibid.

Chapter 7. The Dodgers and Brooklyn's Ethnic Isolation

103 *This was a remarkably*—Historians have long since departed from the comforting notion of American immigration producing a great "melting pot" of acculturation. Ethnic groups maintain their distinctive values and characteristics through the generations. There is an extensive literature on the subject. Some notable examples are: Nathan Glazer and Daniel P. Moynihan, *Beyond the Melting Pot* (Cambridge, Mass., 1963); Thomas Kessner, *The Golden Door: Italian and Jewish Immigrant Mobility in New York City, 1880–1915* (New York, 1977); David M. Reimers and Leonard Dinnerstein, *Ethnic Americans: A History of Immigration and Assimilation* (New York, 1982).

103 *The borough's cultural isolation*—For "Brooklynese," see Geoffrey D. Needler, "Kings English: Fact and Folklore of Brooklyn Speech," in *Brooklyn, U.S.A.,* Rita Seiden Miller, ed. (New York, 1979), 173–83. For an early illustration of Willard Mullins's "Dodger Bum," and an accompanying explanation, see *The Joe Williams Baseball Reader*, Peter Williams, ed. (Chapel Hill, N.C., 1984), 182–85. For Brooklyn's cultural isolation generally, see B. A. Botkin, ed., *Sidewalks of America* (Indianapolis, Ind., 1954).

104 *Brooklyn became the butt*—For Cashmore, see Botkin, ed., *Sidewalks of America*, 20. For the quiz-show anecdote and the more generalized feeling among Brooklyn residents that they were being laughed at, see ibid. and Needler, "Kings English," in *Brooklyn, U.S.A.*, Miller, ed., esp. 173 and 177. For Stengel's observation, see *New York Times*, Sept. 19, 1955.

104 *"The Society for the*—For the society, see Needler, "Kings English," 173–83. For Mencken's confirmation, see Henry L. Mencken, *The American Language: An Inquiry into the Development of English in the United States* (New York, 1963).

105 *This satirical language, so*—For Mullins's Bum, see Williams, ed., *Joe Williams Baseball Reader*, 182–85. For O'Mealia's use of the caricature, see *New York Daily News*, Oct. 5, 1955. Thirty years later, of course, Peter Golenbock entitled his oral history *Bums*.

105 *Stephen King, a Brooklyn*—For King's poem, see "Brooklyn August," in *Into the Temple of Baseball*, Richard Grossinger and Kevin Kerrane, eds. (Berkeley, Calif., 1990), 24–25. For the Erskine anecdote, see Richard Goldstein, *Superstars and Screwballs: 100 Years of Brooklyn Baseball* (New York, 1991), xv.

105 *New York Post columnist*—For Jimmy Cannon, see *New York Post*, Aug. 15, 1952. For Steve Jacobson, see *New York Newsday*, Oct. 23, 1992.

105 *Establishment types habitually and*—John Lardner, "Should It Still Be Brooklyn?," *New York Times Magazine*, Feb. 26, 1956, p. 20. For the Board of Education story, see *Brooklyn Eagle*, Aug. 21, 1953.

106 *The language of the*—William Poster, "'Twas a Dark Night in Brownsville: Pitkin Avenue's Self-Made Generation," *Commentary*, May 1950, pp. 458–67.

106 *It was as much*—For Williams's comment, see Williams, ed., *Joe Williams Baseball Reader*, 184. For the allusion to Dodger fans as vulgar, see *New York P.M.*, Sunday Supplement, Sept. 29, 1946. For Daley, see *New York Times*, April 14, 1949. For Rice's verse, see *New York Sun*, Oct. 2, 1946.

107 *The Times' sportswriters in*—*New York Times Magazine*, Sept. 27, 1953, Sept. 7, 1952, and Feb. 26, 1956, respectively.

107 *Peter Golenbock, with great*—Peter Golenbock, *Bums: An Oral History of the Brooklyn Dodgers* (New York, 1984). This particular quote is on 524, but the sense it conveys forms a persistent theme of the book.

108 *Author Robert Caro blamed*—For Moses's own words, see Robert Moses, "The Battle of Brooklyn," *Sports Illustrated*, July 22, 1957, pp. 26, 27, 49. For Caro's view, see Robert Caro, *The Power Broker: Robert Moses and the Fall of New York* (New York, 1974), 108–9. For a more gentle view of Moses's culpability, see Neil J. Sullivan, *The Dodgers Move West* (New York, 1987), 45–57.

108 *The déclassé image of*—David Shaw, "The Roots of Rooting," *Psychology Today*, Feb. 1978, p. 51.

108 *Class differences were not*—George Will, *Men at Work* (New York, 1990), 240. The two recent community studies are Gerald Sorin, *The Nurturing Neighborhood: The Brownsville Boys Club and Jewish Community in Urban America, 1940–1990* (New York, 1990), and Jonathan Rieder, *Canarsie: The Jews and Italians Against Liberalism* (Cambridge, Mass. 1985).

109 *Gerald Sorin's study of*—For Sorin on Abe Stark, see Sorin, *Nurturing Neighborhood*, esp. 119–25. Sorin reprints a *New Yorker* cartoon caricaturing Stark's famous Ebbets Field sign as "obliquely anti-Semitic." See ibid., 122. Although not strictly a Brooklyn neighborhood study, Peter Levine's *From Ellis Island to Ebbets Field: Sports and the American Jewish Experience* (New York, 1992) is an important new addition to this literature. The book very much deals with Brooklyn neighborhoods, although in a more contained context.

109 *Ball clubs, Ray Robinson*—Ray Robinson, *The Home Run Heard 'Round the World* (New York, 1991), 17–18; Wilfred Sheed, *My Life as a Fan* (New York, 1993), 63.

110 *Linguists in particular in*—See Botkin, ed., *Sidewalks of America*, 464. For Francis Griffiths's essay, see *New York Times*, Aug. 16, 1972. For Geoffrey Needler, see his "Kings English," 176. For Cannon, see *New York Post*, Aug. 13, 1952; *Brooklyn Eagle*, Aug. 17, 19, 1952.

110 *Writing a tongue-in*—*New York Post*, Aug. 13, 1952.

110 *The "borough of churches"*—Ibid.

111 *The Brooklyn Eagle was*—*Brooklyn Eagle*, Aug. 17, 19, 1952.

111 *It was, all in*—Ibid., Aug. 17, 19, 21, 24, 1952.

111 *Predictably, the Eagle's aggressive*—Ibid., Aug. 21, 24, 1952.

112 *A gold-star mother*—Ibid.

112 *The allusions to Cannon's*—Ibid.

112 *In essence, the Dodger*—Ibid.

112 *So if any place*—Curt Smith, *Voices of the Game* (South Bend, Ind., 1987), 108; Roger Kahn, "Dodgers in the Catbird Seat," *Sports Illustrated*, Aug. 5, 1974, p. 39. For a generally more placid view of the impact on Brooklyn of the Dodgers' departure, see Sullivan, *Dodgers Move West*, 107–36, esp. 215–19.

112 *Meat-handed humor was*—For its uncharacteristically snide comment, see *New York P.M.*, Sept. 23, 1946.

113 *A 1954 Brooklyn Eagle*—For the origins of Bedford-Stuyvesant, see *Brooklyn Eagle*, Aug. 16, 1954. Additional neighborhoods were surveyed as well. See ibid., summer and fall 1954. Peter Golenbock's oral histories are especially good regarding both Jackie Robinson's indirect impact in bringing African American fans to Ebbets Field in numbers and the impact of the growing presence of black residents in Brooklyn generally. See Golenbock, *Bums*, 555–61 and passim.

113 *Jews, feeling the pain,*—Ibid., 183–85, 555, 556–61, 580–82; Rieder, *Canarsie*, 90–94.

113 *Another uncomfortable truth was*—Ibid., 94, 133, and passim.

113 *White groups were no*—Alan Lelchuk, *Brooklyn Boy* (New York, 1990), 99; Golenbock, *Bums*, 366.

114 *Eagle columnist Tommy Holmes*—*Brooklyn Eagle*, June 22, 1951; Allen Guttmann, *Sports Spectators* (New York, 1986), 111–13; *New York P.M.*, July 30, 1947.

114 *The Irish were no*—Tommy Holmes's column, *Brooklyn Eagle*, June 22, 1951; Roger Kahn, "In the Catbird Seat," *Sports Illustrated*, Aug. 5, 1974, p. 39.

114 *Although Brooklyn was a*—For the suburbanization of America after World War II and its impact on cities, see Kenneth T. Jackson, *Crabgrass Frontier: The Suburbanization of the United States* (New York, 1985).

115 *Few escaped the sting*—For the generalization about Italians, see Rieder, *Canarsie*, 133; Jerry Della Femina, *An Italian Grows in Brooklyn* (Boston, 1978), 81, 91. For Coplon, the Rosenbergs, and the Jews of Brooklyn, see Chapter 2. For Irish bars in Brooklyn, see Chapter 6.

115 *Peter Levine suggests that*—Levine, *From Ellis Island to Ebbets Field*, 98, 146–47, 243, 269; Deborah Dash Moore, *At Home in America: Second Generation New York Jews* (New York, 1981), 13, 22, 24, 61, 88.

116 *"The city's soul" is*—Lelchuk, *Brooklyn Boy*, 88–89.

116 *Hodges grew up in*—Tom Meany, "When Gil Hodges Slumped, All of Brooklyn Went to Bat for Him," *Colliers*, Aug. 21, 1953, p. 24 and passim; *New York Times*, Aug. 26, 1955; Golenbock, *Bums*, 419.

117 *Both during the 1952*—Ibid.

117 *As happened periodically when*—Ibid.

117 *Public relations exaggeration aside*—See Sullivan, *Dodgers Move West*, 16–19, 33–43, 217–19, and esp. 107–36. While Sullivan ably captures the immediate crisis in Brooklyn as the Dodgers left, the focus of his book then moves to Los Angeles. The crisis, however, persisted.

Chapter 8. Kids' Ball:
The Dodgers and Brooklyn's Boys

119 *"The Great Connors" of*—"The Great Connors" was the name Kevin "Chuck" Connors imprinted on his business cards. His flair for self-promotion was rewarded by frequent attention in the press. See *New York Herald Tribune*, April 8, 1949; *Brooklyn Eagle*, March 1, 17, 21, April 10, 14, 19, 22, 1949.

120 *The Parade Grounds, at*—For a detailed description of the Parade Grounds, see *Brooklyn Eagle*, June 23, 1939. It can be found in the Neighborhood Clippings File, Brooklyn Historical Society.

120 *The Grounds comprised forty*—Ibid.

120 *In 1951, more than*—For the scope of baseball activity on the Parade Grounds, see *Brooklyn Eagle*, July 27, 1951; Neil J. Sullivan, *The Dodgers Move West* (New York, 1987), 109, 128.

120 *Dodger scouts Al Campanis*—For Al Campanis and Arthur Dede scouting the Parade Grounds, see *Brooklyn Eagle*, June 2, 1951, May 18, 1953, June 9, 1954; *New York Times*, March 2, 1953, July 1, 1955. For Joe Torre, Sr., see the *Eagle*, Sept. 3, 1954. Walter O'Malley rejected the Grounds as a possible site for a new Dodger stadium "because of his ostensible concern for the lads who played sandlot ball on the site." Sullivan, *Dodgers Move West*, 128.

121 *The Dodgers shrewdly fed*—See Appendix B.

121 *Some of Brooklyn's young*—The three dominant ethnic groups are examined later in this chapter. George Thomasino and Babe Daskalaksis were the Greeks signed. The Scandinavian was Bob Sundstrom. See respectively *Brooklyn Eagle*, May 14, 1952, Sept. 3, 1954; *New York Times*, March 22, 1950.

While the *Eagle* sometimes mentioned white ethnic derivation in its features on teenage baseball, it never mentioned race or covered Bedford-Stuyvesant, where mostly Spanish and African Americans lived. For John Rucker's signing, see *New York Times*, Aug. 5, 1950. The *Eagle* did not mention it. That discrimination, occasionally at least, spilled over into Ebbets Field. When black newspaper columnist Bill Rowe brought several "Harlem luminaries" to Ebbets Field, he was not permitted to park in the press area, despite his press credentials.

Hank Aaron had a much different take, at least for the Dodger presence outside of New York. "The Brooklyn Dodgers held a tryout camp in Mobile," Alabama, in the early 1950s. "If there was a team that would give a black kid a fair opportunity, it was the Dodgers." Henry Aaron with Lonnie Wheeler, *I Had a Hammer* (New York, 1991), 24.

121 *The Parade Grounds as*—Among the borough boys who played in the majors (at least for a cup of coffee, and not necessarily as Dodgers) after World War II, were Saul Rogavin, Sid Gordon, Cal Abrams, Sandy Koufax, and Mickey Rutner (Jewish); Don McMahon, Bob Grim, Tommy Holmes, Tommy Brown, and Chuck Connors (Irish); Joe Pignatano, Jim Romano, Steve Lembo, Joe Pepitone, Bill Pierro, Bill Antonello, Mario Picone, Frank and Joe Torre, and Ken and Bob Aspromonte (Italian). The figures for 1952 and 1954 were culled from the *Brooklyn Eagle* for those years. From 1950 to 1954, judging only by ethnic name identification, the Dodgers alone signed some forty young men (ten Jewish, thirteen Irish, and seventeen Italians). Only Koufax among them reached the majors. Joe Torre and Bob Aspromonte were signed off the Parade Grounds after 1954, and Ken Aspromonte and Frank Torre before 1950.

122 *Although Pat Jordan was*—See Pat Jordan, *A False Spring* (New York, 1973), 11 and passim.

122 *Those ethnic alumni of*—For the early Brooklyn baseball years of the Aspromonte and Torre brothers, see *Brooklyn Eagle*, July 30, 1953; May 12, Sept. 3, 1954; *New York Times*, March 12, 1955.

123 *Most of the Italian*—See *The Baseball Encyclopedia: The Complete and Official Record of Major League Baseball.* I used the 1974 edition. For glimpses into the Parade Grounds experiences of Joe Pignatano: *Brooklyn Eagle*, Sept. 3, 1954, and *New York Times*, March 13, 1955; Jim Romano: *Times*, Sept. 19, 1950; and Steve Lembo: *Eagle*, May 13, 1952, and *Times*, March 21, 1950.

123 *Antonello's was the most*—For Bill Antonello's Brooklyn years and professional career, see *Brooklyn Eagle*, May 13, Aug. 20, 1952, April 11, 1953; Gene Schoor, *The Complete Dodgers Record Book* (New York, 1984), 24.

123 *Bill Antonello was signed*—Ibid.

124 *This Brooklyn kid seemed*—Ibid.

124 *Charlie DiGiovanna was one*—For biographical information about DiGiovanna see *New York Times*, Aug. 16, 1955. For his political connection, see *New York P.M.*, April 10, 1947. For his double duty as "Penman," see *Times*, Oct. 1, 1955; Duke Snider with Bill Gilbert, *The Duke of Flatbush* (New York, 1988), 34–35.

124 *Charlie's most visible duty*—Ibid.

124 *When The O'Malley announced*—For DiGiovanna's reaction to the Dodgers' departure from Brooklyn, see *New York World Telegram*, Oct. 9, 1957. A clipping of the story can be found in the Neighborhood Clippings Collection, Brooklyn Historical Society. DiGiovanna was voted full shares of World Series purses in 1952, 1953, 1955, and 1956, an incredible amount of money for a batboy to take in. For four of the seven years he had the job, DiGiovanna could have lived off the $5000 to $7000 shares alone. Dodger regulars showed their appreciation for the respite his mighty pen provided them.

125 *The Jewish experience was*—Abrams was one of a generation of ballplayers whose career was interrupted by World War II. He came up to the Dodgers first in 1949, but spent only one full season (1951) with the team. Abrams was traded to Cincinnati early in 1952. For his Brooklyn years, see *Brooklyn Eagle*, April 20, 1949; June 6, July 13, Oct. 2, 1951; *New York Times*, July 15, 1951, June 9, 1952. There is a fine sketch of Abrams's Brooklyn roots in Peter Levine, *From Ellis Island to Ebbets Field: Sports and the American Jewish Experience* (New York, 1992), 96–97, 124–25.

Two other Jewish Parade Grounds products, Saul Rogavin and Sid Gordon, went on from their Brooklyn origins to successful major league careers. Both were given "days" in New York (Abrams was given several) by partisan Jewish locals who, no less than Italians and Irish, played numbers games with their brethren in the big leagues. For Rogavin, see *New York Times*, June 21, 1951, July 21, 1952. For Gordon, see ibid., June 3, 1953; Gerald Sorin, *The Nurturing Neighborhood: The Brownsville Boys Club and Jewish Community in America, 1940–1990* (New York, 1990), 78–80. I am indebted also to a manuscript essay by Irving Saposnik, "To Brooklyn: Again and Again," *Jewish Currents* (March 1995). He makes some interesting points about the Dodgers, Brooklyn, and ethnic immigrant identity: "Unconsciously no doubt, and purely by instinct, we turned baseball into a Jewish game, and the Dodgers into a Jewish team, worshiping them the more they resembled us. . . . We needed the Dodgers, we thought, because they weren't Jewish, but our Jewish needs made them Jewish despite ourselves. And Jewish they remained for as long as we needed them to be."

125 *A great deal has*—For the Murphy story, see Daniel Okrent and Steve Wulf, *Baseball Anecdotes* (New York, 1989), 260.

125 *Others missed the left*—This portrait of Koufax's Parade Grounds start derives largely from two contemporary interviews: *Brooklyn Eagle*, Aug. 17, 1954, and *New York Times*, Aug. 29, 1955. It owes much as well to Peter Levine, *From Ellis Island to Ebbets Field*, 242–45; Peter Golenbock, *Bums: An Oral History of the Brooklyn Dodgers* (New York, 1984), 494–95.

125 *Jerry Della Femina commented*—Jerry Della Femina and Charles Sopkin, *An Italian Grows in Brooklyn* (Boston, 1978), 97.

126 *The Irish American experience*—For Bob Grim, see *New York Times*, April 11, 1954, Sept. 29, 1955.

126 *Bay Ridge's Tommy Holmes*—For Holmes, see *Brooklyn Eagle*, June 20, 1951, June 17, 1952; *New York Times*, Oct. 3, 1951, June 15, 1952.

126 *The ultimate Great Irish*—For Tommy Brown, see *New York Times*, March 8, 1950; *Brooklyn Eagle*, June 8, 1951.

127 *In a Parade Grounds*—For Connors, see *New York Herald Tribune*, April 8, 1949; *Brooklyn Eagle*, March 1, 17, 21, April 10, 14, 19, 22, 1949. For his obituary, see *New York Times*, Nov. 11, 1992. For his election to the Cowboy Hall of Fame, see Kinky Friedman's op-ed piece in ibid., March 18, 1991.

127 *But Connors's first and*—Ibid.

127 *His locker room tour*—Ibid. For Connors's response to Rickey, see Tommy Lasorda, *The Artful Dodger* (New York, 1985), 51. For Connors on Rickey and salaries, see Kevin Nelson, ed., *Baseball's Greatest Insults* (New York, 1988), 116.

128 *It was (maybe) Connors's*—Levine, *From Ellis Island to Ebbets Field*, makes the point that every New York team tried to sign Jewish ballplayers in order to please their many Jewish fans. In a parallel way, of course, the Dodgers took great care of Connors, as they had of Tommy Brown, because he was from Brooklyn. See esp. 119–21.

128 *Dodger-inspired community baseball*—For the Dodger Rookie Team in general, see *Brooklyn Eagle*, Aug. 27, 1952, July 9, Sept. 8, 1954; *New York Times*, July 18, 1953.

129 *That competition complemented high*—Ibid.

129 *The Rookies made the*—Ibid.

129 *Usually though, after the*—Ibid.

130 *To personalize the reality*—For the 1954 Dodger Rookie Team, see *Brooklyn Eagle*, July 9, Sept. 8, 1954. See also Appendix B.

130 *Maybe the Dodger organization*—For Koufax's signing, see *Brooklyn Eagle*, Aug. 17, 1954; *New York Times*, Aug. 29, 1955.

130 *That hope started with*—See Irving Rudd's account of the Brooklyn Amateur Baseball Foundation in Golenbock, *Bums*, 564–69. Immediately after World War II, before there was a Mayor's Trophy Game, BABF was the recipient of the proceeds from an annual home-and-home midseason exhibition series with the Cleveland Indians. See *Brooklyn Eagle*, May 22, June 27, 1949.

130 *Irving Rudd, Dodger P.R.*—Golenbock, *Bums*, 564–69.

131 *BABF needed far more*—*Brooklyn Eagle*, May 22, June 27, 1949.

131 *The entire youth effort*—For good examples of popular conventional wisdom about baseball and juvenile delinquency, see Tommy Holmes's columns in *Brooklyn Eagle*, May 22, June 27, 1949. For the 1957 plea to keep the Dodgers, see Sullivan, *Dodgers Move West*, 18. The idea that baseball built boys' character was not new. Albert Spalding espoused it early in the century. See Peter Levine, *A. G. Spalding and the Rise of Baseball* (New York, 1985), 110–12.

131 *The Classic was first*—For the Sandlot Classic, see *Brooklyn Eagle*, June 2, July 21, 22, 24, Aug. 2, and passim, 1951.

132 *Every major veterans' organization*—Ibid. In 1951, for example, Dodger-oriented bars lent some of their memorabilia to storefront displays advertising the Classic. The Dodgers donated Ebbets Field and paid its groundskeepers, ushers, and organist Gladys Goodding to work the event. Ads published at cut rates appeared in the *Eagle* and in many organization newsletters, all generally "urging the people to attend the game as combatants of juvenile delinquency." *Brooklyn Eagle*, July 24, 1951.

132 *In 1952, for example*—Ibid., June 22, 30, 1952; *New York Times*, June 30, 1952.

133 *A Dodger god was*—See both *Brooklyn Eagle* and *New York Times*, June 30, 1952.

133 *Those BABF events took*—*Brooklyn Eagle*, Aug. 9, 1952.

133 *The money raised at*—Ibid., April 9, 1953. Not everyone was happy. The Bushwicks, the crackerjack Brooklyn semipro outfit, was frozen out of these postwar developments. Max Rosner, head of the Bushwicks, offered in 1948 "to meet the Dodgers in a charity game and was turned down flat." Rosner responded by denouncing the Dodger management to the *Sporting News*. See *New York P.M.*, June 4, 1948.

133 *Yet there is an*—For Rucker's signing, see *New York Times*, Aug. 5, 1950.

133 *Only a small minority*—For Knothole numbers, see *New York Star*, Aug. 12, 1948; *New York Times*, July 19, 1951, July 24, Aug. 18, 1952; *Brooklyn Eagle*, April 14, 1950, Aug. 18, 1952.

134 *The Dodger club provided*—For the 1954 incident, see *Brooklyn Eagle*, May 25, 1954. O'Malley claimed in that year that 300,000 Knothole Club admissions were recorded, but that was an exaggeration. Umpire Augie Donatelli, umpiring at first base, found an opened pen knife near the bag on this occasion. See ibid.

134 *When the Dodgers came*—For Knothole Club sponsorship of the dinner, see *Brooklyn Eagle*, April 19, 1949. For dinner attendance and proceeds, see *New York Times*, March 25, 1953, April 7, 13, 1954; *Eagle*, April 13, 1953.

134 *In 1949, Ralph Branca*—For the 1949 dinner, see *New York Herald Tribune*, April 11, 18, 1949; *Brooklyn Eagle*, April 18, 19, 1949. No question that the 1949 Dodgers made up the most representative team ever to step onto a major league diamond before the 1960s. Levine, *From Ellis Island to Ebbets Field*, 131, quotes columnist Dan Daniel about that 1949 team. He credited Rickey for doing "quite a job building a house of all nations." He described the team as an "American melting pot," reflecting a widely held American perception of immigration in that postwar era.

"With the Jewish Abrams, the Teutonic Reese, Negroes Robinson and Campanella, Polish Miksis and Hermanski, Slovokian [*sic*] Shuba, Italians Furillo and Ramazotti, Italian-Hungarian Branca, Scandinavians Haugstad and Jorgenson, Celtic Kevin Connors and a delegation representing basic American stocks of English, Scotch-Irish ingredients, there is truly a Yankee appeal to the Brooklyn outfit which may win the pennant." To that catalogue of ethnic virtue Daniel might have added Hispanic American Luis Olmo and Armenian American Bud Podbelian. John Cashmore was right.

135 *Despite its deep support*—For background on the Durocher/Knothole Club contretemps, see *New York P.M.*, April 8, 13, 1947; *New York Sun*, March 19, 22, 1947; Damon Rice, *Seasons Past* (New York, 1976), 337; Golenbock, *Bums*, 125.

135 *The scandal did not*—For Powell's statement, see *New York P.M.*, March 2, 1947.

135 *If one possessed such*—For CYO re-entry to the Knothole Club, see ibid., April 11, 1947. A year later, when Leo jumped to the Giants, columnist Tom Meany said it was in the public relations interest of the Dodgers that he was gone. Durocher, Meany said, was a "hot potato." See Meany's column, *New York Star*, July 18, 1948. For two takes on the CYO/Durocher confrontation, see Rice, *Seasons Past*, 337–39; Golenbock, *Bums*, 125–26.

136 *Brooklyn boys, Parade Ground*—*New York Post*, Sept. 13, 1945; Della Femina and Sopkin, *An Italian Grows in Brooklyn*, 98; Golenbock, *Bums*, 222.

136 *Some kids made their*—For Brownsville, see Sorin, *Nurturing Neighborhood*, 191. For Della Femina, see Della Femina and Sopkin, *An Italian Grows in Brooklyn*, 93–94. For Lelchuk, see Alan Lelchuk, *Brooklyn Boy* (New York, 1990), 91. For Podres, see Donald Honig, *The October Heroes* (New York, 1979), 206. For Roth, see Charles Einstein, ed., *The Baseball Reader* (New York, 1980), 271–72.

136 *The true fanatics among*—Woody Allen, *Side Effects* (New York, 1975), 80; Peter Golenbock, *Bums*, 11–12; *New York Times*, Oct. 3, 1955; Lelchuk, *Brooklyn Boy*, 86; Roger Kahn, "Dodgers in the Catbird Seat," *Sports Illustrated*, Aug. 5, 1974, p. 40.

Chapter 9. The Outer Edges of Dodger Memory

139 *Immortalized first by Roger Kahn*—Roger Kahn, *The Boys of Summer* (New York, 1971). For Reese's comment, see Maury Allen, *Jackie Robinson: A Life Remembered* (New York, 1987), 11.

140 *Robinson came to regret*—For Robinson's later expression of his regret about testifying against Robeson, see Jackie Robinson, *I Never Had It Made* (New York, 1972), 95–96. For the reference to Robinson as a "period piece," see Kahn, *Boys of Summer*, 251. Robinson, until the end of his life, could not gain admission to a private golf club, an example of the petty persistence of the race prejudice he continued to face. See William Fugazy's letter to the editor, *New York Times*, Aug. 17, 1990. For Malcolm X's criticism of Robinson, see Martin Duberman, *Paul Robeson* (New York, 1988), 755. For the reference to "Uncle Tom," see Bruce Allen's review of David Falkner's *Great Time Coming: The Life of Jackie Robinson from Baseball to Birmingham* (New York: 1995), in *Civilization*, March–April 1995, p. 80. Faulkner's very positive new biography falls well within the sympathetic model established by the studies of Robinson in the 1980s.

140 *That contest over his*—Red Barber, *1947: When All Hell Broke Loose in Baseball* (New York, 1982), 250–51.

140 *Fixing the ambivalence of*—Ibid.

141 *Yet there is a*—Allen, *Robinson*, 9–11.

141 *Some echoes of that*—For Dave Anderson's column, see *New York Times*, Oct. 25, 1972. For Robinson's funeral and Jackson's eulogy, see ibid., Oct. 28, 1972.

141 *As it always is*—Gerard O'Connor, "Where Have You Gone Joe DiMaggio?," in *Heroes of Popular Culture*, Ray B. Browne, Marshall Fishwick and Michael T. Marsden, eds. (Bowling Green, Ohio, 1972), 92–93.

142 *By the mid-1980s*—Robert Curvin, "Jackie Robinson," *New York Times Magazine*, April 4, 1982.

142 *Maury Allen's biography of*—For Black, Erskine, and Newcombe, see Allen, *Robinson*, 12–13, 163–66, 246, respectively.

142 *A number of significant*—For book-jacket blurbs, see the covers of Allen, *Robinson*, and Harvey Frommer, *Rickey and Robinson* (New York, 1982). For the comment from Jules Tygiel's book, see the back cover of the paperback edition of Tygiel, *Baseball's Great Experiment: Jackie Robinson and His Legacy* (New York, 1984).

143 *In the 1990s, Jackie*—For Garland Jeffreys's recollection, *New York Times*, Jan. 22, 1992. For Jules Tygiel's, see Tygiel, *Baseball's Great Experiment*, vii.

143 *In assailing Clarence Thomas's*—For the reminder that Thomas should remember Jackie Robinson, see Marvin Warren's letter to the editor, *New York Times*, July 23, 1991. For Ken Burns's appraisal, see ibid., April 17, 1992.

144 *For O'Malley, unlike Robinson*—For the Brooklyn Dodger Sports Bar story, see *New York Times*, April 20, May 17, 1990. For Sullivan's assessment of O'Malley's role, see Neil Sullivan, *The Dodgers Move West* (New York, 1987), viii. For Wilfred Sheed's continuing animosity, see Sheed, *My Life as a Fan: A Memoir* (New York, 1993), 90.

144 *In 1957, when Los*—For the lyrics of the Phil Foster song, see "Question Box," *New York Times*, Aug. 6, 1991. Words and music by Roy Ross, Sam Denoff, and Bill Persky.

144 *Within months of the*—For the "Gaelic Machiavelli" and Stoneham quotes, see Arthur Daley, "Will the Dodger-Giant Gold Rush Pan Out?," *New York Times Magazine*, May 11, 1958, pp. 34ff. For the "cold schemer" quote, see Melvin Durslag, "A Visit with Walter O'Malley," *Saturday Evening Post*, May 14, 1960, p. 10ff. For a more dispassionate, scholarly appraisal of the move, see Cary S. Henderson, "Los Angeles and the Dodger War of 1957–1961," *North American Society for Sport History Proceedings and Newsletter*, 1979, unpaged.

145 *The only evolution of*—For alternative views of O'Malley's responsibility for the move, see Robert Caro, *The Power Broker: Robert Moses and the Fall of New York* (New York, 1974), 1018–19; Sullivan, *Dodgers Move West*, 216–17. For Hamill's consignment of O'Malley in the hereafter, see Pete Hamill, *The Invisible City: A New York Sketchbook* (New York, 1980), 138.

145 *Peter Golenbock's oral history*—For Bill Reddy's comments, see Peter Golenbock, *Bums: An Oral History of the Brooklyn Dodgers* (New York, 1984), 530–582. For the impact of the move on the Brooklyn community, see ibid., 582; Stephen Young's letter to the editor, *New York Times*, July 21, 1993; Carl E. Hinds, letter to the editor, *New York Times Magazine*, Sept. 18, 25, 1994.

145 *O'Malley's reputation only worsens*—For Gary Goldberg's perception, see *New York Times*, April 5, 1992. For Jay Feldman, see ibid., July 1, 1990.

146 *Hatred of the O'Malleys*—For the Brooklyn Dodger Sports Bar and Peter O'Malley, see *New York Times*, April 20, May 17, 1990. For Pete Coutros's epithet, see *New York Post*, Oct. 23, 1992. For the petition in the form of doggerel, see the *Times*, May 17, 1990.

146 *Times columnist George Vecsey*—For George Vecsey on the O'Malleys, see his columns in *New York Times*, April 20, 1990, Aug. 1, 1993.

147 *As in the case of*—For the return of the banner and Howard Golden's comment, see *New York Times*, April 20, 1995.

Index

193